Politics and the Theory of Language in the USSR 1917–1938

Politics and the Theory of Language in the USSR 1917–1938

The Birth of Sociological Linguistics

Edited by

Craig Brandist and Katya Chown

ANTHEM PRESS
LONDON · NEW YORK · DELHI

Anthem Press
An imprint of Wimbledon Publishing Company
www.anthempress.com

This edition first published in UK and USA 2011
by ANTHEM PRESS
75-76 Blackfriars Road, London SE1 8HA, UK
or PO Box 9779, London SW19 7ZG, UK
and
244 Madison Ave. #116, New York, NY 10016, USA

British Library Cataloguing-in-Publication Data
A catalogue record for this book is available from the British Library.

Library of Congress Cataloging-in-Publication Data
The Library of Congress has cataloged the hardcover edition as follows:
Politics and the theory of language in the USSR, 1917–1938 : the birth of sociological linguistics /
edited by Craig Brandist and Katya Chown.
p. cm.
Includes bibliographical references and index.
ISBN-13: 978-1-84331-840-8 (hardcover : alk. paper)
ISBN-10: 1-84331-840-7 (hardcover : alk. paper)
ISBN-13: 978-0-85728-948-3 (ebook)
1. Sociolinguistics–Soviet Union–History. 2. Linguistics–Soviet Union–
Philosophy–History. 3. Linguistics–Social aspects–Soviet Union–History. 4. Linguistics–
Political aspects–Soviet Union–History. 5. Linguists–Soviet Union–Biography. 6. Russian
language–Social aspects–Soviet Union–History. 7. Russian language–Political aspects–
Soviet Union–History. 8. Soviet Union–Politics and government–1917–1936.
9. Language policy–Soviet Union–History. I. Brandist, Craig, 1963- II.
Chown, Katya.
P40.45.S65P65 2010
306.440947'09042–dc22
2010004338

ISBN-13: 978 0 85728 404 4 (Pbk)
ISBN-10: 0 85728 404 5 (Pbk)

This title is also available as an eBook.

TABLE OF CONTENTS

Chapter 1

INTRODUCTION

Craig Brandist

While there can be little doubt that the period between the October 1917 Russian Revolution and the outbreak of World War Two saw an extraordinary upsurge in innovative approaches to language in Russia and then the USSR, only isolated examples have reached an Anglophone audience beyond a relatively narrow circle of Slavists. This is especially regrettable since many of the questions that now occupy theorists of language and society were those with which early Soviet linguists grappled, and one can still learn a considerable amount, both positive and negative, from this experience. As the work of what have become known as the Bakhtin and Vygotskii Circles began to appear in translations in the late 1960s, structuralist and then post-structuralist approaches to language became dominant in Western scholarship in the humanities. This movement was led by scholars who often claimed to be giving language due consideration for the first time, and who, polemically, presented previous approaches in caricatured form, as outdated and naïve theorizing that either unwittingly or willingly made common cause with Stalinist totalitarianism. As a result of this, the newly translated Russian texts appeared as exceptions that proved the rule, covertly subverting the official Soviet position and so anticipating, in fragmentary form, the new French-led paradigm. Just as these approaches arose in Europe, so in the United States William Labov led a bold attempt to catalogue and theorise social variations within American English by synthesizing dialect geography, attempts to define language as a social rather than natural science, and US writings on language contact and conflicts of the 1950s into a new discipline that was to be known as sociolinguistics (Koerner 2002). Labov and his followers did not caricature their predecessors in the same way as the post-structuralists, but the boldness of their new formulations combined with the political context of the Civil Rights movement still tended to exaggerate the novelty of these approaches and certainly did not stimulate a search for precursors. By the mid 1980s a veritable boom in Bakhtin studies had been launched, and Mikhail Bakhtin himself, eclipsing the members of the so-called 'Bakhtin Circle', was being held up as the hitherto unacknowledged initiator of a whole range of approaches. It took some time before the problems with the new perspectives became widely acknowledged and sober historical scholarship eroded the inflated claims to individual innovation, leading to a reassessment of the heritage of sociological approaches to language, even after the end of the Cold War had cleared the way for sustained archival research in the ex-USSR.

The current volume presents new materials that were first raised at the conference *Sociological Theories of Language in the USSR 1917–1938*, which took place at the University of Sheffield, UK, in September 2006. The conference was itself a part of a four-year project, *The Rise of Sociological Linguistics in the Soviet Union, 1917–1938: Institutions, Ideas and Agendas*, in the Bakhtin Centre at the same university.[1] The project facilitated extensive archival research in the ex-USSR and collaboration with Russian scholars working in the area, some of whom contributed to the current volume, and has contributed to a changing perspective that was already underway before the project began. One of the main findings of the project has been the multi-dimensional character of the linguistic innovations in the USSR between the two World Wars, which was conditioned by political changes, the rise of new paradigms in linguistics proper, the dynamics of the institutional locus of research, patterns of appropriation of philosophical ideas from abroad and the diverse character of the ethnic composition of the USSR. Not only were these factors always present, but relations within and between each of them were constantly shifting according to the huge socio-political changes that characterized that period. Furthermore, disciplinary boundaries themselves were still in the process of formation and so scholarship about language took place in a wide variety of disciplinary contexts, including what would now be covered by psychology, ethnology, sociology, literary studies and even disability studies and archaeology. Needless to say this volume can do no more than highlight a few aspects of this complexity, but it is hoped that presenting the materials in this way will stimulate further interest in an extraordinarily rich field outside of the narrow confines of Slavic studies, which in many respects maintains some of the conservatism of the Cold War climate in which it developed.

Vladimir Alpatov presents us with a discussion of the way in which Soviet linguists related to the scholarship of the pre-Revolutionary period both within and outside Russia. He shows how the Revolution coincided with the importation of Saussure's new paradigm into Russia, and the way the two factors interacted in the work of different groups of linguists. Four trends are identified: those who rejected the new paradigm and the tasks the Revolution posed for linguists; those who rejected both the old and new paradigms and sought to construct a new Marxist linguistics *ab nihilo*; those who selected one among particular trends as a source for the construction of a new Marxist linguistics; and those who sought to construct a new Marxist linguistics by assimilating and combining aspects from a variety of pre-existing trends. This expands upon Alpatov's earlier work (2000) in which the many claims to having constructed a specifically Marxist linguistics was subjected to scrutiny and found to be seriously lacking in coherence. Linguistic constructions were found to have originated elsewhere and this or that linguist's commitment to Marxism was shown to have only influenced the direction of research and the conception of society of which language was seen as part. Alpatov now shows that linguists related to positivist, idealist and Saussurean linguistics in complex ways, with Marxism influencing the objects of research and the criteria for appropriation of methodology and wider conceptions of language.

Marxism inevitably influenced the conception of society with which linguists worked, and thus of the type of sociology he or she developed. However, it is not always clear that linguists had a sophisticated understanding of Marxism, and quite often general conceptions from positivism or Durkheimian sociology were adopted with Marxist terminology often amounting to little more than a gloss. The dominant form of sociology that developed in postrevolutionary Russia, under the leadership of Nikolai Bukharin, could only be regarded as fully Marxist with considerable reservations. Bukharin's *Historical Materialism: A Popular Manual of Marxist Sociology* (1926 [1921]) presented a brand of positivist Marxism in which technology exerted a determining influence on social development and language was, for the first time in 'Marxist' theory, assigned to the ideological superstructure that arises on the economic base (1926 [1921], pp. 203–6). Despite the fact that Lenin had shown considerable scepticism towards sociology as a discipline and towards Bukharin's understanding of both Marxism and culture (Biggart 1987), and that some of the most talented Marxist theoreticians abroad (Lukács 1925; Gramsci 1971 [1929–35]) heavily criticized Bukharin's work, this formulation was widely accepted by Soviet linguists as the model of Marxism to which their work needed to correspond. Moreover, while Bukharin was quite liberal in his approach to sources from 'bourgeois' thinkers, his conception of culture and science, which derived from the work of Aleksandr Bogdanov, encouraged culture and science to be viewed as class phenomena, with the creation of specifically proletarian versions to be a desideratum of Soviet scholarship. This gave a theoretical basis for the scholarly nihilism that developed among certain Soviet linguists and elsewhere, and for the harassment of scholars who remained open to a wide range of influences, especially at the beginning of the 1930s. As Alpatov shows with reference to linguistics, however, most scholars remained open to pre-Revolutionary and western influences even if they sought to recast those influences in the mould of 'Marxist sociology', and this was particularly true of the former students of the Polish-Russian linguist Jan Baudouin de Courtenay, such as Evgenii Polivanov, Boris Larin, Lev Iakubinskii and Lev Shcherba.

Mika Lähteenmäki examines the notions of sociology found in the work of three prominent Soviet linguists, Rozaliia Shor, Polivanov and Valentin Voloshinov. Of these only the last is well known among Anglophone scholars for his 1929 book *Marxism and the Philosophy of Language* (translated 1973), though a collection of Polivanov's articles has been available in English translation since 1974. Lähteenmäki shows that in her 1926 book *Language and Society* and subsequently, Shor was not only heavily influenced by Saussure (as Alpatov discusses) but also by Durkheimian sociology as adopted by the French sociological school led by Antoine Meillet. Meanwhile, Polivanov and Voloshinov appeared to have a direct relationship to Bukharin's *Historical Materialism*, though neither adopted his perspective in its entirety but sought to cleanse the conception of its mechanistic features and incorporate teleological features into their respective conceptions of language. Furthermore, Lähteenmäki shows that none of the linguists actually made it clear exactly what they understood by 'Marxist sociology', and that this allowed them to emphasise different features at different points in their respective intellectual developments.

A wide range of approaches to the development of a new linguistics was evident during the 1920s when, with certain exceptions, scientific still generally prevailed over statutory authority in determining careers within academic institutions. One certainly needed to pose one's chosen research in terms of relevance to the new social and political environment and, from 1924, this increasingly pertained to the 'building of socialism in one country', but this was a capacious field within which there was little agreement on many fundamental questions. The relationship between social structure and linguistic variation was posed particularly sharply in the 1920s when the conscious construction of standard forms of the languages of the peoples of the former Russian Empire was embarked upon. All national groups had been given the right to be educated in their native language and to communicate with central government in that language, but this often required the selection, systematization and codification of standard forms from a plethora of local dialects, along with the creation of written forms.[2] Even in Russia itself, the rapid process of urbanisation along with the destruction of the old state institutions meant that cities became multi-lingual and multi-dialectal environments. The drive to spread literacy and to form a new public discourse that was not remote from that spoken by the urban population inevitably required attention be given to linguistic and dialectal variation, raising the sociolinguistic problem to attention on a scale hitherto unknown. Most Soviet linguists were concerned with these problems in one way or another. Scholars of oriental languages, like Polivanov and Nikolai Iakovlev, were deeply engaged in language construction, which constantly raised consideration of the sociological dimension of language to a level of primary importance. Others who worked on Russian were constantly concerned with the relationship between standard and non-standard forms.

Particularly important in this regard were the works of two students of Baudouin de Courtenay, Boris Larin and Lev Iakubinskii, who form the focus of attention of Viktoria Gulida's contribution to this volume. Gulida shows that Iakubinskii's influential 1923 article 'On Dialogic Speech' and Larin's work on the linguistic variations of the city (with particular reference to Leningrad) both involve forms of analysis that were to become the basis of Labov's socioliguistics several decades later. Correlations are drawn between today's sociolinguistic concepts and the specific features the Soviet linguists highlighted, revealing how an incipient sociolinguistic theory was developing at the time. In their joint article, Brandist and Lähteenmäki show that it is ignorance of works such as those of Iakubinskii and Larin that has led to the exaggeration of the originality of Mikhail Bakhtin's ideas about language as developed in his essays on the novel of the 1930s, particularly his widely received work 'Discourse in the Novel' of 1934–5. After establishing the conditions within which Bakhtin's essays were written, the authors go on to show that some of the concepts such as heteroglossia (*raznoiazychie*) and polyglossia (*mnogoiazychie*) were already in common usage among linguists in the 1920s. They then go on to discuss Iakubinskii's articles on the formation of the Russian national language of the early 1930s, showing that Bakhtin's account of the linguistic preconditions for the rise of the modern novel closely parallels Iakubinskii's discussion that had been published just a few years earlier. It then becomes apparent that Bakhtin's own originality lies not in his approach to the stratification of language, but his discussion of the way in which the novelist models and exploits that stratification in the composition of works of literature.

Scholarship and Ideology

Like Alpatov, Gulida also shows how ideological pressures impinged on linguists as the decade neared its conclusion, but one might also comment that the development of American sociolinguistics was itself conditioned by the Civil Rights movement, the availability of federal funding to address African-American educational failures, and the development of ethnography spurred by the concerns of the Cold War (Dittmar 1976). One clearly needs to be very careful when posing the relationship between scholarship and ideology unless one propagate what Christopher Hutton calls 'a counter-myth of the "normal situation"... the notion of the disinterested professor, free from external pressures who pursues truth without fear or favour' (Hutton 1999, p. 37).

Even the most deeply ideological brands of Soviet linguistic science were not reacting against scientific objectivity as such but against a doctrine that was, as Habermas puts it, 'inadequately dissociated from the context in which it emerged'. Soviet linguists suspected that 'behind the back of the theory there lies hidden an inadmissible *mixture of power and validity*, and that it still owes its reputation to this' (Habermas 1990 [1985], p. 116). The deeply ideological nature of the heritage of Indo-European philology is now surely beyond question, especially after the work of such figures as Edward Said (1995 [1978]) and Maurice Olender (1992 [1989]), and this should surely give us pause when tackling the most notorious trend in Soviet linguistics of the period, that which was led by the controversial archaeologist and philologist Nikolai Marr. Continuing to apply Habermas's terminology, we can see that Marr attempted an ideology critique of Indo-Europeanism, seeking to show how its 'validity claims' were 'determined by relations of power', especially those of colonialism and imperialism. The truth claims of Indo-Europeanism were disputed with particular reference to languages, such as Etruscan and Basque, that were lodged in the midst of Europe and that proved anomalous to the Indo-European case. For Marr, while it 'presupposes a demythologized understanding of the world' Indo-Europeanism 'is still ensnared by myth' and he does so 'by pointing out a putatively overcome category mistake' (Habermas 1990 [1985], p. 116).[3] Such an argument undoubtedly had a rational core, which is probably why it gained such currency among linguists, philosophers and historians at the time, even if they did not accept Marr's often wild extrapolations from just a few perceptive observations and attempts to fashion a counter-tradition that proved little short of disastrous.[4] Marr was unable judiciously to distinguish between the questionable elements of the Indo-European doctrine and those parts that undoubtedly represented epistemic progress, while his own Japhetic theory was clearly bound up with mythical features the acceptance of which was increasingly bound up with relations of power.

Marrism does not form a central focus of the current collection, partly because it is a large and complex phenomenon in its own right, and one that goes beyond linguistics into anthropology and literary studies, but since it forms an important point of reference we have provided a translation of a particularly useful and systematic summary of its fundamental theses by one of its most significant advocates, Ivan Meshchaninov. This text was published on the eve of fundamental changes in the institutional and ideological context within which Soviet linguistics developed, and the beginning of a relatively short period in which one may justifiably speak about scholarship becoming exceptionally ideologized. In the 1920s Marrism constituted but one trend within Soviet linguistics, though it is clear that many of what one might regard as its legitimate concerns spread beyond its advocates. Alpatov shows how attempts to cling on to the old disciplinary boundaries and research practices were often bound up with hostility to the new regime, which initially sought to undermine the favoured status of Imperial Russian. This undoubtedly contributed to the suspicious or even hostile treatment the old-school linguists received at the hands of their younger opponents, and to the attitude the older linguists adopted towards the 'new paradigm' and 'new regime'. What had come to the fore, and was beginning to be subjected to scrutiny was the fact that ideologies and disciplinary boundaries are by no means mutually exclusive, and this has recently once more surfaced as an issue for researchers in linguistic anthropology such as Susan Gal and Judith Irvine (1995) and Kathryn Woolard (1998).

The Linguistics of Stalinism

After the First Five Year Plan, the political and ideological trajectory of official Soviet culture settled into a conservative channel quite unlike what had preceded it. The focus was now on the development of a unitary state with stable relations between its ethnic components capable of competing militarily with hostile and generally more economically advanced states. By 1934 a systematic reform programme was underway, which was reflected in wider ideological shifts at the highest level and the formation of unitary professional bodies with their conservative orthodoxies (Fitzpatrick 1992 [1975]). In education, the class approach began to be replaced by a focus on a unitary 'peoples of the USSR' (Zhukov 2008 [2003], pp. 72–3), and by 1936 Molotov was addressing foreign journalists, affirming a 'responsibility towards the motherland', advocating 'Soviet patriotism', and raising the possibility of an 'all-Union parliament' (Zhukov 2008 [2003], pp. 124–5). Progressive social reforms of the 1920s were reversed and nationality policy was ever more focused on strengthening central authority at the expense of regional autonomy. In his controversial 2003 book, *A Different Stalin*, the Russian historian Iurii Zhukov (2008 [2003]) argues that this perspective was consistent throughout Stalin's political life, since even when, as Commissar for Nationalities in the period of Lenin's leadership, he deferred to the latter's internationalism, Stalin prized the unity of the state and the priority of Russian interests over all international considerations. According to this perspective, the projected, though unfulfilled, reforms of 1933–7 were the logical outcome of Stalin's coherent leadership, having achieved collectivization and defeated the opposition.[5] Building on his seminal book *Language and Power in the Creation of the*

USSR, 1917–1953, Michael Smith also argues that there was an inner coherence to Stalin's approach to language and the national question despite several turns such as the shift from Latinization of the languages of the peoples of the USSR to the adoption of a Cyrillic alphabet and from initial support for Marr's theory of the movement of all languages towards unity and Stalin's eventual destruction of the dominance of Marrism in 1950. National languages, transcending class distinctions, emerge as the forms through which nations find their existential forms.

Rationalization and the 'Construction of Socialism'

Early Soviet discussions of language often went under the rubric of 'rationalization', and appealed to the urgent drive to rationalize the administrative system and working practices in the face of the catastrophic economic collapse that resulted from World War and then Civil War coming on the back of relative economic backwardness. Surrounded by hostile powers while waiting for the revolution to spread to more advanced economic powers, the drive to make social and economic organization more efficient was urgent, and linguists often presented their work in these terms.

Lenin repeatedly asserted that in order to even reach the threshold at which any talk of the 'construction of socialism' would be more than a utopian fantasy, the necessary economic preconditions would need to be established. While he was clear that such 'construction' would require the establishment of revolutionary regimes in the more economically advanced parts of Europe, he stressed the urgency of rationalizing production in backward Russia, even if this meant the adoption of the principles of scientific management, Taylorism. The Taylor system was in no way presented as an unambiguously positive phenomenon, indeed, in 1914 he had called it 'man's enslavement by the machine' (Lenin [1914], p. 152), but in the new circumstances the Bolsheviks began to find positive aspects to Taylorism. In 1918 Lenin argued the system 'like all capitalist progress' is 'a combination of the refined brutality of bourgeois exploitation and a number of the greatest scientific achievements in the field of analysing mechanical motions during work, the elimination of superfluous and awkward motions the elaboration of correct methods of work, the introduction of the best system of accounting and control, etc' (Lenin 1972 [1918]a). Contrary to the dominant view, adoption of aspects of the Taylor system was not part of an attempt to 'build socialism' in Russia. As Boris Kagarlitsky notes:

> Anyone who reads the statements made by Lenin after 1917 with an unprejudiced mind will easily perceive that what the Bolsheviks saw as their immediate task was not 'the construction of socialist society' but, on

the contrary, the strengthening in Russia of civilization and state capitalism in the German manner, because this state capitalism was 'a complete material preparation for socialism, the threshold of socialism'. (Kagarlitsky 1988, p. 41)

By 'state capitalism' Lenin meant private capitalism under state control, and he was quite clear that this should not be presented as socialism, insisting, against Bukharin and others: 'We... must tell the workers: Yes, it is a step back [from the dictatorship of the proletariat – CB], but we have to help ourselves to find a remedy' (Lenin 1972 [1918]b, p. 301).

   The path from emergency measures considered as regrettable necessities to their being made into a theorized virtue in the 'construction of socialism' finds its elaboration in the work of Bukharin, who consistently failed to distinguish between theoretical abstractions and the reality of the situation in which the Bolsheviks found themselves. In his 1920 book *The Economics of the Transition Period* Bukharin discussed the fundamental threshold between state capitalism and the dictatorship of the proletariat with great clarity, but the valid theoretical distinctions were not contrasted with the reality of the Soviet economy in the middle of the Civil War as bureaucratization accompanied the almost complete disappearance of the working class. On one side, argued Bukharin, was the state as 'collective capitalist', organizing the production of 'surplus value, which the state tries to transform into surplus product' through the 'most complete form of the exploitation of the masses'. The dictatorship of the proletariat, on the other side of the threshold, is the 'collectively organized working class' governing a 'production process for the planned satisfaction of social needs'. Forms of state compulsion in the first case are 'a press that assures, broadens and deepens the process of exploitation', where in the second case it is 'a method for the construction of communist society' (Bukharin 1989 [1920], pp. 138–39). While Lenin worried constantly about the bureaucratic distortions of the state (Lewin 1975 [1968]), Bukharin failed to distinguish between the state structure and the 'collectively organized working class' and as time went on and the bureaucracy increasingly differentiated itself from the working class, this became increasingly problematic. Thus Bukharin viewed those features which Lenin presented as regrettable but necessary 'steps backwards' as progressive virtues: the militarization of labour and one-man management were now understood as condensed forms of workers' control of industry (Bukharin 1989 [1920], pp. 142–49; Gluckstein 1994, pp. 41–48). This tendency went so far that Bukharin could later elaborate Stalin's notion of 'socialism in one country' into a theory of autarchic, state led socialist construction, and even when in prison awaiting execution at the end of the 1930s he could write of Stalin's

Five Year Plans as signifying 'organized society, planned society, the manifestation of the collective will of society as the expression of the totality of individual wills' (Bukharin 2005 [1937], p. 191).

When Bukharin made language part of the superstructure, the formulation not only became part and parcel of Marrism, but was also propagated to students specializing in the human and social sciences from the mid 1920s.[6] Language also became a phenomenon that could be rationalized and made efficient for the construction of socialism. While Lenin, Trotsky and others concerned themselves with the propagation of literacy and the scientific organization of labour they did not make these into elements of an all-encompassing cultural revolution that would accompany the building of socialism in one country (see Biggart 1992). Towards the end of the 1920s state research and educational institutions were increasingly expected to justify their programmes in terms of 'service to the state' and so contributing to the 'construction of socialism', which was ever more connected to economic development rather than the broader social good. Funding was made contingent upon meeting these criteria, with research taking the form of collective projects within which individuals specialized, and greater attention on making research relevant to enterprises.

Again it is very easy to exaggerate the exceptionality of this movement. For comparison one need only mention the development of British higher education over the last decade and a half, summed up by Education Minister Charles Clarke in 2003, when he set as one of his three main goals 'better progress in harnessing knowledge to wealth creation' (Callinicos 2006, p. 12). Former Downing Street adviser Charles Leadbeater put it even more starkly: 'Universities should become not just centres of teaching and research but hubs for innovation networks in local economies, helping to spin off companies for universities, for example. Universities should be the open-cast mines of the knowledge economy' (Callinicos 2006, p. 15). It would be more accurate to view the organizational tendency within Soviet research institutions in the late 1920s as pioneering a role for universities akin to that of modern capitalism, where the imperative for capital accumulation trumps all other considerations. Clearing aside the misleading terms in which cold-war rivals posed the issue, we can see that the interpenetration of capital and the state reached its zenith in the USSR and that it has taken some time for the concentration of capital to reach such a level that it is reflected in the organization of higher education as the state stands in to perform the service roles that the private sector can no longer manage alone. The parallels are striking and even trickles down to trends such as encouraging competition between institutions, the lurching from one target to another even if they are inconsistent with each other, the proliferation of 'champions' for this or that management initiative, and the list could go on.

Nor is the narrowing of the ideological field within institutions that clearly took place as a result of these forms exceptional, since recent research has shown that the Research Assessment Exercise in British higher education has led to a decline of 'heterodox economics' in favour of neo-classical economics as university departments seek to maximise submissions to neo-classical journals that forms the 'diamond list' for that discipline (Lee 2007).

Of course, while this has narrowed the autonomy of academics, few British academics would go so far as to argue their work no longer has intellectual validity. For the same reason we should not simplify the ideological imperative in Soviet intellectual life. Just because intellectuals posed their research in the way that they did does not mean that their work can be reduced to such polemical statements.

Like all academic researchers, Soviet scholars were not solely motivated by a disinterested search for truth, but were at least partially oriented toward the acquisition and accumulation of what Pierre Bourdieu calls 'symbolic capital': authority, prestige, recognition, celebrity and the like. What is important for an analysis of intellectual labour in the period is the way in which this capital could be pursued within a specific institutional setting. Throughout most of the 1920s researchers seeking such rewards were compelled to produce works that could validly claim to be more accurate representations of the world than those of their rivals. In short, the institution channelled social competition in such a way that it resulted in epistemic progress. As Bourdieu notes, in the 'scientific field', 'the struggle [for symbolic capital] takes place under the control of constitutive norms of the field and solely with the weapons approved within the field. The propositions engaged in this struggle recognise each other tacitly or explicitly as amenable to the test of coherence and the verdict of experiment' (2000, p. 111). Scientific authority prevailed over statutory authority in determining the distribution of scientific capital. Yet in Soviet Russia relations between the two forms of authority were particularly fraught in the various fields of the social sciences. As a new bureaucratic ruling class crystallised at the end of the 1920s, the existence of competing discourses claiming truth about the social world was bound to make symbolic powers feel threatened. The bureaucracy increasingly wanted such discourses regulated and subordinated to the prerequisites of its own reproduction. As is generally the case, this external demand found supporters within the field, offering their ideological services to the dominant powers in the form of expert committees or 'scientific ideologies'. Others retreated into a formalism that constituted a gilded cage in which they imprisoned themselves, free to say anything as long as they said nothing about anything essential, or said it in such a form that nothing would escape from the closed circle of the initiated.[7] In any case, as the 1920s wore on, the degree of autonomy of the field narrowed, along with the appeal of the various strategies adopted to negotiate scientific and statutory authority.

If, in the 1920s, socio-political changes and ideological commitments drove progressive developments in linguistic theory and practice, the science-ideology configuration took on a very different form with the 'offensive on the cultural front' which accompanied Stalin's 'Revolution from above' 1929–32. This was the period in which Marrism gained the quasi-official status of 'Marxism in linguistics', but this was perhaps only symptomatic of a deeper shift according to which the boundaries of what Bourdieu (1981) has called the 'specificity of the scientific field' was breached. Kapitolina Fedorova analyses the rhetorical strategies deployed by two avowedly Marxist linguists, Polivanov and Georgii Danilov during this period. What emerges is a generational conflict between the former, an adherent to the idea of Marxism and linguistics both being based on general scientific principles, encountering a younger, less well-trained linguist for whom ideological conformity was the touchstone of the superior argument.

Once the Party institutions had annexed the hitherto relatively autonomous state institutions there was no longer a struggle for authority between the two sectors and professional orthodoxies stabilized. Polemics within Soviet academic life now resembled the game of 'blind man's buff' that Gramsci saw the leaders of a 'governing, totalitarian party' carrying out against ever-present heterodox elements that 'cannot be legally coerced' (Gramsci 1971 [1929–35], p. 149). The Party's attempts to root out the remnants of Trotskyism claimed victims from all trends within intellectual life as accusation and counter-accusation led heavy blows to fall unpredictably. While advocates of a scientific approach to Marxism within Soviet scholarship like Polivanov and the head of the Marx and Engels Institute David Riazanov were repressed (Rotikianskii 1992; Ashnin and Alpatov 1997), so were representatives of the new dogmatic polemics Danilov (Ashnin and Alpatov 1994) and Aptekar´ (Anon. 2003). As the simultaneous loss of Danilov and Aptekar´, shot on the very same day, illustrates, the purges claimed Marrists and anti-Marrists alike.

'Speech Culture'

A specific group of articles of the collection are dedicated to the various attempts to transform the public discourse into a national-popular medium in conditions of urbanization and industrial transformation. There were two sides to this programme: the transformation of the language itself in accordance with what Polivanov called its changing 'social substratum', and the spreading of the evolving standard among the population at large. In their contributions, Vladislava Reznik and Michael Gorham discuss the work of perhaps the most theoretically astute champion of the rationalization of the Russian language, Grigorii Vinokur. In his early work, Vinokur made common cause with the Futurist poets, arguing that such poets acted as the innovators of the new language, weeding out archaisms and combating the degeneration of novelty into cliché. For Vinokur, linguistic science should develop into a utilitarian science, with linguistic technicians systematizing and applying the lessons of the Futurists and guiding the rational organization of language. The Futurist-led journal *Lef* ran a series of articles on Lenin's style of argumentation in 1924, analysing the way in which the late leader used language to deflate his opponents' use of obfuscatory abstractions and inflated rhetoric. This launched a whole trend of research aimed at the renewal of the public discourse, learning from the brilliant oratory of the leaders of the Revolution, particularly Trotsky, Anatolii Lunacharskii and V. Volodarskii. Recordings of the orators were studied by research groups at more than one institute, with students prepared according to new specialisms in engineering the public discourse to avoid stale phrasemongering and the organization of discourse for maximum effect on the listener or reader (Brandist 2007; Brandist 2008; Vassena 2007). This was given theoretical expression in the work of Vinokur who strove for a rapprochement between linguistics and philology in the form of 'linguistic culture'. This attempt to develop a discipline that straddles traditional disciplinary boundaries constitutes another example of the way in which early Soviet studies of language anticipated theories of communication that were to emerge in the West only in the latter half of the twentieth century.

If such attention to language emerged from the bounds of philology, this was certainly not the only discipline. The development of applied psychology in Germany and the United States soon found a very original response within the USSR, led by a Jewish polyglot, Isaak Shpil'rein. In his contribution to the volume, Craig Brandist traces the emergence of Soviet industrial psychology or *psychotechnics* and its turn towards the study of assimilation of linguistic categories as a branch of the psychology of influence. Initially viewing psychotechnics as a neutral trend that could serve as a weapon for either the bourgeoisie or proletariat, Shpil'rein led a group of researchers from the Moscow Institute of Psychology to study the way in which Red Army recruits, many of whom were illiterate when recruited, assimilated the standard language and the rudiments of political education through their lessons. Studying the active and passive vocabulary of soldiers at various points throughout their time in the army, the researchers traced how common points of confusion arose, especially as the result of formulaic and mechanical approaches to instruction. While the research was carried out in 1924 and initial results were well-received, the book was only published in 1928, when the context of reception was much less conducive to revelations of an ideological dislocation between the political leadership and the class in whose name they governed. The study thus stands as a fascinating document of the popular linguistic consciousness of the time and the shifting coordinates within which research was conducted and received.

Together these articles constitute a wide-ranging consideration of early Soviet scholarship about language and society that should alert readers to the multifaceted research of the time and the extraordinarily advanced formulations that emerged. They should help to place better into perspective the achievements of certain scholars of the time whose work has been received as mere exceptions, and of the exaggerated novelty of some more recent trends within social and language study. Yet perhaps, more importantly still, it should draw attention to the complex relations between scholarship and ideology in turbulent times, whether in the extraordinary years of the formation of the USSR, or in our own.

References

Ahmad, A. (1992) *In Theory: Classes, Nations, Literatures* (London: Verso).

Alpatov, V.M. (2000) 'What is Marxism in Linguistics?' in Craig Brandist and Galin Tihanov (eds), *Materializing Bakhtin: The Bakhtin Circle and Social Theory* (London: Macmillan) pp. 173–93.

Anon. (2003) 'Aptekar´, Valerian Borisovich (1899–1937)', *Liudy i sud´by*. Online at http://memory.pvost.org/pages/aptekar.html (accessed 20 March 2009).

Ashnin, F.D. and V.M. Alpatov (1994) 'Georgii Konstantinovich Danilov – odin iz pervykh sovetskikh afrikanistov', *Vostok*, no. 2, pp. 115–121.

Ashnin, F.D. and V.M. Alpatov (1997) 'Iz sledstvennogo dela E.D. Polivanova', *Vostok*, no. 5, pp. 124–42.

Biggart, J. (1987) 'Bukharin and the Origin of the "Proletarian Culture" Debate', *Soviet Studies* no. 39(2), pp. 229–46.

Biggart, J. (1992) 'Bukharin's Theory of Cultural Revolution', in A. Kemp-Welch (ed.), *The Ideas of Nikolai Bukharin* (Oxford: Clarendon Press), pp. 131–58.

Bourdieu, P. (1981) 'The Specificity of the Scientific Field', in Charles C. Lemert (ed.), *French Sociology: Rupture and Renewal Since 1968* (New York and Guildford: Columbia University Press) pp. 257–92.

Bourdieu, P. (2000) *Pascalian Meditations* (Stanford: Stanford University Press).

Brandist, C. (2007) 'Konstantin Siunnerberg (Erberg) i issledovanie i prepodavanie zhivogo slova i publichnoi rechi v Petrograde-Leningrade. 1918–1932gg.', *Ezhegodnik rukopisnogo otdela pushkinskogo doma 2003–2004 gody*, (St. Petersburg: Dmitrii Bulanin), pp. 58–82.

Brandist, C. ed. (2008) *Language and Its Social Functions in Early Soviet Thought (Studies in East European Thought*, no. 60(4)).

Brandist, C. (2008) 'Sociological Linguistics in Leningrad: The Institute for the Comparative History of the Literatures and Languages of the West and East (ILJaZV) 1921–1933', *Russian Literature* LXIII-II/III/IV, pp. 171–200.

Bukharin, N.I. (1926 [1921]) *Historical Materialism: A System of Sociology* (London: Allen and Unwin).

Bukharin, N.I. (1989 [1920]) 'Ekonomika perekhodnogo perioda', in *Problemy teorii i praktiki sotsializma*, (Moscow: Izdatel'stvo politicheskoi literatury), pp. 94–176.

Bukharin, N.I. (2005 [1937]) *Philosophical Arabesques* (London: Pluto Press).

Callinicos, A. (2006) *Universities in a Neoliberal World* (London: Bookmarks).

Dittmar, N. (1976) *Sociolinguistics: A Critical Survey of Theory and Application* (London: Edward Arnold).

Edgar, A.L. (2004) *Tribal Nation: The Making of Soviet Turkmenistan* (Princeton and Oxford: Princeton University Press).

Fitzpatrick, S. (1992 [1975]) 'Cultural Orthodoxies Under Stalin', in *The Cultural Front: Power and Culture in Revolutionary Russia* (Ithaca and London: Cornell University Press), pp. 238–56.

Gal, S. and J. Irvine (1995) 'The Boundaries of Languages and Disciplines: How Ideologies Construct Difference', *Social Research*, no. 62(4), pp. 967–1001.

Gluckstein, D. (1994) *The Tragedy of Bukharin* (London: Pluto Press).

Gramsci, A. (1971 [1929–35]) *Selections from the Prison Notebooks* (London: Lawrence and Wishart), pp. 419–72.

Habermas, J. (1990 [1985]) *The Philosophical Discourse of Modernity* (London: Polity Press).

Kagarlitsky, B. (1988) *The Thinking Reed: Intellectuals and the Soviet State 1917 to the Present* (London and New York: Verso).

Koerner, E.F.K. (2002) 'William Labov and the Origins of Sociolinguistics', *Folia Linguistica Historica* XXII (1–2), pp. 1–40.

Lee, F. (2007) 'The Research Assessment Exercise, the State and the Dominance of Mainstream Economics in British Universities', *Cambridge Journal of Economics*, 31, pp. 309–325.

Lenin, V.I. (1972 [1914]) 'The Taylor System—Man's Enslavement by the Machine', in *Collected Works*, (4th English Edition, Moscow: Progress Publishers), Vol. 20, pp. 152–52.

Lenin, V.I. (1972 [1918]a) 'The Immediate Tasks of the Soviet Government', in *Collected Works*, (4th English Edition, Moscow: Progress Publishers), Vol. 27, pp. 235–77.

Lenin, V.I. (1972 [1918]b) 'Session of the All-Russia C.E.C. April 29 1918', in *Collected Works*, (4th English Edition, Moscow: Progress Publishers), Vol. 27, pp. 279–313.

Lewin, M. (1975 [1968]) *Lenin's Last Struggle* (London: Pluto Press).

Lukács, G. (1925) 'Literaturbericht, N. Bucharin, Theorie des historischen Materialismus. Gemeinverständliches Lehrbuch der marxistischen Soziologie, 1922', *Archiv für die Geschichte des Sozialismus und der Arbeiterbewegung*, Jg. 11, pp. 218–24.

Olender, M. (1992 [1989]) *The Languages of Paradise: Aryans and Semites. A Match Made in Heaven* (New York: Other Press).

Polivanov, E.D. (1974) *Selected Works: Articles on General Linguistics* (The Hague: Mouton).

Rokitianskii, Ia.G. (1992) 'Tragicheskaia sud'ba akademika D.B. Riazanova', *Novaia i noveishaia istoriia*, no. 2, pp. 107–48.

Said, E.W. (1995 [1978]) *Orientalism: Western Conceptions of the Orient* (Harmondsworth: Penguin).

Tolz, V. (2006) 'European, National and (Anti-)Imperial: The Formation of Academic Oriental Studies in Late Tsarist and Early Soviet Russia', in Michael David-Fox, Peter Holquist and Alexander Martin, *Orientalism and Empire in Russia*, (Bloomington: Slavica), pp. 107–134.

Vassena, R. (2007) 'K rekonstruktsii istorii i deiatel'nosti Instituta zhivogo slova (1918–1924)' *Novoe literaturnoe obozrenie*, no. 86, pp. 79–95.

Wollard, K.A. (1998) 'Language Ideology as a Field of Inquiry', in B. Schieffelin, K. Woolard and P. Kroskrity, (eds), *Language Ideologies: Practice and Theory*, (Oxford: Oxford University Press), pp. 3–47.

Zhukov, Iu.N. (2008 [2003]) *Inoi Stalin: Politicheskie reformy v SSSR v 1933–1937gg.* (Moscow: Vagrius).

Archival Source (References to fond/opis´/delo/list):

Tsentral'nyi arkhiv literatury i iskusstv, Sankt-Peterburg, fond 288, Institut sravnitel'noi istorii literatury i iazykov Zapada i Vostoka.

Chapter 2

SOVIET LINGUISTICS OF THE 1920s AND 1930s AND THE SCHOLARLY HERITAGE

Vladimir M. Alpatov

In the second decade of the twentieth century two historical events occurred that were quite incommensurable, but which exerted a decisive influence on the development of the study of language in Russia and then the USSR. The first was the February and October Revolutions of 1917 and the social changes that followed in their wake, and the second was the paradigm shift in linguistics, traditionally connected with the publication of Ferdinand de Saussure's *Cours de linguistique générale* (1916), which also first became known in Russia in 1917.

Of course paradigm shifts do not occur all at once. New ideas of one type or another were announced before Saussure, and in Russia many ideas appeared significantly earlier, with the conceptions of Mikolaj Kruszewski and Jan Baudouin de Courtenay proving especially important.[1] Yet in Russia, as in other European countries, the nineteenth-century linguistic paradigm, based on the recognition of historical linguistics is the only scientific method, and the comparative-historical method as the only rigorous method, continued to dominate the discipline until 1917, and in many respects even longer. One example will suffice. In Russia today, and in the USSR before that, courses in contemporary Russian language maintain a leading place in the training of student philologists, who specialize in Russian. Yet Petr S. Kuznetsov recalled that when on completing his postgraduate studies in 1930, he had to teach a course on the contemporary Russian language, he did not know what to do at first. This was because 'both at University, and as a graduate student, "Russian Language" was understood as the history and dialectology of the language' (Kuznetsov 2003, p.199).

The Revolution did soon change the orientation, however. All the tables of rank that existed previously were no longer valid, and many seemed to be inverted. This also applied to the administrative sphere, and to the received system of social values. Even those who had only recently acquired the titles of academicians and professors were soon to bemoan their fate. There is a recent book (Robinson 2004) that contains much information of this type, based on archival materials: the correspondence of the Second Division of the Russian (formerly Imperial) Academy of Sciences, in which specialists of Russian and Slavonic philology were concentrated. The book is marred by an inadequate distance between the author and his 'heroes', and the frequent absence of necessary correctives to their subjective positions, but it is nevertheless a very valuable source of data about the views of scholars of the old school about the political and scientific events of the 1920s and 30s. I will cite just two instances. Vladimir N. Peretts wrote as early as 1918 'there is no chance of struggling with the unenlightened and illiterate people who are convinced that scholarship, especially that about antiquity [*starina*], is a "bourgeois occupation"' (Robinson 2004, p. 26). And here is Boris M. Liapunov in 1923: 'in Petrograd they are installing the little-known Iakubinskii in the department of linguistics and firing the worthy old professors' (Robinson 2004, p. 49).

For scholars of the old school everything associated with the new regime was unacceptable. But the forces ranged against 'the worthy old professors' were not all of a piece. There were some little-educated people who held all scholarship in contempt that were promoted. Yet there were also those, like Lev P. Iakubinskii, a student of Baudouin de Courtenay, and undoubtedly a significant scholar of the new scientific paradigm, that have still not achieved the recognition they deserve (Brandist 2004). Iakubinskii was 31 in 1923, some thirty years younger than Liapunov, but in other social circumstances he would have still been due for advancement up the steps of an academic career. The Revolution changed the whole hierarchy.

The perception of scholarship as a 'bourgeois occupation' and of the 'bourgeois character' of all intellectuals (then called '*Makhaevshchina*'),[2] was sometimes expressed at lower levels, but it was repudiated by the authorities. On the contrary, the authorities talked about the creation of a new society on the basis of science, according to which it was necessary to formulate a 'new science' based on the ideas of Marxism. This applied to all social and human sciences (in the realm of the natural sciences the repudiation of the earlier science proved unproductive and was quickly abandoned), including linguistics. But of what the 'new science' consisted, was not clear, and various answers to this question were possible in the 1920s. This was especially the case with the sciences that were only 'weakly or remained completely untouched by the hands of the founders – Marx and Engels' (Voloshinov 1995 [1929], p. 218), among which was linguistics.

The positive programmes of scholars were sharply divergent. Some, like Nikolai Ia. Marr, supposed they could construct a science of language anew, but nothing could be built from nothing. Others, to one degree or another, began from the new scientific paradigm, which might be called 'structural' (although the term 'structuralism' was not used in the USSR until the late 1950s). There were also scholars of an intermediate type in the 1920s, that refused the demands of historicism and studied the contemporary language, but who remained connected to the old paradigm in crucial ways. To this group one could assign, for instance, Aleksandr M. Peshkovskii, Dmitri N. Ushakov and Mikhail N. Peterson. There were innovators, who did not accept structuralism and looked for other paths. Finally there were linguists of the old paradigm in the full sense of the term.

The differences between scholarly paradigms appeared simultaneously at several points. They appeared in the very thematic of research: the old paradigm was oriented on the past, and the remote past at that. Scholars of the old school worked either on the very ancient, pre-literate epochs if they were trying to reconstruct proto-languages, or the less ancient, though still rather distant past when, through the study of written documents, they sought to re-establish the historical phonetics and the historical grammar of this or that language. Not only the present, but the recent past remained outside their purview: in courses of the history of the Russian language little was said about the eighteenth century and nothing at all about the nineteenth. These periods demanded a completely different approach: in place of philological analysis, historical stylistics and sociolinguistics were needed. A new discipline – the history of the literary language,[3] based on methods other than historical phonetics and grammar, arose in Russian linguistics only in the Soviet era, in connection with the new paradigm. As far as the present was concerned, only dialectology interested linguists of the old school to any extent (hence Kuznetsov's comment, mentioned above), but more often than not it was from the perspective of linguistic relict forms, supplemented with data from written sources. A self-sufficient interest in contemporary dialects appeared in Russia only in the years leading up to the Revolution, among the most advanced linguists of the Moscow School (Ushakov, Nikolai N. Durnovo). Yet all dialectology of that time was characterized by an interest only in those dialectal features that distinguished a given dialect from the literary language, with no attempt to develop a systematic approach. It stands to reason that the dialectology of that time, like philology as a whole, was vulnerable to the attacks on the 'study of antiquity [*starina*]', over which Peretts grieved. The *Zeitgeist* demanded attention be paid to the present, and that coincided with the demands of the new scientific paradigm.

The two paradigms were not only distinguished by their respective theories and methodologies, but also by their very principles of research. In prerevolutionary Russia the usual type of comparativism that one finds today, according to which the scholar reconstructs proto-forms using data from published dictionaries and the grammars of various languages, was not widespread. It was not only historical linguistics proper (by definition connected to philology), that was based on the independently conducted philological analysis of monuments, but also comparative-historical linguistics. Not only linguistics, but also literary studies had philological roots, and the fact that in Russia today we still have philology faculties in universities and doctors of philology teaching in them is a remnant of this. Vladimir Maiakovskii's comments about poetry accurately characterizes the activity of such scholars: 'Just like the mining [*dobycha*] of radium. To gain just a gram you must labour a year'.[4] The interpretation of such mining either occupied a secondary place, or was considered somehow unscientific. Positivism reached a maximum scale among such scholars. But the new paradigm demanded, above all, a new interpretation of accumulated material. The self-sufficient mining of this material was not prohibited, but it ceased to be a requirement.

Iurii N. Tynianov allegedly recalled one of the academic philologists of the 1910s (most likely the same Peretts) calling the work of all those who worked on literature of the eighteenth century and after 'tra-la-la' [*tru-lia-lia*]. Here the stage of 'mining radium' occupied little time or was superfluous, and so working on plots from recent times seemed somehow 'lightweight' and lacking in professionalism to traditional philologists. To Tynianov and his friends in OPOIaZ (among whom were both linguists and literary scholars),[5] the position of the 'old men' seemed like the science of the past. In the field of ancient Russian literature the primary stage of research, the stage of philological analysis, the offering of conjecture, the restoration of the proto-graph, the correction of the mistakes of scribes etc. demanded so much time that they could not understand the significance of people carrying out this stage of study, say poetics: it could only be 'tra-la-la'. Proper literary, as opposed to philological analysis of ancient Russian literature began only in the middle of the twentieth century, with the work of Dmitri S. Likhachev. For Russian literature of the nineteenth century the first stage could be passed through quickly, and textology had long before been detached from everything else. There were analogous processes in linguistics. Kuznetsov remembered that while working in the manuscript section of the Historical Museum in Moscow in 1926 or 1927 he met Academician Aleksei I. Sobolevskii, who greeted him with the words 'You're working on fine things, young man! I wish you luck'; to which Kuznetsov adds 'young scholars worked with ancient manuscripts rarely in those days' (Kuznetsov 2003, p.179). But Kuznetsov, a scholar of the new paradigm, explains that he and his friend Ruben I. Avanesov were interested in manuscripts as a source of information, and that they paid attention only to the historical phonology of the Russian language.

Avanesov's memoires are also instructive in helping to understand the divergence of old and young linguists, in many cases teachers and students:

> The courteous, high-society G[rigorii] A. Il´inskii approached me and said: 'Let me congratulate you on a very interesting paper, but why was it necessary to write such a long paper about a way of speaking that hardly differs from the literary language?'…. 'Because, you know, you could have told us about just a few differences'. It was a conversation between the blind and the deaf, a conversation between people of different generations, who understood the tasks of their science differently: for the inspiration of our work was the need to reveal the system of language in the fullness of its real functioning. (Avanesov 2004, p.16)

Il´inskii belonged to both the old generation and the old school. The situation was more difficult with Afanasii M. Selishchev, as also recorded by Avanesov. On the one hand he was 'the main teacher', 'our favourite', an example in scholarship and life; on the other hand 'he did not understand or accept the new things in linguistics', including phonology. Avanesov recalls that once he even responded to his teacher rudely after he had 'spoken out against our method quite sharply', which he later regretted (Avanesov 2004, p.16).

Of course one must not conflate the scientific and political positions of the scholars of that time. It suffices to mention Nikolai S. Trubetskoi, an innovator in science, and in many ways a revolutionary, who did not accept the new regime and emigrated. There were, nevertheless, correlations. Linguists of the old paradigm almost always also retained their old positions towards the political events in Russia and then the USSR (though only a few of them emigrated). What in individual and exceptional cases was understood as political conformism, was generally connected with their scientific conformity. Nikolai M. Karinskii was one such example, of whom Kuznetsov's assessment is revealing: 'he was not liked', 'he did not act in a straightforward way', 'he tried to keep in step with the times and explain various linguistic facts socially and economically' (Kuznetsov 2003, p.179). Scientific innovators and young scholars quickly took up the new ideas and very often accepted the new regime, which gave them the possibility to advance and disseminate ideas in keeping with their research.

We are here examining only one aspect of the struggle of ideas in Soviet linguistics of the 1920s and 30s, that connected with attitudes towards the old science that was then often called 'bourgeois', and to which contemporary scholarship abroad could be connected. In the first case we are talking about the dominant paradigm in linguistics of the nineteenth century that developed from Franz Bopp, Rasmus Rask and Jacob Grimm, through

August Schleicher to the Neo-grammarians; Russian scholars of the old generation were their followers. However this could also mean other trends in linguistics of that century, especially those connected with developments of the ideas of Wilhelm von Humboldt, and also contemporary 'bourgeois' linguistics, among which the works of Saussure would certainly stand out. Sometimes the question related to more profound problems, for instance there were arguments over the very division of grammar into morphology and syntax, whether it was justified to begin linguistic research with phonetics and then move on to grammar etc.

One can delineate at least four approaches to the heritage of the science of the past that are closely connected to the general positions of this or that linguist.

1. 'According to the Old Books'

Thus was the leader of the old believers, Dosifei, called upon to live in Musorgskii's opera *Khovanshchina*.[6] This was also the point of departure for scholars of the old school, generally belonging to the older generation, although some younger linguists whose intellectual formation had been in pre-revolutionary times, like the aforementioned Il'inskii and Selishchev (the latter sometimes went beyond the limits of the old paradigm thematically, but not methodologically, as in his well-known book *Language of the Revolutionary Epoch*) sided with them.

The basic principles of the approach of these scholars have already been discussed above. They did not see anything in the old paradigm that needed changing, they did not sense its being in crisis that many recognized in the late nineteenth century, and they related to everything that was new negatively, be it the ideas of the Marrists or those of the phonologists, even those of Trubetskoi. Many clear examples of the opinions of these scholars (philologists, often with linguistic inclinations) can be found in the abovementioned book by Robinson. They did not hide their thoughts in discussions with each other. Here is Peretts writing in 1928 about his intellectual development:

I was drawn towards the verbal life [*slovesnost'*] of the people... but it was only when I had assimilated the evolutionary worldview and noticed the close connection between oral tradition and the written word... that I came to the conclusion that before turning to the study of fairytales, epics, popular drama, pantomimes that one should make ones way towards knowledge of the written tradition. So I began to transfer the centre of my attention to the written monuments of ancient Russia, not without the influence of my dear teacher A.I. Sobolevskii. (Robinson 2004, p. 237)

'The verbal life of the people' was not a traditional theme for the old philological paradigm. Yet as we can see from this evidence, the scholar voluntarily rejected investigations along the new path, and crossed to the most traditional field of study: 'written tradition'.

Moving beyond the limits of historical plots provoked censure, even from one's own. Liapunov could not endorse the very theme of Selishchev's book *Language of the Revolutionary Epoch*: 'Despite all my respect for the erudition and the skill in setting out [his findings] so vividly and interestingly, I am forced to think that in choosing this theme the author was guided by practical considerations' (Robinson 2004, p.182). Aleksandr I. Tomson, a student of Filipp F. Fortunatov, and far from the most conservative of linguists of the older generation, worked on experimental phonetics, far from a traditional field for the nineteenth century, was one of the most forward-looking scholars at the end of that century. But in the 1920s and 1930s he clung to the old positions. Thus, in a letter to Liapunov in 1928 he writes: 'Only he who has for years immersed himself in the solving of particular problems and so can speak from experience, and not with the words of others, has the right to reason about general questions' (Robinson 2004, p.153). This is reasoning typical of a positivist-empiricist. Kuznetsov recalls one conversation with Tomson in 1932: 'Talking to him was exclusively rich in content', wherever the interlocutors agreed, for example, in their negative attitude towards Marr, but, continues Kuznetsov, 'we diverged... in our views on phonology', since for Tomson 'work on the phoneme was unnecessary for linguistics and if it did have any right to exist, then it was in psychology' (Kuznetsov 2003, p. 212). Tomson understood phonology as the 'psychophonetics' of Baudouin de Courtenay, which was not recognized by the follower of Fortunatov, and he did not see any advance of this realm of study in the twentieth century.

It is hardly surprising that scholars of the old school could converge with scholarly innovators when it came to evaluations of Marr, who was unacceptable for the 'old men' both politically and scientifically. For Tomson 'the majority of Marr's comparisons' compelled one 'only to begrudge the paper used' (Robinson 2004, p.169–70). But they also hated the ideas of the linguist innovators. In Robinson's book recollections of N.F. Iakovlev or Iakubinskii are negative, and their scholarly views are not touched upon, and the greatest scholar of the time is resented as 'a certain Polivanov' or 'a not unknown Polivanov', who interested the older generation only when he argued against Marr.

The most extreme conservatives like Il´inskii even considered the ideas of scholars who remained within the old paradigm, but who, here and there, moved beyond its limits, like Fortunatov and Aleksei A. Shakhmatov, unacceptable. In his letter to Liapunov in 1929 Il´inskii writes:

> The linguistic reasoning of Fortunatov and especially Shakhmatov has always, and still does give me a repellent impression. I have a profound antipathy towards their *ultraphonetic* direction, in which morphology plays the role of a worn-out 'Cinderella'. Apart from that, I have always been shocked by A.A.'s [Shakhmatov's – V.A.] extreme weakness for complex and entangled constructions. (Robinson 2004, p.157)

It is clear that Il´inskii criticizes his late older colleagues in as much as they approach the new paradigm, which had, at that time, only begun to be worked out. A leaning towards phonetics, that was subsequently reorganized into phonology, 'for complex and entangled constructions', that is all about interpretations going beyond the bounds of the primary work on facts. Of course Tomson could not relate to his own teacher, Fortunatov, so critically but further developments in scholarship aroused his indignation. In 1934 he wrote to Liapunov about Trubetskoi and Vitol´d Ia. Doroshevskii:

> What does this mean? The search for new paths? Those that deliberately avoid digging deeper. There is only one path, it seems to me: weakness. They cannot cope with the preliminary work by studying accumulated data on the history of languages, especially by comparative linguistics, and so instead of digging deeper they either allow historical fantasizing– marasmus [clearly an allusion to Marrists – V.A.], or play – reasoning without history, classification and so on… It is obvious that their strength is exhausted. Instead of the study of real facts we have a grandiloquent, shameless pouring from an empty vessel into a vacant one. (Robinson 2004, p.175)

The 'game', the 'pouring from an empty vessel into a vacant one' is the same as 'tra-la-la'. In criticizing his scholarly opponents, however, Tomson actually enumerates those principles of which he is sure: the necessity of one's own 'study of accumulated data', the compulsory historical approach and support for 'comparative linguistics'. Work with 'accumulated data' but 'according to the old books'.

The fate of those philologists and linguists who strove to preserve the heritage in an inviolable form was not a happy one. Some, like Il´inskii, were shot; others, like Peretts, died in exile; still others, like Selishchev, spent several years incarcerated. Those who avoided arrest (Sobolevskii, Tomson, Liapunov and others) found problems publishing their works, passing on their knowledge, and continually endured a lack of respect towards their activities from those around them. For people who had enjoyed prestige before 1917, and who were often still capable of working, this was hard to bear. These people had outlived their time. But facts are durable, they knew how to collect them, and many of their works are still used today.

2. There is No 'Bourgeois Sociality'

At the other extreme, as far as attitude towards the scholarly heritage goes, was the popular and influential school of Nikolai Marr in the 1920s and 30s. It repudiated all scholarship carried out outside the school, but it is necessary to distinguish between their particularly extreme declarations and the real content of their activities, including those of Academician Marr himself. Not everything was built from nothing, and in Marr's work there were a number of formulations that were far from new, and which most often came from scholarship of the early nineteenth century avoiding later developments in linguistics (Sériot 1999, p.139–67). Yet both Marr and his followers, who were called 'podmarki', were generally people with no linguistic education, who announced they were 'Marxists in linguistics', declaring a complete denial of 'bourgeois Indoeuropeanism' (which is what the Marrists called any study of language except Marr's 'new theory of language', regardless of its method or theme). Marr himself set this tone: 'I know very well those noble, selfless, Indoeuropeanist-linguist workers, among whom Indoeuropean linguistics itself is the flesh and blood of obsolete bourgeois sociality, built on the oppression of the peoples of the East by Europeans and their murderous colonial policy' (Marr 1934 [1924], p.1).

He evaluated Il´inskii's book *Proto-Slavonic Grammar* in a similar vein, not allowing it to be published:

> Il´inskii's work is the result of his many years of work, not going beyond the limits of the school of formal-comparative linguistics in either his material or interests, and standing entirely on the ground of idealist linguistics. As a consequence, Il´inskii's work can in no way be recommended as a practical aid in the study of Slavonic languages, and it is, consequently useless to print it… This book would clearly convince not only the reader with a special interest in language, but even the reader from the masses of the inability of the formal-comparative method to solve the most important problems of linguistics and the hopelessness of the cul-de-sac into which this method has led what is known as 'Slavic studies' [*slavianovedenie*]. (Quoted in Robinson 2004, p.165).

The 'podmarki' also denounced 'formal-comparative linguistics'. The most noise was made by the followers of Marr like Valerian B. Aptekar´, who had no specialist education, or those former members of the old school who had defected to the Marrist camp, the most active of whom was the former director of a pre-revolutionary grammar school Nikolai S. Derzhavin. Here is a comment by Aptekar´ about 'bourgeois linguistics' from 1934: 'At the present time there is nothing that can come from its prolonged and tortured agony. It has to die along with the bourgeois sociality that gave rise to it, clearing the way for the Marxist-Leninist theory of language that is being built in our country' (Aptekar´ 1934, p. 56–7). Aptekar´ even called Saussure the author of 'sacred writing for the contemporary epigones of comparativism' (Aptekar´ 1934, p. 61), and this is what Derzhavin had to say: 'The sunset of the reign of comparativism here is inescapable, it is increasingly turning into scholasticism. It is increasingly becoming locked up in its invented schemes, divorcing the facts of language from its bearer, the person and his life' (quoted in Robinson 2004, p.150). 'It is insufficient to simply be a scholar, one must become a scholar-worker, i.e. a scholar imbued with the ideology of the working class, its urge and its mood, its will unbending before the internal and external difficulties, in order to be able to spread the ideas of manual workers (*orabochit´*) in science (quoted in Robinson 2004, p. 361). Another Marrist, Iosif K. Kusik´ian, wrote in the same spirit: 'The existence of the prejudice that a linguist is one who works on the phonetics and morphology of this or that language has not seemed strange until now, It is necessarily clearly and distinctly to declare that in our situation, it is he who has assimilated the methodology of dialectical materialism that can work in linguistics and even more so, language building' (Kusik´ian 1931, p. 78).

Such scholarly nihilism removed the whole problematic of the scholarly heritage altogether, and could hardly be taken seriously by scholars regardless of their attitude towards Soviet power. Consequently, far from everyone in the Marrist camp thought in this way; the most significant scholars in the camp had a quite different approach, as we shall see from the example of Vasilii I. Abaev.

At the same time, there were some linguists, outside the Marrist camp, who said things that converged with the dilettantes, but who were stressing their loyalty to the authorities, among whom were prominent scholars belonging to the new paradigm. The greatest Russian Mongolist Nikolai N. Poppe wrote in 1933 that Indo-European theory was 'reactionary', and that we have 'other goals and tasks' (Poppe 1933, p. 23). Poppe was an educated and complex scholar, whose research practice was quite unlike such threatening declarations. His later fate puts his sincerity in some doubt, however: in 1942 he defected to Nazi Germany and then emigrated, but in his memoires (Poppe 1983) published in the United Sates in his declining years he spoke out sharply about the Soviet regime.

The fate of Derzhavin was quite different. In the changed social situation of the 1940s he had stopped declaring the 'proletarianization' of science, and was insisting on an attentive attitude toward the heritage of Russian scholarship. There is some evidence that even Marr's attitude to the 'Marxist' components of his theory was not quite as it seemed. Though unconditionally sincere in his belief in his 'Japhetic dawn', when he was abroad he announced: 'when you live among wolves, you have to be like a wolf' (Sköld 1929, p. 84). Authors could make declarations about 'agony' or about 'scholar-workers whether they were quite uneducated, or insincerely and according to convention; the first could contribute nothing positive while the second leaned upon declarations, in their research or otherwise, that repudiated scholarship. Such declarations had only two real results. Firstly, they denied any scholarly critic a position from which to denounce them: this is what Marr did, he could turn around any scientific fact he did not like. Secondly, it was possible to achieve organizational ends, as was the case with the publication of Il'inskii's book. The struggle against 'Indoeuropeanism' was, almost always used as a cudgel that was brought down on the heads of the linguists of the old school in the late 1920s and early 1930s, but scholars working in the new paradigm were on the whole in a better position as long as they did not come into conflict with Marr.

3. The Acceptable and the Unacceptable

For serious scholars of the 'new science', the question of which 'heritage we renounce' and which we retain, was posed quite differently.[7] Some elements that were more or less acceptable could be found in the linguistic trends of the past and/or the present. All such scholars were united in decisively rejecting the linguistic scholarship of the late nineteenth century, including that of pre-Revolutionary Russia: extreme positivism, empiricism, a fear of generalization and 'a worship of "facts", understood as something firm and unshakable', in the words of Valentin N. Voloshinov (1995 [1929], p. 218).

As we have already noted, the idea of a 'new science' could be understood in various ways, and this affected attitudes towards the heritage. Alongside scholars who were inclined to bring Marxism and the new linguistic paradigm together, about whom we shall say more below, were others who pursued other trends, and were receptive to the tradition of von Humboldt. Apart from the already well-known book of Voloshinov (1995 [1929]), one should also mention the works of Abaev that were published in the 1930s, and especially his 1934 article 'Language as Ideology and in a Technical Sense', which has recently been republished as part of a collection of his articles (Abaev 2006).

Abaev was a student of Marr, siding with the Marrists in the 1920s and 30s, but always maintaining his own particular position. He did not reject the structural analysis of language, but regarded it as inadequate since it touched upon only one side of language – 'language in a technical sense'. Apart from language as a technical medium there is also 'language as ideology'. The form of language relates to technical features, while semantics relates both to technical and ideological aspects. Technical semantics answers the question 'what is expressed by this or that element of language?' Ideological semantics, on the other hand, answers the question 'in what way is it expressed? This mode depends on worldview, the ideology of people who are using language (Abaev 2006 [1934], p. 29). By 'language as ideology' Abaev had in mind much of what is now called 'the linguistic picture of the world', an idea that has some affinity with Marrism, but which is to a greater degree based on the ideas of von Humboldt. This approach also conditioned Abaev's stance towards the linguistic heritage.

In an article of 1933 he counterposed the 'initiators': von Humboldt, Bopp, Georg Curtius, August Schleicher to those who have developed linguistics subsequently (excluding, it stands to reason, Marr):

> The scholarship of the initiators is the scholarship of a rising class with the following qualities: courage of thought, breadth of vision, and a highly developed capacity for generalization. Subsequent linguistics, like that of the Neogrammarians and the 'sociological' school (meaning Saussure and Meillet – V.A.) is, on the contrary, the scholarship of a declining class with a type of scholarship that is characterised by an unrestrained tendency towards cowardly and wingless hairsplitting. And when we speak about the bourgeois heritage, for us von Humboldt and Bopp are unconditionally more valuable than Brugman and Meillet, just as in philosophy Hegel is higher than Wundt, in literature Goethe is higher than Meterlinck, in music Beethoven is higher than Strauss. Even given all their muddle, these 'old men' possessed enough breadth and depth of philosophical thought to see that language is a unity, a unity of form and content, having specific qualities and laws... They were thinkers in the full sense and not guild professorial-grammarians.[8] They were not afraid to pose 'fundamental' questions when their research led to these. The Neogrammarians were simply afraid of difficulties, and in order to avoid them, they pronounced that the fundamental questions on which the initiators had bravely worked and thought through either did not exist or, were not the object of linguistics in any case (Abaev 2006 [1933], p. 29).

Abaev linked Saussure with the Neogrammarians and judged him harshly, pronouncing him to be 'prattling on about language being a "social phenomenon"', but unable to understand its nature (Abaev 2006 [1933], p. 19).

Abaev did recognize that the 'initiators' were sometimes inaccurate when dealing with facts and that their work held glaring contradictions, which the Neogrammarians could sometimes correct. In essence he argued that a more accurate description of facts may have no connection with a more accurate explanation. Such a point of view was the diametrical opposite of that of Tomson or Il'inskii. What seemed 'weakness' or 'lightweight' to Tomson or Il'inskii, for Abaev was 'breadth and depth of thought', and what for the former was the only acceptable scholarly method to the former was seen as 'pointless hairsplitting' by the latter. It is worth noting that although Abaev's activity as a linguist was exceptionally long (almost eighty years!), he retained the ideas of his early publications even later. In an article of 1965, for instance, he repeats the same harsh evaluations of the Neogrammarians and Saussure, now adding Louis Hjelmslev and Noam Chomsky, and contrasting them with von Humboldt (Abaev 2006 [1965]).

In general one can say that such an approach fitted and was widespread in the USSR in the 1920s and 30s, and sometimes later. This attitude towards the heritage of the past was modelled on the evaluations by Marx and Engels, who contrasted the politicians and thinkers of the enlightenment and romanticism, when the bourgeoisie was a rising class, with their 'crushed' contemporaries. Such a point of view dominated the history of philosophy throughout the Soviet period; the philosophers preceding Marx and Engels, beginning with the philosophers of antiquity and ending with those immediately preceding Marxism, Hegel and Feuerbach, were always regarded as great thinkers and studied seriously. However, non-Marxist philosophers of a later period were considered ideologists of a 'declining class', and were harshly criticized and slighted. Other advocates of Marxist linguistics, especially the group Iazykfront, compared Hegel and von Humboldt, praising von Humboldt (however the extreme Marrist Aptekar´ demanded the work of von Humboldt also be discarded (Belevitskii 1931, p.13–14)). Abaev's delineation was the most widespread version of such ideas in linguistics.

Voloshinov approached and evaluated the history of linguistics differently, although he also regarded von Humboldt highly.[9] He divided all existing linguistics into 'individualistic subjectivism' and 'abstract objectivism'. The first category included von Humboldt and his followers, especially Karl Vossler, the second category included everyone else (the Neogrammarians are consigned to a category having a 'mixed or compromise character' (Voloshinov 1995 [1929], p. 277), though the features that bring it close to 'abstract objectivism' seem more essential). The majority of schools and trends are only mentioned briefly in the book. In general Saussure's ideas are analysed as the clearest example of 'abstract objectivism', and the ideas of Vossler and his school as an example of 'individualistic subjectivism'.

Voloshinov's assessment of 'abstract objectivism', especially its Saussurean variant, is particularly harsh:

> The problem of the real data of linguistic phenomena, as a specific and unitary object of study is addressed incorrectly. Language as a system of normatively identical forms (Saussure's *langue* – V.A.) can not serve as a basis for understanding and explaining linguistic facts in their life and becoming.... On the contrary, it leads us away from the living, becoming reality of language and its social functions. (Voloshinov 1995 [1929] p. 284).

'Individual subjectivism', above all Vossler's school (there is not a single reference to its founder, von Humboldt) is considered differently. The evaluation of this school is very high, especially given it was losing popularity by 1929. It is called 'one of the most powerful movements in contemporary linguistic thought' (Voloshinov 1995 [1929], p. 316). The Humboldtian trend itself, according to Voloshinov, 'having rejected the route of positivism, has once again achieved a powerful blossoming and breadth in its understanding of its tasks in Vossler's school' (Voloshinov 1995 [1929], p. 262). There is no one among contemporary linguists that is treated more positively in the book (the mentions of Marr may be considered positive, but they are few in number and do not touch upon the basis of his theory).

Such high regard does not indicate a complete acceptance of the ideas of Vossler and Leo Spitzer: such shortcomings as the 'individual' component, an inclination towards the individual psyche and an underestimation of communication and dialogue are recognized. Nevertheless, the verdict is also softened here, 'Certain Vosslerians (Spitzer and Otto Dietrich – V.A.) are beginning to approach the problem of dialogue and, consequently, moving towards a more correct understanding of verbal interaction' (Voloshinov 1995 [1929], p. 311). In his later article 'On the borders of poetics and linguistics', the Vossler school is treated much more critically (Voloshinov 2000 [1930], p. 497–98), but it still stands higher than Saussure's school, which is called 'the most formalistic variety' of 'deeply reactionary thinking' (Voloshinov 2000 [1930], p. 490).

The attempt to mark out the Vossler school among trends within western linguistics (which Vossler himself called idealist) and, moreover, to incorporate their ideas into 'Marxist linguistics' was unique in Soviet linguistics and received support neither from the supporters of Marxist scholarship, nor linguists of the new paradigm.

There were some linguists who thought it necessary to develop a new, Marxist linguistics using the ideas of Saussure, albeit cleansed of their 'idealist' features. Such was the case with the first prominent woman linguist, who was particularly active in the 1920s and 1930s, Rozalia O. Shor. It was on Shor's initiative, and under her editorship, that Saussure's *Cours* was first published in Russia. Her review of Voloshinov's book was characteristic, for here she evaluated the two trends in linguistics in exactly the opposite way to the book she criticized. According to Shor, Vossler's conception is 'an apology for illogicality and irrationality', his ideas are 'radically alien' to us, but many propositions of Saussure irrefutable, and his theory, subject to 'radical restructuring', may be suitable for the construction of Marxist linguistics (Shor 1929, p. 154). However, Shor's commitment to Saussure was combined with an endorsement of Marr's ideas, for which she was criticized by Evgenii D. Polivanov (1931, p. 7–8). One might also mention Aleksandr A. Reformatskii's verdict that Shor 'was by nature an eclectic, flirting with Marrism' (Reformatskii 1970, p. 25).

4. Don't be Obscurantists

The most judicious approach to the problem of the linguistic heritage in those years was offered by the greatest of the Soviet linguists who was striving to construct a Marxist linguistics, Polivanov. He laid out his position on the matter in his speech against Marr in 1929 at the dispute in the Communist Academy, that was published only relatively recently (Polivanov 1991), and in his book (more precisely, a collection of articles) *For a Marxist Linguistics* (Polivanov 1931). First of all, he argued, 'In order to work out a Marxist linguistics, faithfulness and Soviet loyalty are not enough, rather one needs to have linguistic and methodological preparation' (Polivanov 1931, p. 4).

As a counterbalance to the Marrists, who were trying to reject the whole heritage of 'bourgeois scholarship', Polivanov wrote something quite different:

I do not at all deny the bourgeois character of the whole past history of our science. All the science that was created in bourgeois society can be called bourgeois science and may well display internal features of its social nature. But there is no other science but the bourgeois variety, it did not exist at all, and still, even today, does not exist in the west. This applies equally to linguistics, to astronomy, to the theory of probability, to ornithology etc. etc. Our task is as follows: we must be convinced that this or that scientific discipline can establish a series of irrefutable propositions. Once we start to prove to ourselves that this is the case (for which we need particular knowledge from that particular specialism), then we not only can, but must reckon with the undeniable achievements of bourgeois science – and we must do so....We must acknowledge the existence of the microscope, and that whole bacteriological fauna discovered by means of that microscope, even though its inventor (Anthony van Levenhoek – V.A.)

was a Dutch trader, a bourgeois being through and through, who may well be ideologically completely alien to us. If under the pretext that it is a 'product of bourgeois science', we build our own science without all the relevant types of bourgeois-scientific achievements or simply sweep them aside (i.e. not wanting to know) or refuse them (because it is a product of the bourgeois world), we not only do not create any new, our own, science, but simply become obscurantists. This was understood very well by Lenin, who warned against such stubs as proletarian culture and proletarian science. (Polivanov 1931, p.15)

Polivanov thus stood up for the right to utilize the results of comparative linguistics, which was rejected not only by the Marrists in those years: 'The need to mention the comparative method here is simply because it is the most fruitful method for achieving results, and so its significance is real and undeniable' (Polivanov 1931, p.10).

At that very time Polivanov was himself actively pursuing comparative linguistics, striving to broaden traditional research both thematically (the study of familial connections between non-Indoeuropean languages) and methodologically (inner reconstruction, the development of typology as a 'compass' in the search for relations), and leading on to broader conclusions. He also observed that Marxist linguistics has to take account not only of the factual results of 'bourgeois science', but also its methods and theoretical approaches. 'One may consider linguistics already to be a materialist [science] from the time of Schleicher' (Polivanov 1991, p. 537). 'I would not say that the best of our linguists of the last generation were entirely silent about the social aspect [of language]' (Polivanov 1991, p. 539). Among the scholars who in one way or another examined this aspect of language he nominated Saussure, Meillet, Charles Bally, Joseph Vendryes, Otto Jespersen, and Vossler (Polivanov 1968, p.184). This includes almost all the most prominent western scholars of the time who went beyond the framework of the Neogrammarians. He had paid attention to 'several sociological schools of contemporary western-European and American linguistics' (including Saussure's school), 'which *could be useful* for the construction of Marxist linguistics' (Polivanov 1931, p. 3). One thus needs to look for points of convergence with a wide variety of approaches and not with just one of them.

Unlike Shor, however, Polivanov did not regard Saussurean linguistics as the most essential. Following on from the above quotation about the various schools of linguistics, he writes:

But it does not follow that one should exaggerate the importance of the sociological trend in foreign linguistics, and it especially does not follow, in the USSR, where the previous generation left us a much more valuable heritage in the abovementioned sense, than the contemporary west... Saussure's posthumous book, which was seen as a discovery, contained literally nothing new in the posing and broadening of general linguistic problems in comparison with what long ago was obtained by Baudouin de Courtenay and his school. (Polivanov 1931, p. 3–4)

Though Baudouin de Courtenay was not a Marxist while his student Polivanov fought for a Marxist linguistics, many of the latter's works bear the marks of the influence of his teacher, and he always acknowledged that fact. The Baudouin de Courtenay school continued to develop in the 1920s and 30s, and even later, to which belonged Lev V. Shcherba, Iakubinskii and Boris A. Larin. Of these it was probably Polivanov who remained most faithful to his teacher, while striving to go further.

Thus, some scholars of the 1920s and 1930s regarded the science of the nineteenth century as an indisputable authority and did not want to change any of its principles. Others rejected this scholarship in its entirety. A third group divided this scholarship into more or less 'correct' trends, taking account of some ideas and completely rejecting others. A fourth group, like Polivanov, singled out something valuable in a wide variety of linguistic trends and tried to use it for the development of a new conception. We can now see that this last approach was the most productive in scholarly terms.

Translated by Craig Brandist.

References

Abaev, V.I. (2006 [1933]) 'O foneticheskom zakone', in *Stat'i po teorii i istorii iazykoznaniia* (Moscow: Nauka), pp.16–26.

Abaev, V.I. (2006 [1934]) 'Iazyk kak ideologiia o iazyk kak tekhnika', in *Stat'i po teorii i istorii iazykoznaniia* (Moscow: Nauka), pp. 27–44.

Abaev, V.I. (2006 [1965]) 'Lingvisticheskii modernizm kak degumanitatsiia nauki o nauke', in *Stat'i po teorii i istorii iazykoznaniia* (Moscow: Nauka), pp.108–31.

Alpatov, V.M. (2005) *Voloshinov, Bakhtin i lingvistika* (Moscow: Iazyki slavianskoi kul'tury).

Aptekar', V.B. (1934) *N.Ia. Marr i novoe uchenie o iazyke* (Moscow: AN SSSR).

Avanesov, R.I. (2004) 'Vladimir Ivanovich Sidorov' in S.N. Borunova and V.A. Plotnikova (eds) *Otsy i deti Moskovskoi lingvisticheskoi shkoly* (Moscow: Institut russkogo iazyka), pp. 13–19.

Belevitskii, S (1931) 'O chëm shël spor?', *Iazyk i revoliutsiia*, no. 1, pp.11–20.

Brandist, C. (2004) 'Voloshinov's Dilemma: On the Philosophical Roots of the Dialogic Theory of the Utterance', in C. Brandist, D. Shepherd and G. Tihanov (eds.), *The Bakhtin Circle: In the Master's Absence* (Manchester: Manchester University Press), pp. 97–124.

Iartseva, V.N. (ed., 1990) *Lingvisticheskii entsiklopedicheskii slovar'*, (Moscow: Sovetskaia entsiklopediia).

Kusik'ian, I.K. (1931) 'Ocherednye zadachi marksistov-iazykovedov v stroitel'stve iazykov narodov SSSR', *Prosveshchenie natsional'nostei*, nos. 11–12, pp. 72–79.

Kuznetsov, P.S. (2003) 'Vospominaniia', *Moskovskii lingvisticheskii zhurnal*, no. 7(1), pp.155–250.

Marr, N.Ia. (1934 [1924]) 'Ob iafeticheskoi teorii', in *Izbrannye raboty* vol. 3 (Moscow and Leningrad: Gosudarstvennoe sotsial'no-ekonomicheskoe izdatel'stvo), pp.1–34.

Polivanov, E.D. (1931) *Za marksistskoe iazykoznanie* (Moscow: Federatsiia).

Polivanov, E.D. (1968 [1929]) 'Krug ocherednykh problem sovremennoi lingvistiki' in *Stat'i po obshchemu iazykoznaniiu* (Moscow: Nauka), pp.178–86.

Polivanov, E.D. (1991) 'Problema marksistskogo iazykoznaniia i iafeticheskaia teoriia' in *Trudy po vostochnomu i obshchemu iazykoznaniiu* (Moscow: Nauka), pp. 508–42.

Poppe, N.N. (1933) *Lingvisticheskie problemy Vostochnoi Sibiri* (Moscow and Irkutsk: AN SSSR).

Reformatskii, A.A. (1970) *Iz istorii otechestvennoi fonologii* (Moscow: Nauka).

Robinson, M.A. (2004) *Sud'by akademicheskoi elity: Otechestvennoe slavianovedenie (1917-nachalo 1930-kh godov)* (Moscow: Indrik).

Sköld, H. (1929) *Zur Verwandtschaftslehre: die Kaukasische Mode* (Lund: Hakan Ohlsson).

Sériot, P. (1999) *Structure et totalité. Les origins intellectuelles du structuralisme en Europe central et orientale* (Paris: Presses universitaires de France).

Shor, R.O. (1929) 'Retsenziia na knigi Voloshinova, *Marksizm i filosofiia iazyka*', *Russkii iazyk v sovetskoi shkole*, no. 3, pp.152–4.

Voloshinov, V.N. (1995 [1930]) 'O granitsakh poetiki i lingvistiki' in M.M. Bakhtin, *Freidizm: Formal'nyi metod v literaturovedenii: Marksizm i filosofiia iazyka: Stat'i* (Moscow: Labirint), pp. 487–514.

Voloshinov, V.N. (1995 [1929]) 'Marksizm i filosofiia iazyka' in *Filosofiia i sotsiologiia gumanitarnykh nauk* (St. Petersburg: Asta Press), pp. 216–380.

Chapter 3

'SOCIOLOGY' IN SOVIET LINGUISTICS OF THE 1920–30s: SHOR, POLIVANOV AND VOLOSHINOV

Mika Lähteenmäki

1. Introduction

By the late 1920s the idea that language is a social phenomenon and various linguistic phenomena can be given a sociological explanation had become a commonplace in Soviet linguistics. Several reasons for the 'sociological turn' can be found. Firstly, the dramatic social and economic changes caused by the Revolution were reflected in the Russian language, thus making it evident that language and society are intimately connected. Secondly, many Soviet linguists – like scholars in other academic disciplines too – felt the urge to develop a new Marxist approach to the study of language as opposed to earlier 'bourgeois' theories of language (for discussion, see Alpatov 2000, Brandist 2005). In most cases the growing interest in 'the questions of language and society' meant the study of social dialects and linguistic changes that took place in the Russian language after the Revolution. Thirdly, linguistics became a socially significant discipline in the construction of the new Soviet state, because many linguists were engaged in the creation of alphabets for different languages which did not hitherto have a written form. Fourthly, one certainly should not underestimate the role of the 'climate of opinion' (see Koerner 1987) – the special emphasis on language as a social fact at the beginning of the 20th century – in the formation of the early Soviet sociology of language.

The early sociological approach to the study of language is frequently – albeit mistakenly – equated with the idea of the class character (*klassovost´*) of language only (see Desnitskaia 1974). It is based on the assumption that language is a superstructural phenomenon which, either directly or indirectly, reflects the characteristics of the socioeconomic basis. The most radical version of the idea of the class-nature of language was held by Nikolai Marr

(1864–1934) who maintained that the class-structure of a given society determines not only the social stratification of a language but also its actual linguistic structures and typological features. However, while many linguists subscribed to the idea of the class-character of language, they did not accept Marr's extreme position. As emphasised by Viktor Zhirmunskii (1891–1971), the idea of the class-character of language was endorsed 'simultaneously with Marr and independently of him' (Zhirmunskii 1964, p. 101) by many contemporary linguists including Zhirmunskii himself who held more refined views regarding the interconnectedness of language and society (see, Zhirmunskii 1936).

The present article examines the development of the concept of 'sociology' and its different understandings in the new intellectual and ideological climate of Soviet linguistics in the late 1920s and early 1930s. It focuses on Rozaliia Shor's (1894–1939) (re)interpretation of Ferdinand de Saussure (1857–1913) and the French sociological school, Evgenii Polivanov's (1891–1938) views on the social nature of language evolution and Valentin Voloshinov's (1895–1936) sociological approach to the study of language. The aim of the discussion is to demonstrate that irrespective of the sometimes dogmatic nature of the construction of a Marxist linguistics in the Soviet context, there existed a diversity of views regarding language and the role of 'sociology' in the description and explanation of linguistic phenomena which differ from the dominant view according to which the 'social' would amount to *klassovost'*.

2. Sociology and Soviet Marxism

From the mid-1920s many Soviet linguists took it for granted that language is a social phenomenon which has to be studied using a sociological methodology. Irrespective of the apparent consensus regarding the very nature of language, there was no unanimity regarding what kind of sociology linguistics should be based on. The situation did not change much even in the late 1920s and early 1930s when Marr's 'New Theory of Language' became the dominant trend in Soviet linguistics. In most cases authors who insisted on the necessity of a sociological account of language were not explicit about what they actually meant by 'sociology'. Accordingly, the notion of sociology remained implicit, and their theoretical background assumptions have to be extrapolated from their characterisations of the relation between language and society. This also holds true of those linguists who were actively engaged in the creation of new 'Marxist linguistics'. As Vladimir Alpatov (2002) has pointed out, in the 1920–30s Soviet linguists developing a sociological approach to the study of language held different political views and the degree in which they were actually committed to Marxism varied significantly.

That many linguists failed to explicate their understanding of 'sociology' or 'Marxist sociology' may, at least in part, be explained by the fact that in the 1920s, the history of sociology as an independent academic discipline was still relatively short. For instance, Emile Durkheim (1858–1917) who is generally considered as one of the founding fathers of classical sociology was the first professional French sociologist and was appointed to a Chair of Sociology in Paris in 1913. As regards the institutional status of sociology in Russia, at the beginning of the 20th century sociology was not taught as an independent subject in Russian universities and there was only one chair of sociology, at the Psycho-Neurological Institute in St. Petersburg (Weinberg 2004, p. 1). This did not mean, however, that Russian intellectuals would have been ignorant of the contemporary developments in the Western sociological thought. On the contrary, thanks to extensive translation of the works of various German, French, British and American sociologists, the ideas discussed by the representatives of Western sociology exerted significant influence on the formation of sociology in Russia (Weinberg 2004, p. 1). The institutional status of sociology was gradually consolidated, and by the late 1910s sociology had become a more or less independent academic discipline in Russian universities, which increasingly offered special courses to university students.

After the October Revolution, the understanding of the concept of sociology, as well as the institutional status of the discipline, were bound to change. However, the Revolution did not have an instant effect on sociology. Earlier 'bourgeois' sociological theories were replaced by a Marxist theory of society only gradually and the institutional status of sociology in Soviet-Russian universities did not change instantly (Weinberg 2004, p. 4). The Soviet regime was well aware of the acute demand for specialists in Marxist philosophy, and in order to rectify this problem several new educational establishments were founded, including The Communist Academy (1918) and The Institute of Red Professors (1921). A key figure in the development of Soviet Marxism and historical materialism was Nikolai Bukharin (1888–1938) who had been characterised by Lenin as 'a most valuable and major theorist of the Party' whose 'theoretical views can be classified as fully Marxist only with great reserve'[1] (Lenin 1966 [1922], p. 595). Bukharin's influential 1921 textbook *Teoriia istoricheskogo materializma* which went through several editions became a central work on Soviet Marxism, and its ideas were widely discussed until the early 1930s.

For the purposes of the present article, it is important that in his discussion of the place of sociology among other academic disciplines Bukharin identified historical materialism with Marxist sociology: 'it is the general theory of society and the laws of its evolution, *i.e.*, sociology' (Bukharin 1969 [1921], p. 15).

In his attempt to transform historical materialism into Marxist sociology Bukharin drew from various sources including Max Weber (1864–1920), George Simmel (1858–1918), Robert Michels (1876–1936) and Aleksandr Bogdanov (1873–1928). He subscribed to a mechanistic view of society according to which the system generated by the natural socioeconomic laws dominates the individual who is given a passive role (Swingewood 1984, p. 219). Bukharin's theory of social equilibrium was influenced by Bogdanov's tektology *inter alia* in that both Bukharin and Bogdanov argued for a 'systems approach' that would abolish the barrier between natural and social sciences (Susiluoto 1982, p. 80). Thus, following Bogdanov Bukharin maintained that sociological phenomena are governed by laws akin to natural laws from which it follows that they can be explained and predicted by using the methods of natural sciences.

In his discussion of the relation between the socioeconomic basis and the superstructure Bukharin maintained that all societies develop according to natural socioeconomic laws and the changes in the socioeconomic basis of a society causally effect the superstructure, which refers to all social phenomena 'erected on the economic basis' including such established systems of ideology as art, religion and science as well as non-systematised everyday thoughts and feelings belonging to social psychology (Bukharin 1969 [1921], p. 208). Although superstructural phenomena are determined by the socioeconomic characteristics of a society, Bukharin carefully emphasised that the superstructure also reflects back and exerts influence on the socioeconomic basis (Bukharin 1969 [1921], p. 228). Thus, on one hand, changes in the superstructure can be seen as effects caused by changes in socioeconomic factors and productive forces of a particular society, but, on other hand, superstructural phenomena can have a causative effect on the socioeconomic basis.

Bukharin's views on the evolution and functions of language were influenced by the philologist Ludwig Noiré (1829–1889) who had been characterised by Bogdanov as 'a Marxist of comparative philology having no idea of Marxism' (Bogdanov 1995 [1918], p. 245). As its title suggests, Noiré's *Der Ursprung der Sprache* (1877) dealt with the question of the origin of human language and the author emphasised the fundamental role of labour and goal-oriented social activity in the development of language. In addition to Bukharin, Georgii Plekhanov (1856–1918) and Bogdanov, Noiré's linguistic ideas were well-known among Soviet linguists in the 1920–30s and influenced, for instance, Marr's views on the development of human language. Bukharin emphasised the social origin of human language and was first to allocate it – together with thought – to the superstructure, characterising them as 'the most abstract ideological categories of the superstructure' (Bukharin 1969 [1921], p. 203). According to him, language 'grows out of production, develops under the influence of the social evolution, *i.e.*, its evolution is determined by the natural law of social evolution' (Bukharin 1969 [1921], p. 228). Thus, he subscribed to a deterministic stance according to which there are natural laws governing social and economic development which are causally effective at the level of superstructure. As regards the interrelation of language and thought, Bukharin (1969 [1921], p. 204) defined thought as 'speech minus sound' and insisted that thought is equally social in its nature and its development cannot be separated from the development of human language. For him, the social nature of thought is based on the assumption that processes of thinking are symbolic activity and symbols are, by definition, social. Bukharin characterised the act of thinking as 'combining concepts' which are represented in the form of word symbols (Bukharin 1969 [1921], p. 204). This clearly suggests that thought is not based on abstract universal categories, but on categories provided by the language spoken in this or that society at a given stage of its socioeconomic development. This view was then developed into the idea of the class-character of language endorsed by many Soviet linguists.

Despite Bukharin's central role, his mechanical views and scientism were criticised both in the West and the Soviet Union. Western critics of Bukharin included Antonio Gramsci (1971) and Georg Lukács the latter of whom argued that Bukharin's view of sociology as science is undialectical and close to 'bourgeois, natural-scientific naturalism' (Lukács 1966, p. 29). In the Soviet Union the critique of Bukharin's views reached its culmination during the discussion between the 'mechanists' and 'dialecticians' which broke out in the mid-1920s (see Iakhot 1991).[2] The 'dialecticians', represented by Abram Deborin (1881–1963) and his followers, gained victory over the 'mechanists' in a long-lasting battle at the Second All-Union Conference of Marxist-Leninist Scientific Institutes that took place at the Communist Academy in 1929. Unlike Bukharin who identified Marxist sociology with historical materialism, the Deborinites subscribed to a Hegelian interpretation of dialectical materialism and insisted that historical materialism is to be seen as a constitutive element of dialectical materialism only. In distinction from the 'mechanists' according to whom philosophical principles are generalisations based on the results of special – mainly natural – sciences, the 'dialecticians' saw historical materialism as a set of abstract logical categories that constitutes the methodology of sociology. Despite the victory of Deborinites in 1929, the discussion of the status of historical materialism and the Marxist understanding of sociology continued in 1930–1931 when Deborin was accused of Hegelianism and 'menshivising idealism'. The fact that Marxist theorists were unable to decide whether Marxist sociology amounts to a theory or methodology and to define the relation of historical materialism and Marxist sociology may explain why the representatives of the early Soviet sociology of language felt reluctant to define their notion of sociology in positive terms.

3. Shor and the French School of the Sociology of Language

In the mid-1920s when the need for a new sociological approach to the study of language became urgent, the ideas of the representatives of the French sociology of language were regarded as a potential basis for the further development of the sociology of language in the Soviet context. The significance of the French linguistic tradition for the formation of the early Soviet sociology of language has been emphasised by Agniia Desnitskaia (1981, 1991) according to whom Antoine Meillet's (1866–1936) *Linguistique historique et linguistique générale* was widely read in the 1920–30s (Desnitskaia 1991, p. 478). On the other hand, Desnitskaia (1981, p. 82) points out that the interest of Soviet linguists was directed mainly to the concrete linguistic material presented in Meillet's book, while his theoretical considerations based on Durkheimian sociology did not arouse significant interest among Soviet linguists.

Among linguists inspired by the French sociological school was the Moscow-based linguist Shor who discussed and popularised Saussure's and Meillet's linguistic views in her writings. The aim of Shor's 1926 book *Iazyk i obshchestvo* ('Language and Society') is, in her own words, to give an account of the 'latest achievements of the Western scientific thought in the area of sociology of language'. Her account of the general linguistic theory was based on the works of Saussure, Meillet, Charles Bally (1865–1947) and Edward Sapir (1884–1939). Shor's book was written according to a popular-scientific genre and, therefore, does not represent a detailed and critical discussion of the ideas of the above-mentioned linguists, but amounts to a rather general and positive sketch of their ideas.

After giving numerous concrete examples of language change and social differentiation within different languages Shor (1926, p. 140) argues that the social and cultural-historical nature of the linguistic sign makes it possible to give a common causal explanation of the various changes that take place in a language. When language is seen as a social fact, it follows that language changes cannot be explained by psycho-physiological or physical laws, as was assumed earlier, but by referring to other social facts only. For Shor (1926, p. 141), the most important factor explaining a language change is the structure of society, because any change in the structure of a society will necessarily – either directly or indirectly – cause a change in language. It should be pointed out that Shor's account is non-Marxist in the sense that she does not try to explain the interrelation of the structure of a society and language in terms of the interaction between the socioeconomic basis and the superstructure, as in the case of Bukharin. On the contrary, Shor seems to subscribe to Durkheim's realist view according to which social structures – which may not be directly observable– underlie social action and are causally effective exerting coercive power on the behaviour of individuals. This suggests that she finds Saussure's position according to which language is 'a product inherited from preceding generations' which cannot be modified at will (Saussure 1959 [1915], p. 71) perfectly plausible. A similar characterisation of the significance of Saussure is given by another Moscow linguist Mikhail Peterson (1885–1962) in his 1927 article *Iazyk kak sotsial'noe iavlenie* ('Language as a Social Phenomenon') in which he argues that Saussure managed to establish the social nature of language as well as the dependence of the language change on social factors (Peterson 1927, p. 9).

It is noteworthy that while the reception of Saussure's and Meillet's ideas by Shor and Peterson was mainly positive, linguists based in Leningrad were less convinced about the theoretical novelty and significance of Saussure's and Meillet's works. According to Lev Shcherba (1880–1944), many ideas discussed in Saussure's seminal book had already been well-known to Leningrad linguists from the writings of Jan Baudouin de Courtenay (1845–1929) and, for them, Saussure's ideas seemed less groundbreaking than to Shor and Peterson (Shcherba 2004 [1945], p. 49). Exactly the same point was made by another student of Baudouin, namely Polivanov who emphasised that main ideas of the European and American sociological schools had been anticipated by Baudouin de Courtenay (Polivanov 1931, p. 3–4). It should be emphasised that Shor's and Peterson's early accounts of Western sociological linguistics were by no means enthusiastic. For instance, Peterson concludes his article *Iazyk kak sotsial'noe iavlenie* by saying that the sociology of language has not been adequately developed, and rightfully (Peterson 1927, p. 18). What they basically argued – together with Polivanov – was that contemporary achievements in Western sociology of language might be fruitful for the further development of the sociological approach to the study of language. However, in her later writings, Shor took an extremely critical attitude towards the representatives of the French sociology of language as well as towards those who had popularised their ideas in the Soviet Union, including her own 1926 book *Iazyk i obshchestvo*.

While Shor's earlier works did not make explicit pretences to constituting a Marxist linguistics, in her 1931 booklet *Na putiakh k marksistskoi lingvistike* ('Ways to Marxist Linguistics') she criticised representatives of contemporary Soviet linguists for their unorthodox Marxist views and also made concessions to Marr's 'New Theory of Language'. In this work, Shor critically examines the problem of the 'bourgeois heritage' in linguistics and also pays attention to the role of 'bourgeois sociology' in contemporary developments in Soviet linguistics. Unlike Desnitskaia, who argued that the theoretical contribution of the French sociological school remained rather insignificant, Shor (1931, p. 18) insisted that Saussure's theory of language which can be characterised as a manifestation of Durkheim's sociological ideas in linguistics was influential and attracted many

Soviet linguists with its tendency towards sociologism.[3] Among the followers of Saussure she mentions Peterson, Grigorii Vinokur, Ian Loia and criticises her own 1926 book which, in her own words, was 'an eclectic construction with obvious concessions to the un-Marxist and un-dialectical understanding of the society and class' (Shor 1931, p. 27). While in her earlier writings Shor saw Saussure's theorising on language as an important contribution, in 1931 she was more sceptical about the potential of 'bourgeois sociology' represented by the Swiss linguist and his followers: 'No, it is necessary to rebuild from the very beginning, from the very foundations!' (Shor 1931, p. 30).

The critique of Saussure in Shor's later writings was most likely conditioned by the First Five-Year Plan (1928) and the 'ideological offensive' which had profound social and cultural ramifications in the quest for orthodox dogma in different disciplines. This is supported by the fact that later in the 1930s she promoted the translation of works by Saussure, Meillet, Joseph Vendryes (1875–1960), and Sapir despite her earlier criticism of Western 'bourgeois' linguistics.[4] It is likely that Shor's criticism of Saussure's 'sociologism' may have also been motivated by the contemporary critique directed against Durkheim's view of society as an abstract holistic entity which is not divided into social classes. Shor argued that by reducing 'sociological' to 'collective-psychological' Saussure repeats Durkheim's mistakes by isolating language from its social basis and studying it as an abstract social entity (Shor 1931, p. 19). Quoting F. Telezhnikov, a contemporary Soviet critic of Durkheim's sociology, Shor (1931, p. 19) pointed out that while Durkheim succeeded in establishing a causal link between a particular social phenomenon and the social environment, he ignored the causal relation between the productive forces and social phenomena. What is more, it is easy to see that there was a gradual shift in her writings towards Marr's ideas and even his rhetorical strategies and the style of argumentation, which is explained by the fact that the position of Marrists had become significantly stronger in Soviet linguistics by 1931. While in her 1930 review of the collection *Iafetidologiia i marksizm* ('Japhetidology and Marxism') Shor (1930, p. 201) still argued that Marr's definition of 'class' was un-Marxist and the class-language is mistakenly equated with group-language, which also was a common mistake in the Western sociology of language, only a year later she stated that 'the most serious and original constructions in the area of material linguistics we find in the works of the Academician N. Ia. Marr' (Shor 1931, p. 27).

4. Polivanov: The Social Dimension of Language Evolution

While Polivanov has generally been regarded as one of the most important names in the history of Soviet linguistics, the linguistic ideas of the convinced Marxist and member of the Communist Party were criticised as non-Marxist, especially after the notorious 'Polivanov discussion' that took place in Moscow at the Communist Academy in February 1929 (see Polivanov 1991a [1929]). As regards his own evaluation of Soviet linguistics, in 1928 he wrote that 'some of our linguists have mastered Marxist ideology and Marxist methods of research' (1974a [1928], p. 57), while in the preface to *Za marksistskoe iazykoznanie* (For Marxist Linguistics), which appeared three years later, Polivanov stated that to date there is no such a thing as Marxist linguistics. He also made a distinction between 'Marxist linguistics' and 'materialistic linguistics' arguing that linguistics since August Schleicher can be characterised as materialistic, while Marxist linguistics is based on the use of the categories of historical or dialectical materialism in the interpretation of linguistic facts (Polivanov 1991a [1929], p. 537). In his view, the development of a Marxist approach to the study of language must be based on a proper linguistic and methodological training which allows one to elicit objective linguistic facts which must *then* be given a Marxist interpretation. According to Polivanov, linguistic research must be based on a careful analysis of facts, while 'a linguist can approach the research material without thinking altogether what Marxism has to say about it'(Polivanov 1991a [1929], p. 512).

Unlike Marrists who attacked earlier linguistic traditions and thought that the construction of a Marxist linguistics must start from the denouncement of the achievements of 'bourgeois linguistics' or 'Indo-Europeanism', Polivanov emphasised that a Marxist approach must be based on 'indubitable facts and premises which are given by linguistics as a natural science' (Polivanov 1974d [1929], p. 177). Thus, Polivanov did not see the earlier historical-comparative and Neo-Grammarian schools and a new Marxist approach as mutually exclusive, but insisted that in linguistics there cannot be 'assertions opposing Marxism' and 'the results attained by linguistics as a science of natural history remain completely acceptable for the representative of Marxist ideology as well' (Polivanov 1974a [1928], p. 57).

In Polivanov's view, the primary task of Marxist linguistics was the study of the social dimension of language which had been neglected by the earlier linguistic tradition focusing on language as a natural historical phenomenon. Marxist linguistics cannot be identified with 'materialistic linguistics' as Marrists maintained, but it amounts to 'sociological linguistics' which – together with natural historical approaches – provides a better understanding of the nature of linguistic evolution. According to Polivanov, language should be studied as a collective work activity and described 'from the point of view of the general number of consciousnesses for which the given system to some degree or another is identical'(Polivanov 1974c [1929], p. 170). Here, we find an interesting combination of Noiré's views on the role of labour in the evolution of human languages and Saussure's idea that social langue is not complete in any individual, but 'exists perfectly only within a collectivity' (Saussure 1959, p. 14).

While Polivanov saw historical-comparative and Neo-Grammarian schools as invaluable sources of linguistic facts, he was more sceptical regarding the potential role of the contemporary Western sociological approaches in the development of a Marxist linguistics. On the one hand, Polivanov admitted that in European and American linguistics there existed several sociological schools which 'might be useful' for the development of Marxist science of language', although language has, as a rule, been studied 'as a property of some kind of abstract individual' apart from the collective which uses the language (Polivanov 1974d [1929], p. 175). On the other hand, he carefully emphasised that their significance should not be exaggerated. For Polivanov, the European and American sociological schools were not particularly novel and insightful, because most of the general linguistic problems discussed by their representatives had already been elaborated by Russian and Polish linguists (Polivanov 1931, p. 3)[5]. Polivanov held that the general linguistic tradition – represented e.g. by Baudouin de Courtenay – may turn out to be more fruitful for the development of a Marxist approach to the study of language (Polivanov 1931, p. 4). Thus, he concluded that from the fact that a theory of language calls itself a sociological theory it does not automatically follow that it would contribute to the development of a Marxist linguistics (Polivanov 1974d [1929], p. 197).

In Polivanov's view the social nature of language has important bearings regarding the explanation of linguistic facts. In his view, language evolution is a teleological process and the possibility of teleological explanation is based on the social nature of language (Polivanov 1974d [1929], p. 173). From the teleological nature of language evolution it follows that in addition to linguistic facts of the preceding generations, which are considered as causes of the evolution, one is also allowed to refer to 'the necessary consequences dictated to the given chronological stage of the language by facts of the economic order' (Polivanov 1974d [1929], p. 173) in the explanation of language evolution. That Polivanov accepts the existence of teleological processes in language evolution and sees a particular stage in the development of a language as the *telos* sets him apart from Bukharin (1969 [1921], p. 30) according to whom the development of social and natural phenomena is based on causal laws, while teleological explanations amount to 'expressions of religious belief and cannot explain anything'.

Despite the fact that Polivanov acknowledged the importance of socioeconomic factors in language evolution, he also emphasised that Marxist linguistics is not exhausted by establishing the pragmatic dependence between economic and linguistic facts which belong to the superstructure (Polivanov 1991b [1929], p. 560). In his view, it would be possible – even in principle – to establish a correlation between the socioeconomic situation of a society and concrete linguistic facts. Polivanov also rejected the notion of class language or class dialect endorsed by 'vulgar sociologists' and preferred a more neutral term 'dialect of a social group'. Polivanov compared 'vulgar' sociological explanations which aim to reduce linguistic facts into the socioeconomic characteristics of a society to those racial theories which tried to explain the characteristics of German phonetic system in terms of the national psychology of the German nation (Polivanov 1974d [1929], p. 174). In Polivanov's view, the influence of socioeconomic factors on language is causal but still indirect: various social changes affect the contingent of language users, that is, the social substratum of a particular language or dialect (Polivanov 1974b [1931], p. 90). The change in the social substratum, in turn, affects the communicative needs of a community which will finally result in a language change.[6]

Thus, Polivanov saw language as simultaneously a both natural historical and social phenomenon, which means that language evolution is governed by both natural historical and socioeconomic laws. Natural historical laws, for instance, sound-laws are intrinsically linguistic laws, while socioeconomic laws are extra-linguistic and thus can affect language only indirectly by regrouping the social substratum of a particular language. Socioeconomic laws cannot change the direction of a particular natural historical process in the evolution of a language, but they determine whether particular process will take place in a language in the first place (Polivanov 1931, p. 141). This view was criticised by Shor (1929, p. 140), who accused Polivanov for holding orthodox Neo-Grammarian views according to which language evolution is governed by natural historical laws, while socioeconomic factors only change the conditions in which verbal interaction takes place and, therefore, affect language only indirectly.

Polivanov argued for Marxist linguistics, but did not elaborate his own understanding of Marxism or Marxist sociology in any detail. He insisted that Marxist linguistics must be non-dogmatic in its nature, that is, it must base itself on purely linguistic facts which are independent of the theory and philosophical commitments. From Polivanov's methodological empiricism it follows that in a genuinely Marxist approach to language it is 'important not to start from Marxism, but to arrive at Marxism on the basis of the investigation of facts' (Polivanov 1991b [1929], p. 559). Polivanov's methodological position seems to resemble Bukharin's view according to which historical materialism must be based on and compatible with the latest developments in natural sciences. They both seem to assume that various social phenomena can be analysed by using methods stemming from the natural sciences. However, as demonstrated above, Polivanov's idea of the teleological nature of language evolution differs from Bukharin's mechanistic view according to which the relationship of basis and superstructure is based on causal laws and, that teleological explanations therefore have no place in Marxist sociology.

5. Voloshinov: Sociology and the Philosophy of Language

While Shor and Polivanov identified themselves as linguists, Voloshinov defined his research area as 'the philosophy of language'. In the preface to his 1929 book *Marxism and the Philosophy of Language* – which was characterised by Shor as representing 'a quasi-Marxist philosophy of language' based on German idealistic neophilology (Shor 1931, p. 34) – Voloshinov stated that prior to his own attempt to apply the Marxist sociological method to the study of language, 'there is not as yet a single Marxist work on the philosophy of language' and nothing of an 'elaborated nature has been said about language in Marxist works devoted to other, related fields' (Voloshinov 1986, p. xiii). Voloshinov's bold remarks on the current state of Marxist approach to the study of language were in stark contrast with those of Polivanov who, on the one hand, acknowledged the significance of the works of Marx and Engels and, on the other hand, gave contemporary developments in Soviet linguistics their due. The aim of Voloshinov's book was to outline 'the *basic directions* that genuine Marxist thinking about language must take' and also to define 'the *methodological guidelines*' for a Marxist account of concrete linguistic phenomena (Voloshinov 1986, p. xiii). In Voloshinov's view, this task was complicated by the fact that earlier works on Marxism – even those by Marx and Engels – rely on the positivistic category of mechanic causality and have failed to account for the material nature of ideological phenomena, including language (Voloshinov 1986, p. xiv). Voloshinov was also sceptical about the achievements of Soviet theorists of Marxism and argued, for instance, that Plekhanov's works on literature are practically irrelevant for the task of his book.

Voloshinov's discussion of the social nature of language cannot be separated from his consideration of ideological phenomena in general and the question of their relation to the socioeconomic basis. For him, the relationship of basis and superstructure 'is closely linked with questions of philosophy of language at a number of crucial points' and boils down to '*how* actual existence (the basis) determines sign and *how* sign reflects and refracts existence in its process of generation' (Voloshinov 1986, p. 17, 19). Voloshinov saw ideological phenomena as a part of the superstructure which reflect and refract the characteristics of the socioeconomic basis. His understanding of the relationship of basis and superstructure significantly differs from that of Bukharin and Plekhanov who saw 'social psychology' as a link between the socioeconomic basis and various superstructural phenomena. Bukharin (1969 [1921], p. 209) criticised the notions of 'popular spirit' and *Zeitgeist* replacing them with 'social psychology' defined as 'a certain psychology in the *individual*' produced by the mutual interaction between individuals which does not exist 'between men but in the brains of men' (Bukharin 1969 [1921], p. 209). Voloshinov rejected this view, held by Bukharin and Plekhanov, because it failed to grasp the material nature of ideological phenomena assuming 'the guise of a metaphysical or mythic concept' characteristic of the notions of 'popular spirit' and *Zeitgeist* criticised by Bukharin in the first place (Voloshinov 1986 [1929], p. 19).

Voloshinov does not refer to Bukharin, but he finds the notion of social psychology endorsed by the leading Soviet theorist of Marxism idealistic and argues for a materialisation of the notion. By this Voloshinov means that 'social psychology' is not to be seen as an inner property of an individual psyche, but as something that has a material existence in the form of verbal utterances. In this, Voloshinov distinguishes between two types of ideology, namely 'life-ideology' and ideology proper. Life-ideology – which roughly corresponds to Bukharin's 'social psychology' – refers to 'the whole aggregate of life experiences and the outward expressions directly connected with it', whereas ideology proper designates those spheres of symbolic activity which can be characterised as established systems of ideology (e.g. art, ethics, law) (Voloshinov 1986, p. 91). In distinction from Bukharin, who regarded language – as well as thought – as a part of the superstructure, Voloshinov does not explicitly place language in the superstructure nor does he identify language with any element of ideology. On the contrary, language becomes the very material of which all superstructural phenomena are made (Brandist 2002, p. 76). As opposed to other ideological phenomena, Voloshinov grants language with a special status of 'a master code' making other sign systems used in different spheres of ideology mutually translatable (Tihanov 1998, p. 607). Thus, language is a universal semiotic medium which makes possible the interaction between life-ideology and ideology proper as well as between different spheres of ideology proper.

As regards language, Voloshinov holds that linguistic changes are causally related to changes that take place in the socioeconomic basis. However, he insists that causality must not be understood in terms of mechanic causality. In his view, it is impossible to explain an isolated fact by trying to establish a connection between it and the basis, because 'every domain of ideology is a unified whole which reacts with its entire constitution to a change in the basis' (Voloshinov 1986, p. 18). For him, the social and functional stratification of a language derives from productive relations and the socio-political situation of a society. In other words, the socioeconomic formations and the class-structure of a society determine the forms of verbal communication and changes in the socioeconomic basis will eventually result in a linguistic change:

> *social intercourse is generated* (stemming from the basis); *in it verbal communication and interaction are generated; and in the latter, forms of speech performances are generated; finally, this generative process is reflected in the change of language forms.* (Voloshinov 1986, p. 96)

Voloshinov's understanding of the relationship between the socioeconomic basis and ideological phenomena in terms of 'non-mechanic' causality is remarkably similar to that of Polivanov, for they both argue that there is no direct causal link between socioeconomic characteristics of a society and concrete linguistic features. Both Voloshinov and Polivanov hold that changes in the socioeconomic situation of a society affect language indirectly by conditioning the range and forms of social interaction between individuals.

Voloshinov, like most contemporary Soviet linguists, acknowledged the fundamental role of 'the class struggle' in the historical becoming of a language. However, the most significant departure from the dominant idea of the class-character of language is that Voloshinov does not accept the idea that in a capitalist society there is a multiplicity of contrasting class-languages which would actually be different languages. According to Voloshinov,

> Class does not coincide with the sign community, i.e., with the community, which is the totality of users of the same set of signs for ideological communication. Thus, various different classes will use one and the same language. (Voloshinov 1986, p. 23)

Voloshinov (1986, p. 23) insists that different social classes do not speak different languages but use a common language. For him, the social differentiation within a class-society is reflected in the multiaccentuality of linguistic signs. In this view, a linguistic sign amounts to 'an intersecting of differently oriented social interests', and the way in which extradiscursive reality is refracted in the sign is determined by competing ideological purviews within a linguistic community. Voloshinov's idea of a linguistic sign as a refraction of language-independent reality commits himself to a realist ontology which clearly separates him from Bakhtin's neo-Kantian idealism (Brandist 2002, p. 76). An important ramification of the multiaccentuality of the sign is that not only outer speech but also inner speech and hence thought are characterised by the intersection of differently oriented social accents. Voloshinov's position significantly differs from that of Marr and his followers who equated language and thought with ideology and held that a particular social group possesses a unified class-language and way of thinking, because the structure and evolution of language and thought are determined by the characteristics of the socioeconomic basis.

Despite Voloshinov's frequent use of Marxist terminology in the first part of his book, he basically equated the 'Marxist approach' with a 'sociological approach', which was also the case with Polivanov (Alpatov 2005, p. 208). Although he emphasised the importance of his contribution to Marxist study of language, Voloshinov nevertheless failed to explicate his understanding of Marxist sociology and its implications for the study of language. While in the first part of the book he characterised the understanding of the relation of basis and superstructure as a necessary prerequisite for a Marxist theory of language, elsewhere in the book there is no macro-level analysis of the interaction between social structures and linguistic phenomena. On the contrary, Voloshinov's discussion of verbal interaction is mainly based on a micro-analysis of the dialogical relations between the interlocutors in a concrete context. This is also reflected at the textual level: while the first part of the book is characterised by frequent use of Marxist terms, in the second and the third part which deal with linguistic issues the Marxist terminology is practically nonexistent (Alpatov 2005, p. 207). With the exception of odd references to Plekhanov and 'classics of Marxism', Voloshinov does not explicate his understanding of Marxism and Marxist sociology. However, his discussion of ideology and social psychology reveals that he distances himself from Plekhanov's and Bukharin's version of Marxism. Given that in 1929 Marxism had already transformed in to an official dogma in the Soviet Union, it is easy to understand why Voloshinov was consigned into oblivion.

6. Conclusion

It can be argued that the 'sociological turn' that took place in Soviet linguistics in the late 1920s is of outmost importance from the point of view of the metatheory of the study of language. As opposed to earlier views of linguistics as belonging to psychology or the natural sciences, linguists began to view their own discipline as a primarily sociological discipline which was naturally reflected in the methodology of linguistic research. This also holds true for Polivanov who called for a sociological approach but also insisted on the importance of the natural historical laws established by the comparative-historical and Neo-Grammarian schools for the understanding of the evolution of language. However, notwithstanding the great importance Soviet linguists attributed to a new 'Marxist' approach in the 1920-30s, such epithets as 'social', 'sociological' and 'Marxist' were used in somewhat different meanings. As the different interpretations of the 'social nature' of language by Shor, Polivanov and Voloshinov demonstrate, even those linguists who explicitly called for a Marxist approach to the study of language remained implicit or felt reluctant to explicate what they actually meant by 'Marxist sociology'.

Bibliography

Alpatov, V. M. (2000) 'What is Marxism in Linguistics?', in C. Brandist and G. Tihanov (eds.) *Materializing Bakhtin: The Bakhtin Circle and Social Theory* (Houndmills: Macmillan), pp. 173–193.

Alpatov, V. M. (2002) 'Filologiia i revoliutsiia', *Novoe literaturnoe obozrenie*, no. 53, pp. 199–216.

Alpatov, V. M. (2005) *Voloshinov, Bakhtin i lingvistika* (Moscow: Iazyki slavianskikh kul´tur).

Bogdanov, A. A. (1995 [1918]) 'Metody truda i metody poznaniia', in S. S. Gusev (ed.) *Russkii pozitivizm: Lesevich, Jushkevich, Bogdanov* (St. Petersburg: Nauka), pp. 241–258.

Brandist, C. (2002) *The Bakhtin Circle: Philosophy, Culture and Politics* (London: Pluto Press).

Brandist, C. (2005) 'Marxism and the Philosophy of Language in Russia in the 1920s and 1930s', *Historical Materialism*, vol. 13, no. 1, pp. 63–84.

Bukharin, N. (1969 [1921]). *Historical Materialism: A System of Sociology* (Ann Arbor: The University of Michigan Press).

Day, R. B. (1976). 'Dialectical Method in the Political Writings of Lenin and Bukharin', *Canadian Journal of Political Science/Revue canadienne de science politique*, vol. 9, no. 2, pp. 244–260.

Desnitskaia, A. V. (1974). 'Kak sozdavalas´ teoriia natsional´nogo iazyka', in N. F. Belchikov (ed.) *Sovremennye problemy literaturovedeniia i iazykoznaniia* (Moscow: Nauka), pp. 398–415.

Desnitskaia, A. V. (1981). 'O traditsiiakh sotsiologizma v russkom iazykoznanii', in *Teoriia iazyka, metody ego issledovaniia i prepodavaniia* (Leningrad: Nauka), pp. 79–87.

Desnitskaia, A. V. (1991). 'Frantsuzskie lingvisty i sovetskoe iazykoznanie 1920–1930-kh godov', *Izvestiia Akademii Nauk SSSR, Seriia literatury i iazyka*, vol. 50, no. 5, pp. 474–485.

Gramsci, A. (1971) *Selections from the Prison Notebooks*, ed. and transl. by Q. Hoare and G. N. Smith (London: Lawrence & Wishart).

Iakhot, I. (1991) 'Podavlenie filosofii v SSSR (20–30-e gody)' *Voprosy filosofii*, no. 9, pp. 44–68.

Iakubinskii, L. P. (1986 [1931]) 'F. de Sossiur o nevozmozhnosti iazykovoi politiki', in *Izbrannye raboty: iazyk i ego funktsionirovanie* (Moscow: Nauka), pp. 71–82.

Joravsky, D. (1961) *Soviet Marxism and Natural Sciences* (London: Routledge and Kegan Paul).

Koerner, K. (1973) *Ferdinand de Saussure: Origin and Development of his Linguistic Thought in Western Studies of Language*, Schriften zur Linguistik, vol. 7 (Braunschweig: Vieweg).

Koerner, K. (1987) 'On the problem of "influence" in linguistic historiography', in H. Aarsleff, L. Kelly, H.-J. Niederehe (eds.) *Papers in the History of Linguistics: Proceedings of the Third International Conference on the History of the Language Sciences* (Amsterdam and Philadelphia: John Benjamins), pp. 13–28.

Lenin, V. I. (1966 [1922]) 'Letter to the Congress', in *Selected Works*, vol. 36 (Moscow: Progress), pp. 593–596.

Lukács, G. (1966) 'Technology and Social Relations', *New Left Review*, vol. 1, no. 39, pp. 27–34.

Lähteenmäki, M. (2006) Da crítica de Saussure por Voloshinov e Iakubinski, in C. A. Faraco, C. Tezza, G. de Castro (ed.) *Vinte ensaios sobre Mikhail Bakhtin* (Petrópolis: Editora Vozes), pp. 190–207.

Medvedev, P. N. (1978 [1928]) *The Formal Method in Literary Scholarship: A Critical Introduction to Sociological Poetics* (Baltimore and London: Johns Hopkins University Press).

Noiré, L. (1877) *Der Ursprung der Sprache* (Mainz: Victor von Zabern).

Peterson, M. N. (1923) 'Obshchaia lingvistika', *Pechat' i revoliutsiia*, vol. 6, (Moscow: Gosudarstvennoe izdatel'stvo), pp. 26–32.

Peterson, M. N. (1927) 'Iazyk kak sotsial'noe iavlenie', *Uchenye zapiski Instituta iazyka i literatury*, vol. 1, pp. 5–21.

Polivanov, E. D. (1931) *Za marksistskoe iazykoznanie* (Moscow: Federatsiia).

Polivanov, E. D. (1974a [1928]) 'Specific Features of the Last Decade, 1917–1927, in the History of Our Linguistic Thought', in *Selected Works: Articles on General Linguistics*, trans. D. Armstrong, ed. A. A. Leont'ev et al. (The Hague and Paris: Mouton), pp. 57–61.

Polivanov, E. D. (1974b [1931]) 'Where Do the Reasons for Language Evolution Lie?', in *Selected Works: Articles on General Linguistics*, trans. D. Armstrong, ed. A. A. Leont'ev et al. (The Hague and Paris: Mouton), pp. 81–92.

Polivanov, E. D. (1974c [1929]) 'The Problem of Marxist Linguistics and the Japhetic Theory (Résumé of a Report)', in *Selected Works: Articles on General Linguistics*, trans. D. Armstrong, ed. A. A. Leont'ev et al. (The Hague and Paris: Mouton), pp. 169–170.

Polivanov, E. D. (1974d [1929]) 'The Sphere of Immediate Problems in Contemporary Linguistics', in *Selected Works: Articles on General Linguistics*, trans. D. Armstrong, ed. A. A. Leont'ev et al. (The Hague and Paris: Mouton), pp. 171–178.

Polivanov, E. D. (1991a [1929]) 'Stenogramma 4 fevralia 1929 g. "Problema marksistskogo iazykoznaniia i iafeticheskaia teoriia" ', in *Trudy po obshchemu i vostochnomy iazykoznaniiu* (Moscow: Nauka), pp. 508–543.

Polivanov, E. D. (1991b [1929]) 'Programmno-metodologicheskii ekskurs. Fragment stat'i 1929 g.', in *Trudy po obshchemu i vostochnomy iazykoznaniiu* (Moscow: Nauka), pp. 508–543.

Radwańska-Williams, J. (1993) *A Paradigm Lost: The Linguistic Theory of Mikołaj Kruszewski*, Studies in the History of the Language Sciences, vol. 72 (Amsterdam: John Benjamins).

Saussure, F. de (1966 [1916]) *Course in General Linguistics* (transl. W. Baskin) (New York: McGraw-Hill).

Shcherba, L.V. (2004 [1945]) 'Ocherednye problemy iazykovedeniia', in *Iazykovaia sistema i rechevaia deiatel'nost'* (Moscow: URSS), pp. 39–59.

Shor, R. O. (1926) *Iazyk i obshchestvo* (Moscow: Rabotnik Prosveshcheniia).

Shor, R. O. (1929) 'Paradoksal'naia ortodoksal'nost'', *Literatura i marksizm*, no. 2, pp. 139–149.

Shor, R. O. (1931) *Na putiakh k marksistskoi lingvistike* (Moscow and Leningrad: Gosudarstvennoe uchebno-pedagogicheskoe izdatel'stvo).

Swingewood, A. (1984) *A Short History of Sociological Thought* (London: Macmillan).

Susiluoto, I. (1982). *The Origins and the Development of Systems Thinking in the Soviet Union: Political and Philosophical Controversies from Bogdanov and Bukharin to Present-Day Re-Evaluations.* Annales Academiae Scientiarum Fennicae, Dissertationes Humanarum Litterarum, vol. 30 (Helsinki: Suomalainen tiedeakatemia).

Tihanov, G. (1998) 'Vološinov, Ideology, and Language: The Birth of Marxist Sociology from the spirit of *Lebensphilosophie*', *The South Atlantic Quarterly* vol. 97, no. 3/4, pp. 599–621.

Voloshinov, V. N. (1986 [1929]) *Marxism and the Philosophy of Language* (Cambridge, Mass: Harvard University Press).

Weinberg, E. A. (2004) *Sociology in the Soviet Union and Beyond* (Hants: Ashgate).

Zhirmunskii, V. M. (1936) *Natsional'nyi iazyk i sotsial'nye dialekty* (Leningrad: Khudozhestvennaia literatura).

Zhirmunskii, V. M. (1964). 'Problemy sotsial'noi dialektologii', *Izvestiia Akademii Nauk SSSR, Seriia literatury i iazyka*, vol. XXIII, no. 2, pp. 99–112.

Chapter 4

THEORETICAL INSIGHTS AND IDEOLOGICAL PRESSURES IN EARLY SOVIET LINGUISTICS: THE CASES OF LEV IAKUBINSKII AND BORIS LARIN

Viktoria Gulida

An examination of the legacy of two Russian linguists of the early Soviet period, Boris Alexandrovich Larin (1893–1964) and Lev Petrovich Iakubinskii (1892–1945), shows that their interest in 'living vernacular speech' (*'zhivaia razgovornaia rech''*), so typical of the sociolinguistic approach to language study, served as a source of genuine inspiration that led them to a novel approach to Russian language studies in early Soviet linguistics. It also provided them with what largely constituted their source of data – everyday language, mostly spoken (or transcribed spoken language) and all language varieties rather than just the standard one.

Representatives of the first generation of Soviet linguists, Boris Larin and Lev Iakubinskii advanced the sociological paradigm in Russian linguistics in the beginning of the 20th century while simultaneously pursuing traditional lines of research. They had been educated as linguists by, *inter alia*, Jan (Ivan) Baudouin de Courtenay, a linguist of exceptional abilities and a person of liberal values, active civic orientation and political awareness, and by Aleksei Shakhmatov, who imbued them with his love for 'living speech'. Both Larin and Iakubinskii lived and worked in Leningrad; their professional paths crossed at Petrograd-Leningrad University and the Herzen Pedagogical Institute, the institutions where they worked in various capacities in the 1920–1930s, and at seminars at ILIaZV (*Institut sravnitel'noi istorii iazykov i literatur zapada i Vostoka* (Institute for Comparative History of the languages and Literatures of the West and East), which promoted creative thought and new research.

Iakubinskii's interests lay in the history of Russian and comparative Slavonic studies; he was an early member of OPOiAZ, the Society for the Study of

Poetic Language. Larin's pursuits included various areas of Slavonic language studies, Lithuanian and Sanskrit. They were both fortunate enough to survive the harsh 1930s, dying from natural causes in times when many others did not (although Iakubinskii's death may have resulted from the privations of the blockade of Leningrad). The articles discussed in detail in the present paper were written in the 1920s, when sociolinguistics in Russia was on the rise. Some ten years later the trend was curtailed, with sociolinguistic studies of urban dialectology and modern standard Russian resuming only in the 1960s.

Lev Iakubinskii

In Iakubinskii's article 'On Dialogic Speech' ('*O dialogicheskoi rechi*', 1923) and Larin's 'On the Linguistic Study of the City' and 'On the Linguistic Characteristics of the City (some presuppositions)' ('*O lingvisticheskom izuchenii goroda*', '*K lingvisticheskoi kharakteristike goroda (neskol'ko predposylok)*', 1928) several profound insights into the systemic nature of the relationship between the social conditions of speech production and use, and their linguistic outcomes were developed. Viewing language in society as a heterogeneous phenomenon motivated both early Soviet and modern Anglo-American sociolinguists to transcend the limits of traditional linguistics in determining both research areas and methods. Compare, for instance, Larin's passionate rejection of 'those who ignore social dialects ...and keep talking of thousand styles of Standard Russian, striving to save the dogma of the single common national language' (Larin 1961, p. 370) with Labov's later protest against linguists of Saussurian tradition working 'with one or two informants in the quiet of their studies or analyzing their own knowledge of the *langue*' (Labov 1970, p. 98).

Based on astute observations of the everyday speech around him, conversations with people at home and at work, and subtle introspection, Iakubinskii's article 'O dialogicheskoi rechi' is, essentially, a description of the process of speech interaction in all the complexity of its categories, components, modes of realization and situational constraints. It addresses the following set of problems:

- how verbal interaction is socially organized;
- how it is culturally shaped;
- how the exchange of information is conducted and what factors determine the success of the exchange;
- what non-verbal features of an utterance are involved in its understanding and in what way speech is affected by the speaker's emotional state.

Iakubinskii's interest in dialogue was stimulated by two main factors: a belief that it is in this activity that the phenomenon of 'language' comes to the fore,

Language is seen as an aspect of human behaviour in groups, where one 'organism' interacts with other 'organisms'. Iakubinskii argues that the conditions of speech interaction (the situational context) are in the long run responsible for creating new community codes with their distinct repertoire of words, phonemes, morphology, syntactic constructions, meanings and rules of language use.

It is worth noting that Iakubinskii's reference to 'organisms' is a clear indication of his familiarity with Jean-Gabriel Tarde's (1843–1904) views on the fundamental link between modes of communication and social formations. In fact, a significant proportion of his course on speech evolution which he taught during his work at the Institute of the Living Word (*Institut zhivogo slova* (1918–1924) in Petrograd, was based on the 'subjective sociology' approach developed by Tarde. Iakubinskii's discussion of the borderline between an unorganized crowd and the organized participants of a Komsomol meeting, to which we shall return below, can be traced back to the discourse around subjective sociology.

Iakubinskii describes his stance as radically new for and different from traditional linguistics:

'The study of language as a product of the context of an interaction must form the basis of contemporary linguistics' (1986 [1923], p. 18); '…traditional linguistics is helpless when facing facts' (1986 [1923], p. 22). He goes on to explain, that linguists of a Neogrammarian orientation found the functional approach to language study unimportant for dialectology. Even a subtle phonetician like A.I.Tomson (1860–1935) made no distinction between the language of school and literature, and that of administration, etc.[1] Iakubinskii also objected to the lack of attention paid to the distinction between the syntax of spoken language and that of literary texts (fiction, *belle lettres*) in school grammar books of the period and viewed the teaching of the syntax of 'the Russian language' to young students as involving a 'confusion of concepts' if it was based on such material. Placing 'the Russian language' in inverted commas here (1986[1923], p. 21–22) suggests that he found the idea of the homogeneous language unacceptable.

Iakubinskii identified two distinct basic varieties of speech (following the appreciation of the distinction among early Soviet linguists), the distinctive features of which can be summarized as follows:

Dialogue natural		Monologue artificial
face-to-face interaction	versus	*distanced*
basic, spontaneous		*advanced, prepared*
elliptical, short, stereotyped		*elaborated*
pragmatic		*poetic*

Here dialogue is understood as a rapid exchange of short, spontaneous, elliptical remarks, an almost physiological reaction, i.e. automatically evoked by a stimulus (the exchange performed as an 'ideo-motor act'), with speech formulas that are stereotyped and a purpose which is strictly pragmatic. A monologue, on the other hand, presupposes longer, non-spontaneous, prepared passages delivered at a slower pace. A distance between language users in space or time involves writing, and writing requires self-awareness because the interlocutors then go through the process of appraising the result of their speech production by criteria the nature of which is similar to literary composition (for example, repeating the same word is poor style, and expressing oneself in an inadequately clear fashion is frowned upon). Linguistically, writing generates more complex syntax, rounded explicit sentences, and the purpose of writing may be poetic, i.e. disengaged from any directly pragmatic purpose.

In Iakubinskii's opinion, the opposition of these basic forms of speech is tied to a number of factors of a psychological, social, cultural and linguistic nature. Considered *psychologically*, speech is contrasted to writing as a process lacking in premeditation or self-awareness ('*govorit, chto popalo*'), and is contrasted to a non-spontaneous, prepared, process in which the language user exercises control over his or her speech production. Interestingly, the criterion of control over one's speech was employed by Labov to measure intra-speaker stylistic variation (Labov 1975[1970], p. 152).

The *social factor* comes into the picture by relating monologue to the *speaker's status*, seen as a mark of power ('the powerful will be listened to…'). Thus, by contrast, dialogue should be embedded in relations of solidarity. Another social factor is the *familiarity of settings*, since the basic dialogue is more likely to occur in a familiar setting. The distinction between a heavy reliance on the mental operation of choice and having no recourse to choice can be regarded as the *psycholinguistic* factor at work.

Initially, Iakubinskii contrasted dialogue as a natural activity to monologue as an artificial one. When more discursive genres were considered, such as *beseda* (informal discussion), an unhurried exchange of well-formulated remarks, *tost* ('toasting'), an exchange of short clichéd speeches during social events and some other speech genres, this opposition turned into a gradual scale of phenomena, which are culturally shaped and in this sense 'artificial' compared with Iakubinskii's initial view of dialogue as an elementary, almost automatic activity. Later he conceded that the dialogue is no less 'a product of culture' than monologue.

Yet it is difficult to escape the feeling that there must be something underpinning this common association of spontaneity with dialogue. It seems likely that it has to do with the degree of discipline in the organization of speech interaction. The process of speech interaction is a series of exchanges, 'turn-taking', to employ Schegloff and Sacks' terminology (Schegloff & Sacks 1999[1973]).[2] The exchange can be rule-governed in an orderly way, for example, in public situations of speech events such as court hearings, school classes, meetings, or less so, as in conversations at work, with friends and the like. A dialogue may appear totally un-organized, as in the type of dialogue Iakubinskii felt to be natural, that is with speakers freely butting in and shouting as they become excited. Iakubinskii's example of a meeting of a group of young workers, where everybody starts speaking simultaneously, and the din ('*galdezh*') becomes so bad, that the participants have to stop and have someone utter an organizationally key phrase: 'Let's appoint the chair who'll lead the meeting', is an instance of a borderline case in the discussion of 'the natural and the artificial'. And yet, if a loud and unruly informal conversation can go on, that is, the utterances are comprehended and responded to, then we are dealing with an organized process, however unappealing. Clearly, it is not carried out according to the standards of 'middle-class' conversations and generally reserved behaviour, but these may happen to be some other community rules.

According to this view *any* dialogue is organized in some way if it is to function as a speech event. The rules of organization may vary widely, as is demonstrated in some recent studies: middle class New York Anglo-Saxons and Jewish speakers of English at a Thanksgiving dinner sounded equally shocking to one another, with differences of more and less 'organized' behaviour just being their *typical interaction styles*, part of their ethnic sociolinguistic codes (Tannen 1999[1981]). One may understand why young post-revolutionary Russians appeared rather unorganized, but to believe that there can be a dialogue or any other kind of talk, for that matter, without any organization, would be fundamentally mistaken: speaking as social activity is constituted by certain rules. The rules are of two kinds – constitutive and regulative. This distinction was suggested by John R. Searle (Searle 1986, p.152): the first type, such as etiquette rules, regulate the behaviour that had existed prior to their introduction; and the other kind generate new forms of behaviour. A speaker is usually aware of regulative, etiquette type of rules In evolutionary terms, however, dialogue is prior to monologue, and is in that sense elementary, as Iakubinskii rightly felt it was.

If a speech community tends to use elementary dialogue to the exclusion of other interaction forms, it may become its distinctive communicative style. Iakubinskii quotes Lev Shcherba's observations of a typical interaction manner among the Muskau villagers (speaking a Muzhakow dialect of Sorbian languages of east Germany), from his book 'Vostochno-luzhizkoe narechie' (published in 1915 in St. Petersburg): 'I have never observed the villagers here use monologues, exchange impressions… just these short replies', joining in with Scherba's stress on the essentially dialogic nature of language (1986[1923]p. 31).

The *distant mode* of communication is contrasted to *face-to-face* interaction, which is influential in shaping a speech variety. The face-to-face type makes it possible to achieve adequate communication by resorting to a highly reduced type of code, using elliptical phrases, deictic words rather than names, etc. The verbal component plays a less important role in *situated interaction* because the facial movements, gestures, body language available to the listener can aid the interpretation of conversational meanings. A nod, a gesture, a look away are involved in the creation of local meaning. Iakubinskii offers a rich description of what intonation and voice quality can contribute to rendering speaker's meaning directly or through modification of the utterance. From the very beginning the tone and timbre of the speaker's voice makes the listener adopt a particular attitude to whatever is to follow and treat it as crucially important or otherwise, joking or serious, trustworthy or worthy of suspicion. An important detail here is that estimations of this kind will be made below the level of consciousness (Iakubinskii 1986 [1923], p. 26–27).

It is now an established concept of and a subject for study in discourse analysis that body posture, the direction of gaze, movements of one's hands, seeing other people making small movements according to the speaker's emphasis on a particular part of his or her utterance are all part of the communicatively organized space and are functional in the creation of local meaning. To illustrate, consider, for example, a transcription system for full representation of all vocalizations and movements connected to speech in the studies of child language acquisition (Ochs 1999[1979]), or systems signaling the alignment of speaker frames in conversation (Kendon 1999). Interlocutors' facial expressions indicating interest or the lack of it, a greater or lesser degree of attention, excitement or boredom as well as interjections with similar effect are important factors in the progress of conversation, and are termed in discourse studies as second channel signals.

Modern, technologically mediated communication adds more examples of distant modes of interaction producing their own varieties to those given by Iakubinski: e-mails, text messages, Internet-chat are developments of telephone conversations and writing notes (to individuals) during a lengthy public meeting. The significance of the *channel of communication* is obvious in these instances of speech modes.

Albeit indirectly, the style of interaction depends on the proximity (cultural, social, and/or communicative) of the interlocutors. A large portion of Iakubinskii's article is devoted to the crucial issue of the perception and understanding of utterances in conversation. Iakubinskii is fully aware that there is more to speech perception than merely identifying verbal meanings; he introduces the concept of 'apperception masses', which one may understand as a speaker's cognitive perceptual resources. These include the topic of conversation, one's awareness of the type of speech event (telling a joke, expressing an opinion, in terms of speech genres) – both are engaged in 'the whole internal and external experience of the listener', as he puts it. One's 'experience' is made up of two parts: the permanent (world knowledge) and the current, pertaining to the situation of the conversation. The current element, the 'orientation' (*ustanovka*), is responsible for the 'activation' of one's permanent 'package'. (Tannen and Wallat 1999 [1987]). In fact, Iakubinskii's concept of 'apperception masses' may be understood as covering such notions as *frames, scripts, scenarios*, as well as what Gumperz terms *contextualizers* (Gumperz 1997[1982], p. 396). These early insights into what has become part of the modern cognitivist and interactional paradigms are genuine evidence of the linguist's talent.

In simple words and using everyday examples of misinterpreted and misheard utterances, Iakubinskii demonstrates how the listeners' ways of thinking or feeling define their perception of another person's speech. People are capable of hearing only some part of the sound content of a reply or ignore it altogether:

(I am yelling from my room) 'Oh, it's really freezing today!' – ' It's ten o'clock already'

'Have you bought the paper today?' – 'No, it's too early'

They hear what is 'in line with their thinking at the moment' or what is most probable in the settings the talk occurs in, or for a phase in the deployment of the conversation. In the first example the first question in the morning will be about time, which explains the answer; in the second – the listener is thinking about putting on the samovar, because it's normally done at 9 o'clock in the evening (Iakubinskii 1986 [1923], p. 44).

It matters, Iakubinskii insists, whether one is hungry, or what time of the day it is at the moment of talking, who the interlocutor for the interpretation of speech is. In his romantic way Iakubinskii discusses at length the issue of total mapping of speakers' cognitive and socio-cultural background, which – in case of Kitty and Levin's conversations, from L. Tolstoy's *Anna Karenina* – is brought about by love. Again, the issue of problematic interpretations and their causes is now a large research area in the studies of miscommunication.

Thus, in his analysis of speech-related factors and their effects upon the form and meaning of utterances Iakubinskii succeeded in covering both *factors of immediate context* and *factors of the greater socio-cultural context* that contribute to perception and interpretation of meaning in interaction.

In more recent terms, the taxonomy of the fundamental factors of speech variability identified by Iakubinskii in his comparison of dialogue and monologue have, in part, become scalable parameters of research in microsociolinguistics, and are comparable with the parameters conditioning stylistic variation and, in part, of levels of conversational inference and contextualization process in Gumperz's model for interactional sociolinguistics. Iakubinskii's ideas about the connection between situational speech variability and the formation of functional language varieties, discussed above, is also a valuable insight as it contributes to a unified view of the as yet separate micro– and macro-linguistic areas of sociolinguistic research.

Boris Larin

In his work of the 1920s Boris Larin focused on the living speech of urban communities . He was driven by the potential he saw in this material for constituting a third major area of language research, after the standard language and regional dialects. Study of urban speech could, he hoped, yield results as crucial for the development of language theory as those from regional dialectology had proven to be for the advancement of comparative linguistics. He proceeded from the following positions:

- investigation of the non-standard varieties that are in contact with the standard language is imperative for obtaining a realistic account of the formation of standard Russian and its development;
- specific patterns of the social organization of city life are bound to generate specific linguistic units and ways of language use as well as patterns of communication;
- the multilingual[3] nature of city life and the language competence of city dwellers is a prototype for future solidarity of the global community, which will be brought about by the world revolution.

Larin considered the language of large cities, in which he included 'urban folklore, non-canonical types of written language, the conversational speech of various social groups of the urban population' (Larin 1928a, p. 301) to be the least linguistically covered area in linguistics, not only in Russia, but also throughout Europe. Objecting to current scholastic discussions about the factors influencing 'the evolution of the 'literary' language' he urged linguists to move on to collecting real language data on the subject (Larin, 1961, p. 370). Larin's belief was that standard language, no longer an urban variety as it acquires national functions, continues to develop through permanent interaction with the non-standard idioms surrounding it. Larin holds that the history of literary Russian is a series of successive stylistic 'lowerings' due to the influence of non-standard varieties and of the urban koine ('gorodskoe prostorechie') (Larin 1928a, p. 302). Moreover, in the first stages of its formation (from the end of the fifteenth to the mid seventeenth century) standard Russian was shaped by the interaction of 'high' written forms and the language spoken by lower level state administration officers (*pod'iachie*). (Larin 1961, p. 370–2).

The 'blindness' of traditional linguists towards the language of the city was a logical outcome of the standard language *versus* regional dialects research paradigm which recognised only these two varieties. With a condescending connotation, '*meschansky govor*' [a low middle class accent, – V.G.] of the city was explained away as 'intermediary lingos between proper dialects and *literaturnyi Russkii* [literary Russian).' (1928a, p. 303). As far as their linguistic content was concerned, these varieties were treated as collections of deviations from either the standard or a dialect variety. But in Larin's opinion these varieties were language idioms in their own right, socially and linguistically distinct, and deserving a systematic approach (Larin 1928a, p. 310–312). This was a position he felt the need to defend.

During fieldwork expeditions with students of Leningrad University[4] he supervised a group observing the speech of Leningrad and Borovichi, a small town close to Leningrad. The informants included such diverse members of the urban community as unemployed Leningrad workers exchanging jokes on a tram, young people with little education aspiring to be writers, or members of ethnic minorities struggling to fill a questionnaire in formal Russian.

Larin was brilliantly resourceful in finding ways of investigating the 'living speech' of any epoch, including the medieval Muscovy ('Moskovskaia Rus'), in the sixteenth and seventeenth centuries. Various social groups of a Russian medieval, city such as *posadskie* ('residents of Russian medieval market quarters'), *prikaznye* ('junior administrative staff in medieval Rus') , *remeslenniki* ('craftsmen'), etc, were bound to have their characteristic dialects but their speech would be unlikely to be transcribed, and even if it was transcribed, it would be 'normalised'. One particular type of legal document – confessions of people accused of slandering, or plotting against the tsar or his family, had to contain their exact words since the crime was essentially linguistic. So the scribes who usually avoided recording suspects' dialectal features for fear of being 'beaten with long sticks' if their texts did not conform to Moscow style, had to be precise in such cases (Larin 1961, p. 379).

To supply more material on the actual phonology and wording of spoken Russian of the sixteenth to the mid-eighteenth centuries (the period of the formation of standard Russian) , Larin, inventively, turns to foreigners' accounts of spoken Russian, such as James's notes from the Arkhangelsk region and the records of Ludolf from Moscow (Larin 1946, p. 357). He found that a foreigner's ear oriented towards 'deciphering' a spoken word and insensitive to stylistic overtones of alien speech proved to be a precise instrument for recording pronunciation.

It is interesting, that Larin's approach towards the standard language was very much in line with its current placement in sociolinguistics as just one functional variety among others. Structurally, any variety would fit the purpose, however the standard one is 'richer', has more 'items' due to the functions it performs (due to its fortune in history). Not disputing its importance, both present-day and early Soviet linguists gave their due to non-standard varieties by joining with Charles Bally in describing the standard language as a 'crust of ice' over the living stream (Larin 1928a, p. 307).

The social structure of the urban population, its varied means and patterns of communication and the co-existence of various cultures within the larger community is a highly complex social reality and a challenging field for sociolinguistic patterning. Hence, the sociolinguistic objective of identifying social groups and their language varieties proved a far more complicated task when dealing with city codes than with regional dialects.

A major factor of urban life (*'byt goroda'*) is the *co-existence* of several social groups in close contact (Larin 1928a, p. 303). The inevitable linguistic effects of the contact are borrowings and mixing. Every community is in possession of several language varieties as people belong to several language communities. For example, a group of peasants from Saratov region who have served in the Navy and are Party members, would use their dialect while speaking to co-villagers, a 'simple city speech', *prostorechie* to people nearby, maritime professional language while on board ship, and standard Russian in a Party meeting (1928a, p. 304). Every member of the group is, then, a user of two or more codes. The borderlines between the varieties, whether inter-speaker (between groups) or intra-speaker (in the speech of a single speaker) must inevitably be blurred.

Larin suggested novel criteria for identifying language varieties. He refuted the 'dogma of a required list of morphological or phonetic peculiarities' (Larin 1928a, p. 312), as proclaimed by traditional dialectologists, in favour of systems involving characteristics of another kind. The argot used by Leningrad workers is a good example here.[5] The two men are chatting:

'Where are you working now?' – 'At Mars field. Got a job painting ceilings' – and both laugh heartily. To understand the argot meaning of this exchange - 'I am unemployed', one has to drill through several layers of semantic overtones: Mars field, apart from being a city place name, was at that time a place for the homeless and outlaws; painting ceilings is a job that does not pay well; the ceilings of Mars field are, in fact, open sky. An outsider could have made some sense of this conversation at the standard lexical semantic level; the second semantic code, with its special meanings of Mars field and ceilings, is the second code but the essence of the argot, its richness is in the speaker's reference to both in his/her meaning making.

Larin argues that urban argot is typically a product of two language varieties merging, one more common, the other of a more special type. While having many linguistic items in common with, for instance, standard Russian or the city koine (as a more common variety), it belongs to a different semantic system, tied to the context of use. The system consists of alternating between the argot elements and those of a more common code, and hinges upon the speakers' familiarity with the context of use and their awareness of the other code (Larin 1928a, p. 310–312).

This is a new and an entirely original criterion for identifying a language variety in a close contact type of language situation. By introducing it, Larin breaks away from the traditional requirement of specifying a set of individually distinct phonetic, morphological and lexical features as constituting a language variety; in the absence of these, argot was seen as merely a list of deviations from the standard, a deficit system. This was an approach of which Larin was strongly critical in his polemics with French social linguists.[6] Larin contended that argots (or any other mixed varieties, for that matter) are constituted by unique combinations of linguistic elements and their structured patterns, rather than by a set of elements. In adopting this position he prepared the next step, introducing a quantitative approach to the task of distinguishing urban varieties. Argot is 'as mixed a dialect as the standard language, and its difference from the standard language is quantitative, not qualitative' (Larin 1928a, p. 310). Indeed, the study of varieties such as these will require 'highly sophisticated methods'. This insight and the methods Larin developed anticipated those that later appeared in Labov's research into stratified speech variation – specifically, in his finding that the distribution of relative frequencies of a sociolinguistic variable correlates with social class stratification (Labov, 1997 [1972] p. 174).

Urban speakers (and, to a lesser degree, some village speakers) are *bi–* or *trilingual* owing to his or her membership in several speech communities (Larin 1928a, p. 304). In the 1920s the types of bilingualism could be generalized as: an intellectual having command of standard Russian and a foreign (world) language; a less educated citizen speaking his or her native dialect and a more common variety and/or national language, and a villager speaking his or her native regional dialect as well as some knowledge of standard Russian (if for political education only).

Bilingualism was the central issue in discussions of the ideologically loaded concept of a 'global language', which many expected to emerge as a logical consequence of the imminent global revolution and the unity of the proletariat. Larin's stand against the idea was firm: monolingualism is a reflection of the village type of the language situation, of living in a small isolated community with one language for all; the world of the future will be built like a big city, with communities and their languages in contact. The normal condition for everyone is to be bilingual (Larin1928b, p. 191–194).

Evidently proceeding from the notion of perfect bilingualism, Larin finds the current level of city bilingualism poor. Speakers of structurally related Ukrainian or Belarussian, or speakers from Odessa are fairly easy to understand but likely to make stylistic deviations from standard Russian norms, especially phonetic. Here are some of Larin's observations of the attempts to use standard Russian by a number of non-Russian speakers:

'At a public dispute on Meierkhold's version of the *Auditor* :

Мы жив'ем в очэнь тяжолые врэм'я со срэтствами *[16]*...Я не знаю, куда он ыдет, т. Мэйерхольт. Зачэм эти пастанофкы ыс шкафамы ыс корэльской берозы *[17]*.

(*My zhiv'em v ochen' tiazholye vrem'a so sretstvami ... ia ne znaiiu, kuda on ydet...Zachem eti pastanofky ys shkafamy ys korelskoi berozy*).

The speaker is from Odessa and his Russian is self taught. That a strongly deviant kind of language, such as this should be acceptable on a public occasion points to the weakness of 'our public standards', comments Larin (1977 p. 197)

Others, like Latvians, commit heavier errors by confusing grammar categories and word usage. A Latvian, whose father was educated in Moscow and Riga, says, describing differences of his mother tongue from standard Russian:

...на латышском литерат. яз. есть большая различие между материнским. Есть уезды где говорят таких слова которые давно изчезли как, напр. *Ziergs sieris, duris* и даже интунация других буква изменяется, окончание большое часть на материнском стречается а,е, а литерат. больше i, а.

(...*na latyshskom literaturnom iazyke est bolshaia razlichie mezhdu materinskim. Est uezdy gde govorat takikh slova kotorye davno izchezli, naprimer, Siergs sieris, i dazhe intunaziia drugikh bukva izmeniaetsa okonchanie bolshoe chast na materinskom strechaetsa a,e, a v literat. bolshe i, a*). (Larin, 1977 p. 198)

Demonstrating the differences between different errors, Larin suggests a clear plan for investigating interference as determined by linguistic factors such as the structural proximity of one's native tongue to standard Russian, as well as social prestige factors to motivate speakers' will to acquire normative competence in either code. These will be a 'linguistically differentiated cultural milieu' that will provide one with a feeling for the norm and make non-standard speech unacceptable. To make perfect bilinguals of city people, i.e., perfect code-switchers, in Larin's opinion, will require both linguistic research and state language policy.

At the time when Larin began working on the collection of data (from 1924) describing and modelling the linguistic situation of a large city, Leningrad was in the midst of rapid urbanization. Demographically, this meant a major influx of villagers from around Leningrad, as well as from all over Russia, into the city, and a 'fluid situation' at workplaces with an annual turnover of up to 30 % of the workforce. There were hardly any stable work collectives or time for permanent social ties or habits to form. Linguistically, this involved the co-presence of numerous dialects and structurally foreign interlanguages (imperfectly learned language varieties) of people mastering Russian, hence the excessive variability of language forms with no shared norms of usage.

Larin emphasised the importance of stable work teams, of collectives as social conditions conducive to the formation of coherent language idioms. Shared accommodation and strong ties among their members promote developing common linguistic features ('*tesnaia bytovaia spaika obuslovlivaet iazykovuiu assimilaziiu*') (Larin1928a, p. 306). The candidates for this type of living conditions and solidarity relations will be students or soldiers, sailors, or workers of the same factory. Free professions and individual entrepreneurs were unlikely to generate specific linguistic repertoires. This description of social relations and dense communication practice leading towards uniform linguistic habits strikes one as very similar to the concept of networks as discussed by Milroy (2003[1987], p. 117–118). Contrasting the type of relations typical of soldiers, students or permanent work teams, with more individualistic activities and social relations seems to correspond to Milroy's contrast between strong and multiplex network ties versus weak and monoplex ones. Both Milroy and Larin stress the norm enforcing function of strong networks.

The issues of urban dialectology discussed here are just a few of those analysed in Larin's papers on urban dialectology. For a comprehensive list of major themes see Brandist (2003, pp. 217–218).

This period in the development of the city language is pictured by Larin in rather dramatic terms: 'Language parties – imperial chauvinism', 'the desperate struggle of language parties', 'intense struggle on all routes of human activity in the city' – all of them related to class strife, which is perfectly understandable in the political context, but does not seem to be borne out by the linguistic data. It is people who fight, not languages. Languages interact, and borrowing and mixing is not the same as fighting, in human terms. A prediction stating that 'The fierce fighting among language parties is, of course, an unavoidable phase on the road to language varieties becoming allocated to distinct domains and every speaker turning into a 'perfect polyglot'' sounds somewhat too forceful for an academic.

Although a great stylist, Larin gives no indication that these phrases are used metaphorically. In his description of the Strasbourg site of language strife he outlined a gloomy perspective for French and Alsatian. Yet both languages have, in fact, survived, evolving a pattern of peaceful code-switching, even if with considerable overlapping. As shown in a recent study of code-switching in Strasbourg (Gardner-Chloros 1997), the availability of the choice between the two codes enhances the richness of their speakers' politeness strategies, with no unduly strain of their speaking activity.

The stylistic switch from the 'scientese' of an academic text to Soviet public meeting rhetoric, from cautious suppositions to planning (the notorious 'five-year' plans) cannot be explained other than by a pressing need to align with the rhetoric of the period, i.e. of political control over social and even natural forces. Language progress is not to be subject to the play of natural elements or the 'chance of history' (Larin 1928b, p. 193).

The two of Larin's articles discussed in this paper are a vivid illustration of how the political regime exercised pressure in the academic context. The first article written in 1926 and published two years later concentrated on urban linguistic diversity and ways of its investigating, although it contained slightly apologetic statements such as 'even big cities are at cross-roads of language disunity (*razdroblennost'*) ...' (Larin 1928 a, p. 309). The second article, written in 1928 (when state language policy began promoting a unified Russian language at the expense of a plurality of social dialects, abounds in the rhetoric of dialect strife and downplays the diversity issue in favour of the considerations of future linguistic uniformity, revealing the pressure to demonstrate loyalty to regime in professional terms. The author is sadly admitting that '... our language situation is still far from the global scale aspirations, typical of our era' (Larin 1928 b, p. 297). Other linguists, including Iakubinskii (1986 [1931]), made even stronger statements of the same nature.

Early Soviet linguists were engaged in three types of task: those inherited from traditional linguistics; those needed by the young Soviet state – all real and linguistically promising, and those imposed by ideology, pseudo-tasks to bridge ideologemes (myths) and research (reality). The third made a poor case for an honest scientific judgement: instead of playing the role of a research foundation for language policy decisions, it served the purpose of providing theoretical cover for (*podvesti teoreticheskuju bazu*) language policy in the USSR. This is where the 'equilibristics' of the later period of Soviet linguistics described by I. Kreindler (1985) comes in. There is no denying that ideological pressures were an integral part of early Soviet sociolinguistics.

One cannot but admire the intellectual power and insight of these early Russian sociolinguists, who, relying on a limited amount of observation over a short period, were able to identify several of the most promising sites for sociolinguistic investigation and give shape to relevant tasks and conceptualizations. Many of these would later be corroborated in research relying on the rigorous methods and fully-fledged theories of modern sociolinguistics.

References

Brandist, Craig. 2003 The origins of Soviet sociolinguistics. In *Journal of Sociolinguistics*, no. 2., Oxford: Blackwell, 213–232.

Gardner-Chloros, Penelope. 1997 Code-switching: language selection in three Strasbourg department stores. In *Sociolinguistics. A reader and coursebook* Ed-s N. Coupland and A. Jaworsky, London: Macmillan Press, 361–376.

Gumperz, John. 1997 [1982] Interethnic communication. In *Sociolinguistics. A reader and coursebook* Ed-s N. Coupland and A. Jaworsky, London: Macmillan Press 395–408.

Iakubinskii Lev P. 1986 [1931] F. de Sossiur o nevozmozhnosti iazykovoi politiki. In L.P. Iakubinskii, *Izbrannye raboty: iazyk I iego funktsionirovanie*. Moscow: Nauka,71–82.

Iakubinskii Lev P. 1986 [1923] O dialogicheskoi rechi. In L.P. Iakubinskii, *Izbrannye raboty: iazyk i iego funktsionirovanie*.Moscow:Nauka, 17–59.

Kendon Adam 1999 [1979] The negotiation of context in face-to-face interaction. In *The Discourse Reader*. Eds A. Jaworski and N. Coupland. London, New York: Routledge, 367–377.

Kreindler Isabelle. 1985 The Non-Russian languages and the Challenge of Russian: The Eastern versus the Western Tradition. In *Sociolinguistic Perspectives on Soviet National languages. Their past, present and future*. Mouton de Gruyter, Ch 6, 345–368.

Labov William 1997 [1972] The Social Stratification of (r) in New York City Department Stores. In *Sociolinguistics. A reader and coursebook* Ed-s N. Coupland and A. Jaworsky, London: Macmillan Press 168–178. Quoting *Labov, Sociolinguistic patterns*, Philadelphia, 43–54.

Labov William 1975 [1970] The Study of Language in its Social Context. In translation. In *Novoe v lingvistike*, Moscow: Progress, 96–182.

Larin Boris A. 1977 [1956] Avtobiografiia. In *B. A. Larin Istoriia russkogo iazyka i obshchee iazykoznanie (Izbrannye raboty)*. Moscow: Prosveshchenie, 214–215.

Larin Boris A. 1977 [1928b] K lingvisticheskoi kharakteristike goroda (neskolko predposylok). In *B.A. Larin Istoriia russkogo iazyka i obshchee iazykoznanie (Izbrannye raboty)*. Moscow: Prosveshchenie. 189–199.

Larin Boris A. 2003 [1928a] O lingvisticheskom izuchenii goroda. In *B. A. Larin Filologicheskoe nasledie*, St. Petersburg: Izd. S. Peterburgskogo universiteta, 301–313.

Larin Boris A. 2003 [1946] O zapisiakh inostrantsev kak istochnike po istorii russkogo iazyka. In *B.A. Larin Filologicheskoe nasledie*, St. Petersburg: Izd. S. Peterburgskogo universiteta, 353–366.

Larin Boris A. 2003 [1961] Razgovornyi iazyk Moskovskoi Rusi. In *B.A. Larin Filologicheskoe nasledie* , St. Petersburg: Izd. S. Peterburgskogo universiteta, 370–380.

Milroy Lesley. and Gordon Matthew 2003 Sociolinguistics. Method and interpretation. Oxford: Blackwell, 116–136.

Ochs Elinor 1999 [1979] Transcription as theory In *The Discourse Reader*. Eds A. Jaworski and N. Coupland. London, New York: Routledge, 167–183.

Searle John/Translation: D. Serle 1986 In *Novoe v zarubezhnoi lingvistike*, vyp.17, Moscow: Progress Publishers, pp. 151–169.

Schegloff Emanuel and Sacks, H. 1999 [1973] Opening up closings. In *The Discourse Reader*. Eds A. Jaworski and N. Coupland. London, New York: Routledge, pp. 263–275.

Tannen Deborah and Wallat, C. 1999 [1987] Interactive frames and knowledge schemas in interaction: examples from a medical examination/interview. In *The Discourse Reader*. Eds Jaworski Adam and Coupland Nicolas London, New York: Routledge, 346–367.

Tannen Deborah 1999 [1981] New York Jewish conversational style. In *The Discourse Reader*. Eds A. Jaworski and N. Coupland. London, New York: Routledge, 459–474.

Chapter 5

EARLY SOVIET LINGUISTICS AND MIKHAIL BAKHTIN'S ESSAYS ON THE NOVEL OF THE 1930s

Craig Brandist and Mika Lähteenmäki

In recent years, determined and rigorous historical scholarship has begun to undermine the aura of exceptionality that surrounded the image of Mikhail Bakhtin. Where this figure was once held to be the initiator of an improbably wide range of intellectual trends, it has now been clearly established that Bakhtin was particularly influenced by German language philosophers, whose work he adapted to the cause of the theory and history of the novel. Research has often revealed that rather than being a remarkable innovator, Bakhtin adopted ideas that were current at the time but have now receded from the view of scholars, suggesting a reassessment of various aspects of intellectual history is needed. With certain notable exceptions, however, the Soviet context has been less thoroughly examined, and this is nowhere clearer than in the lack of attention paid to Bakhtin's debt to early Soviet sociolinguistics. In Russia in particular, Bakhtin has frequently been seen as an 'unofficial' thinker who opposed, and developed his views on language, culture and literature in isolation from the contemporary, 'official' Soviet scholarship. Consequently, the nature of the interaction between the thinkers who comprised what is now generally referred to as the 'Bakhtin Circle' and contemporary Soviet linguistics and philosophy of language has generally been neglected and even treated as a non-issue. One reason for this may be that it is generally assumed the ideas follow on from those delineated in Valentin Voloshinov's 1929 book *Marxism and the Philosophy of Language,* which has often been ascribed to Bakhtin himself. There is, however, a qualitative difference between the linguistic ideas in Voloshinov's texts and those in Bakhtin's essays of the 1930s, not least the discussion of the historical development of language and discursive relations within society and the modelling of these features in the novel as a genre.

While Voloshinov's work facilitated the transformation of Bakhtin's early phenomenology of intersubjectivity into the account of discursive relations we find in the latter's 1929 Dostoevskii book, both works present largely synchronic analyses quite distinct from that found in Bakhtin's 1934 essay 'Slovo v romane' ('Discourse in the Novel', hereafter DiN) and after.

The present article analyses the formation of Bakhtin's conception of the social and ideological stratification of language, as discussed in DiN and supplemented in his other essays on the novel of the late 1930s. Our aim is to question the claims regarding the exceptional originality of Bakhtin's linguistic views by demonstrating that the idea of language as socially and ideologically stratified phenomenon which underlies Bakhtin's celebrated concept of heteroglossia was current in Soviet linguistics in the 1920–30s. We will focus on the 1930–31 articles by Lev Iakubinskii whose views on the linguistic diversity and the formation of national languages are perhaps the closest to Bakhtin's conception of language. Despite the fact that Bakhtin's account of linguistic diversity and the social stratification cannot be reduced into the works by the early Soviet sociolinguists, it will be argued that a historiographical analysis of Bakhtin's views necessitates a serious reassessment of his contribution.

Problems with Bakhtin's Texts

One of the problems in analysing Bakhtin's now famous essays on the novel of the 1930s is that the published versions of the texts were not prepared for publication by the author himself and, therefore, the references or absences thereof that we find in the texts are insufficient guides to the sources of the ideas discussed there. DiN provides a particularly clear example of the problem. It was completed by Bakhtin in 1934–35 in Kustanai, Kazakhstan, where he had been living since 1930 after his sentence to ten years on Solovetskii Islands had been commuted to six years of internal exile. Despite his efforts, Bakhtin failed to get the essay published in the 1930s and it only appeared in print some forty years after its completion. The essay was first published in the 1975 Russian collection *Voprosy literatury i estetiki*, although two chapters of it had appeared in the periodical *Voprosy literatury* already in 1972. However, it appears that Bakhtin's manuscript of DiN was not published as it is but 'with cuts', certain passages being editorially excised from the manuscript prior to its publication, as is revealed in the editorial commentaries on Bakhtin's working notes dating from the early 1950s (Gogotishvili 1996, p. 575). Bakhtin's working notes, now published as 'Dialogue II', which were written in 1952 when DiN was still unpublished, contain Bakhtin's conspectus of the essay. In this conspectus we find an explicit reference to Iakubinskii's 1923 article 'On Dialogic Speech' (Bakhtin 1996, p. 225) which is discussed in Gulida's contribution to the present collection. The absence of the reference to Iakubinskii in the published version of DiN suggests that it may have been among the items that were editorially removed. A comparison of Bakhtin's conspectus and the published version of DiN shows that the reference to Iakubinskii's article 'On Dialogic Speech' was most likely excised from the following passage of the published version in which Bakhtin evaluates contemporary accounts of dialogue proposed by linguists:[1]

> This open orientation toward the listener and his answers in everyday dialogue and in rhetorical forms has attracted the attention of linguists. But even where this has been the case, linguists have by and large gotten no further than the compositional forms by which the listener is taken into account; they have not sought influence springing from more profound meaning and style. (Bakhtin 1975 [1934–5], p. 93; 1981 [1934–5], p. 280)

Bakhtin's evaluation of Iakubinskii's article is apt, for the latter mainly discusses dialogue as a specific compositional form, whereas the semantic and stylistic, not to mention philosophical implications of the concept fall outside the scope of his article.

Elsewhere in DiN, Bakhtin's characterisation of contemporary linguistics is often marked either by caricature or a relative lack of appreciation for the finer points of the subject. For instance, at one point (1975, p. 88–89) he argues that such phenomena as the dialogical nature of the utterance and social stratification of language have remained 'almost completely' beyond the scope of linguistics and the philosophy of language. He admits – without giving any references – that in recent decades these phenomena have begun to attract the attention of linguists who have nevertheless failed to acknowledge the wide-ranging significance of these phenomena in different spheres of the life of discourse. Bakhtin (1975 [1934–5], p. 89; 1981 [1934–5] p. 275) also argues that linguists view the influence of languages on each other as 'socially unconscious' processes. This critical evaluation of contemporary linguistics must be regarded as incorrect in so far as Iakubinskii is concerned, especially with regard to his articles on the formation of the Russian national language of the early 1930s, to which we shall return. Moreover, in his critique of Saussure, Iakubinskii (1986 [1931]) challenges Saussure's position according to which language cannot be changed at will and argues that conscious interference in a language is indeed possible (for discussion, see Lähteenmäki 2006).

In addition to Iakubinskii's article on dialogue, the manuscript of DiN also contained a reference to Nikolai Marr which was editorially removed from the published version.[2] If we add to this the observation that Bakhtin was extremely cavalier about quoting his sources even before any editorial intervention, then the absence of references to Soviet linguists in no way suggests a hostility toward

Soviet linguistics of the period. Taken together, this evidence suggests that Bakhtin consciously tried to relate his work to the contemporary linguistic discussion in the Soviet Union, even if his knowledge of that field was, at that time, somewhat limited. What is more, Bakhtin made some efforts to get DiN published, making a trip to Moscow in 1936 in order to pass the manuscript to his friend Matvei Kagan for his comments and for assistance in finding a publisher for the article (Konkin and Konkina 1993, p. 215). This clearly suggests that Bakhtin's linguistic ideas cannot be regarded as 'unofficial' in the sense that they would be diametrically opposed to the contemporary Soviet linguistic scholarship, but that he was seriously engaging with it and sought to contribute to it. The impression of an 'unofficial' scholar standing aloof from the field was created later, by deliberate editorial decisions to excise references to the works by contemporary Soviet linguists and which obscured the appropriate intellectual context of Bakhtin's linguistic views.

Bakhtin's Conception of Language in the 1930s

According to Bakhtin (1975 [1934–5], p. 72; 1981 [1934–5], p. 259), the principal aim of DiN is 'to overcome the division between abstract "formalism" and abstract "objectivism" in the study of the artistic word. Form and content are united in the word, understood as a social phenomenon, social in all spheres of its life and in all its moments – from the sound image to the most abstract semantic strata'. This idea is said to define his whole emphasis on the 'stylistics of genre' in which stylistic phenomena are to be linked to the 'social modes in which the word lives' and the 'great historical destinies of genres'. He argues that this can only be achieved by approaching the stylistics of the novel from a sociological point of view, which also involves considering language and verbal discourse as social phenomena. Bakhtin (1994 [1929], p. 9) had argued for a 'sociological method' already in the 1929 *Problems of Dostoevsky's Art* (*Problemy tvorchestva Dostoevskogo*) in which he insists that a literary work is an 'immanently sociological' phenomenon. Bakhtin's considerations were tightly bound in with the collective research project on sociological poetics that members of the Bakhtin Circle Pavel Medvedev and Voloshinov worked on at ILIaZV in the late 1920s, as shown by the fact that Bakhtin's monograph was published in the same series with other products of the project on sociological poetics (Brandist 2007). However, in DiN the sociological approach is combined with a historical perspective for the first time.

The same can be said for Bakhtin's approach to language. According to Bakhtin's 'sociological' point of view, a language does not represent a monolithic neutral system of linguistic forms, but is to be seen as a stratified social and ideological concreteness associated with various, often clashing, worldviews. This idea had also been touched upon in the 1929 Dostoevsky book where Bakhtin argues that 'every social group in every epoch has its own sense of discourse [*slovo*] and its own range of discursive [*slovesnyi*] possibilities' (Bakhtin 2000 [1929], p. 99).[3] In DiN, however, this argument is combined with an emphasis on the dynamic nature of a language as a social phenomenon which is constantly in the process of becoming and shaped by centripetal and centrifugal forces. Thus, a national language is simultaneously characterised by its unifying tendencies and striving for stratification and differentiation.

In his discussion of the linguistic diversity within a community Bakhtin introduces the concepts *raznorechie* and *raznoiazychie* in order to account for the social and ideological stratification of a national language. *Raznorechie* refers to the co-existence of a multiplicity of various struggling language-forms – e.g. social registers, professional discourses and so forth – associated with certain ideological points of view. *Raznorechie* is counterposed to the category of the unitary language, that has crystallized 'in the real, but nevertheless relative unity of the dominant conversational (everyday) and literary language' (Bakhtin 1975 [1934–5], p. 84; 1981 [1934–5], p. 270). For Bakhtin, social stratification of language is not primarily a linguistic phenomenon but has to do with the existence of a multiplicity of different ideological purviews within a linguistic community. From this it follows that *raznorechie* – unlike *raznoiazychie* – 'may not violate the abstract-linguistic dialectological unity of the common literary language' (Bakhtin 1975 [1934–5], p.103; 1981 [1934–5], p. 290), although different social language-forms are often characterised by particular phonetic, grammatical and lexical features.

Raznoiazychie, in turn, designates language plurality, that is, the presence of multiple dialects and languages, which differ according to certain linguistic features, within the confines of a particular linguistic community. An example of language plurality would be a linguistic situation of an illiterate peasant who used Church Slavonic to pray to God, sang songs in another language and spoke to his family members in third language (Bakhtin 1975 [1934–5], p.108; 1981 [1934–5], p. 295). *Raznoiazychie* can become *raznorechie* only, if different language-forms (e.g. regional dialects) distinguished by overt linguistic features come to represent specific ideological points of view. Thus, language plurality becomes *raznorechie* when the peasant eventually realises that the languages he uses are not just different languages, but also associated with different ideological systems and approaches to the world which 'contradict each other, and cannot peacefully co-exist alongside each other' (Bakhtin 1975 [1934–5], p.109; 1981 [1934–5], p. 296). For Bakhtin, linguistic communities are characterised by *raznorechie* and even *raznoiazychie*, whereas the idea of a totally homogeneous monolingual society must be regarded as an idealisation. He also argues that the speaker of a language does not experience her own language as a neutral medium but as a stratified conglomerate of competing ideological points of view.

Common Arguments

While Bakhtin's idea of the social stratification of language has often been invoked to suggest his exceptional insight and innovative thinking about language, the idea of social stratification of language was widely discussed in Russia by the late 1920s and early 1930s. Consider, for instance the following passage from Baudouin de Courtenay's article 'Language and Languages' ('Iazyk i iazyki') that appeared in Polish as early as in 1904:

> One and the same tribal or national language can play the roles of a state, administrative, clerical, school, literary, scholarly language etc. Everyday language is distinguished from 'noble' and elevated language, the popular language is distinguished from that of the 'educated class' etc… languages of certain artisans, professions (the language of actors, for instance) may arise, along with those of particular social classes, languages of women and of men, of different age groups… (Boduen de Kurtene 1963 [1904], p. 740)
>
> Human language, or speech, reflects various worldviews and moods of both individuals and whole groups of people. (Boduen de Kurtene 1963 [1904], p. 79)

Here, Baudouin de Courtenay outlines two basic components of Bakhtin's notion of *raznorechie*, namely that a national language is a socially and functionally stratified whole and that language reflects the worldviews of individuals or groups of individuals. The idea that social differentiation within a society is reflected in linguistic differentiation was again discussed by Rozaliia Shor in her 1926 book *Language and Society* (*Iazyk i obshchestvo*):

> [I]f language is a social phenomenon, if it is the necessary precondition and tool of social intercourse, if the environment within which and through which language is maintained and passed on is social environment, then it is obvious that any kind of social differentiation must find itself reflected in linguistic differentiation. (Shor 1926, p.100)

And we can find a discussion of the relation of literary language and *raznorechie* that closely resembles that of Bakhtin in a text published at the same time as Bakhtin's essays on the novel: Viktor Zhirmunskii's 1936 book *National Language and Social Dialects* (*Natsional'nyi iazyk i sotsialnye dialekty*):

> Alongside the language of the ruling classes, which is the ruling language of a given society, there are other social dialects; various peasant dialects, colloquial speech of the middle class, the dialectally coloured language

of workers. On the whole, the characteristic feature of the linguistic development of capitalist society is its essential diglossia [*dvuiazychie*]: the unitary language of the ruling class (the 'common', 'national', 'literary' language – the terminology is insufficiently settled) is in contrast with the territorially scattered dialects of subordinate social groups. (Zhirmunskii 1936, p. 6)

As these examples show, different aspects of social stratification and differentiation of language were widely discussed in Russian/Soviet linguistics. 'The questions of language and society', as they were called, had become a central research topic thanks to the many sociological problems that were raised by the need to address the national and colonial questions bequeathed to the new regime by its Tsarist predecessors. As Marxist theory was brought to bear on language policy, the development of approaches that could establish the connections between linguistic and social variations gained special importance. By the time Bakhtin's essays on the novel were written such considerations constituted a part of the general climate of opinion among linguists.

The same can be said of the idea of centrifugal and centripetal forces in the development of language in society. Baudouin de Courtenay and Aleksei Shakhmatov, discussed the struggle between centripetal and centrifugal forces as crucial factors in the history of a language. Baudouin (1963 [1870], pp. 47–77, 58–60) discussed this in his inaugural lecture at St. Petersburg University as early as 1870, and Shakhmatov (1915, pp. xlvii–xlviii) revived the idea in 1915. In a 1929 article on the methodology of Soviet folklore, the veteran orientalist and folklorist Sergei Ol'denburg argued that 'interactions between different social milieux are phenomena no less important than those between races or peoples' and that 'to the tendencies toward differentiation are always opposed the tendencies toward unification'. Furthermore, Ol'denburg argued that awareness of this was leading to a breaking down of the 'artificial distinction between popular and non-popular' literature (quoted in Howell 1992, p. 173).

Lev Iakubinskii's Articles 'The Class Structure of Contemporary Russian Language' 1930–31

While many of the ideas regarding the social nature of language that we find in Bakhtin's essays were thus quite commonplace at the time they were written, there is one source in which we find most of them all together: a series of articles about the 'formation of the common-national language of bourgeois society from the dialects of the feudal epoch' on the basis of the 'Marxist understanding of the social-historical process' published by Iakubinskii. The articles appeared in Maksim Gor'kii's prominent journal *Literaturnaia Ucheba* in

1930 and 1931 and were given the collective title 'The Class Structure of Contemporary Russian Language' ('Klassovyi sostav sovremennogo russkogo iazyka'). A year later they were published in book form as *Essays on Language For Workers of Literature and For Self-Education* (*Ocherki po iazyku dlia rabotnikov literatury i dlia samoobrazovaniia*). As the title of the collection suggests, these articles were of a popular-scientific [*nauchno-populiarnyi*] nature, and were originally contributions to a journal connected to Gor'kii's educational programme the aim of which was to educate new writers according to the principles of socialism (See Dobrenko 2002, pp. 324–34). Accordingly, Iakubinskii's articles were not written for specialists in language studies, and he often presented his views in an oversimplified and pointed way which in some respects makes them prone to criticism. In this respect, the articles written by Iakubinskii in 1930–31 are similar to the articles by Voloshinov that appeared in the same periodical, for both occasionally suffer from oversimplification and a polemical tone. However, in both cases the articles nevertheless contained sophisticated analyses that are worthy of attention today, and they were probably the first to discuss the formation of the Russian national language in correlation with the formation of the national market as discussed in Lenin's landmark 1899 (second edition 1908) study *The Development of Capitalism in Russia*.

The starting point for Iakubinskii's account of the social and ideological differentiation within language is the contention that language has two fundamental functions from which all subsequent functions arise: '1) language as a medium of intercourse and 2) language as ideology'. While this distinction must not be erased, 'in no cases must these fundamental functions be separated from one another: in all its phenomena language fulfils both these functions at once'. Iakubinskii argues that the application of Marxism to language science reveals that 'a language is a unity of these functions', and allows the linguist to show how, at various stages of a society's development, these two aspects 'enter into contradiction'. This contradiction is determined by socio-economic circumstances and acts as the 'inner motor' of a language's development (Ivanov and Iakubinskii 1932, p. 62). Here we already have an argument that anticipates Bakhtin's (1975 [1934–5], p. 72; 1981 [1934–5], p. 259) aim to 'to overcome the divorce between an abstract "formal" approach and an equally abstract "ideological" approach' in the study of the artistic discourse.

Iakubinskii treats the historical vicissitudes of the national language and ideological differentiation as two sides of a single problem. Form of communication and ideological content are to be understood as united (but not fused) in language. It is this feature that fundamentally distinguishes Iakubinskii's argument from the class reductionism of the 'class character' of language advanced by Marr. For Iakubinskii, the development of national languages in capitalist societies, which involves linguistic unification and standardization of 'a language as means of intercourse', reveals the contradiction based on the 'class differentiation of a language as ideology':

> The same capitalism that maximally differentiates language as ideology strives to transform it into an all-national inter-class means of intercourse. In this way language, having taken shape in capitalist society, is characterised by the intensification of that internal contradiction that we mentioned above. This contradiction may be formulated as the contradiction between the commonality of language as a means of intercourse (form), and the class differentiation of language as ideology (content). (Ivanov and Iakubinskii 1932, pp. 62–3)

This dialectic of 'form' and 'content', so understood, is the methodological premise of Iakubinskii's detailed and sophisticated account of the formation of the Russian national language.

For Iakubinskii, language-as-ideology in a capitalist society bears features characteristic of all stages of its development as sedimented strata. On the one hand, language-as-ideology is the realm of what the neo-Kantians called 'objective validity', that is, 'the inescapable form of our cognition', but developed 'according to the level of the formation [*obrazovanie*] and differentiation of the superstructural world'. Iakubinskii explicitly points to Marr's semantic paleontology at this point, arguing that at the beginning of its existence as an 'independent form of ideology' language was 'one of the forms of existence for the majority of other ideologies (religious, juridical, scientific, political and so on)'. On the other hand, language-as-ideology is also the embodiment the socio-specific worldviews of different social groups. The history of class society is therefore the history of class ideologies engaged in a struggle that reaches a peak under capitalism, when a common language-as-medium-of-intercourse becomes 'the form of existence of different class consciousnesses (psychologies)' (Ivanov and Iakubinskii 1932, p. 62).[4] This process is further elaborated in Iakubinskii's account of the historical formation of the Russian national language.

The Formation of the Russian National Language

Iakubinskii's historical account begins with an examination of the language of the peasantry under feudalism, where society was divided into a 'series of linguistic regions corresponding to feudal estates [*pomest'é*]'. These regional dialects were not monolithic, however, because 'the population of a feudal estate could include within its structure a series of primordial economic groups'. The resultant variations within feudal dialects were, and here Iakubinskii follows Marr closely, 'relics of the preceding stage of society'.

In general, however, feudal linguistic relations were characterized by regional 'boundedness' and 'enclosure'. In feudal society 'peasants spoke differently in different regions, and within a region common characteristics naturally emerged, although they could also retain distinct characteristics inherited from preceding epochs'. (Iakubinskii 1930a, p. 85).

With the uneven development of capitalist relations within the framework of a feudal society, linguistic relations began to change. These new relations were first apparent within a growing town, where from its inception the population is to some extent a mixture of people from various feudal estates. A certain 'common conversational language' arose as a result, 'reflecting the characteristics of the varied dialects of settlers'. The language of each separate town was, however, formed in the grasp of intensifying inter-urban relations, on the basis of the conversational language of the largest centre(s) of the society. This forms the nucleus of the common-national [*obshchenatsional'nyi*] language, which develops as the bourgeoisie concentrated wealth in fewer and fewer hands, centralised production and thus the population, and brought about political centralisation. Paraphrasing Marx's comments on the nature of the peasantry as a class in the *Eighteenth Brumaire of Louis Bonaparte*, Iakubinskii argues that 'linguistic sociality becomes ever less like that sack of dialects that it was under feudalism'. Giving earlier schematic accounts of centrifugal and centripetal forces within language some sociological concreteness, Iakubinskii argues that the formation of the national language is a 'tendency [*tendentsiia*], (a striving [*stremlenie*]) to commonality', the progress of which depends on factors such as the arrival of new peasants with their own dialects, the stage of capitalist development, and the size of the capitalist centre. More importantly, however, the urban population is divided into classes and a stratum of 'professional intellectuals': 'the degree of commonality of the language of various social classes ... is different. Different classes generalise their language to various degrees depending on the extent to which they are compelled to do so by their objective class interests and on how much this generalisation is permitted by the objective political conditions in which the given social class develops'. The proletariat has an interest in generalising its language, but being politically subordinate, exploited and oppressed, it is unable to become a 'class for itself'. The contradictions of capitalism thus both drive and limit the development of a common national language (Iakubinskii 1930a, pp. 86–88)

Public Discourse and its Genres

Iakubinskii argues that the 'capitalization' of linguistic relations is crucially tied to the development of 'public discourse' [*publichnaia rech'*], which is to be distinguished from conversational language in terms of possible numbers of participants and length of utterance. Reiterating a point from his 1923 article on dialogic discourse, Iakubinskii argues that 'conversation is the exchange of short rejoinders (dialogue)' while the utterances of 'public discourse' are 'extended, lengthy, monologic' (Iakubinskii 1986 [1923] §4).[5] Public discourse is also more likely to be written. Platforms for public discourse only really arise as a result of the 'capitalisation' of linguistic relations, for 'public discourse begins to "flourish" in parliament and at court, in higher education institutes and at public lectures, at rallies and congresses; even the square becomes its platform':

> Parliamentary discourse, a diplomat's address to a conference, a statement in a dispute or at a rally, a political speech, the discourse of a lawyer or prosecutor, agitational speech on the street etc. etc. These are genres of public discourse characteristic of capitalism as opposed to feudalism, regardless of the fact that we find their embryos under feudalism. Capitalism speaks publicly incalculably more and in a different way than feudalism. Public speaking under feudalism is narrowly specialised, limited by the narrow domains of sociality; public speaking under capitalism pretends to universality; it wants to be as universal a form as conversational language... In accumulating the various genres of oral public discourse, capitalist sociality also accumulates corresponding written genres. (Iakubinskii 1930a, p.89–90)

While capitalism develops a wide variety of genres of public discourse and aims to transform them into universal forms of verbal interaction adopted by all members of a particular society, it simultaneously restricts the access of much of the population to those genres. This necessarily leads to an unequal distribution of linguistic resources within a society and, consequently, the idea of having a common unified language shared by all classes remains a myth, for the conflict created by the class-structure of a capitalist society sets limits to the unifying tendencies (Iakubinskii 1930a, p. 92). In a capitalist society there cannot be a common unified language so long as there are different social classes: 'the identity of the language of the different social classes of a given nation could only come about with the destruction of these classes' (Iakubinskii 1930b, p. 62).

Iakubinskii's use of the term 'discursive genre' is precisely akin to that of Bakhtin in the essays of the 1930s and then in the early 1950s. However, while Iakubinskii developed a substantive socio-historical account of the revolutionary changes brought about within discursive relations by the development of capitalism in Russian, Bakhtin integrated his considerations of discursive genres into an 'ideal' literary history. Although Voloshinov had used the term sparingly in 1929,[6] Bakhtin provides a historical treatise of the question in his articles of the 1930s. His concern with this category reaches a peak in 1951–3, in the essay 'Problemy rechevykh zhanrov' (Problems of Discursive Genres), which was written in response to Stalin's attack on Marr in June 1950. Here we learn that Bakhtin regards discursive genres as typical forms of utterance. While Bakhtin undoubtedly developed the idea by drawing on his knowledge of the theory of genre in artistic literature, it retained the sociological force that it was given by Iakubinskii in his work of the 1930s. Thus, in the 1951–3 essay he argues that discursive genres are 'drive belts [*privodnye remni*] from the history of society to the history of language', a metaphor used about language by Marr but here transferred to Iakubinskii's category.[7]

Linguistic Unification and Discursive Differentiation

In his 1940 article on the 'Prehistory of Novelistic Discourse', Bakhtin describes the significance of the breaking-down of the Athenian city-state's linguistic isolation as a precondition for the rise of the significant parodic genres that are the precursors of the modern novel. Only with the coming of *mnogoiazychie*, a pluri-lingual environment (polyglossia), can 'consciousness be completely freed from the power [*vlast'*] of its own language and linguistic myth. Parodic-travestying forms flourish in conditions of *mnogoiazychie*, and only under such conditions can they be elevated to completely new ideological heights' (Bakhtin 1975 [1940] p. 61; 1981 [1940] p. 426). This account – together with DiN – is a clear example of how Bakhtin integrated the sociology of language developed in Russia in the 1920s and 1930s into an ideal history of literary form.

While the term itself is considerably older, '*mnogoiazychie*' was used to refer to the co-presence of different national languages within a single city by Iakubinskii's colleague Boris Larin in a paper delivered at ILIaZV in 1926 and published in 1928 (Larin 1928). Two years later appeared Iakubinskii's analysis of how the 'common-urban language' penetrated the ranks of the peasantry and led to a self-conscious approach to language. Iakubinskii also argued there that linguistic parody was a key form in the struggle of languages that resulted from the breakdown of 'feudal fixity'. Iakubinskii investigates '1) how the peasantry accommodates itself to the conversational language arising in capitalist society and 2) how the peasantry joins the process of the transformation of public discourse into the universal form of intercourse on the basis of its new genres (that are alien to feudalism)' (Iakubinskii 1930b, p. 51). This dual problem leads to three theses: a) The peasantry's assimilation of the common-urban language is an uneven process depending on the variety of social groups in a given village, the distribution and character of capitalist centres and the penetration of market forces into villages generally; b) the process of assimilation is not linear as a result of peasant resistance to the common-urban language and consequently c) assimilation is to a large degree a conscious process on the part of the peasantry. It is thesis c) that we are most concerned with here. According to Iakubinskii, the peasantry's move towards the common-urban language is a 'conscious act':

> By counterposing the common-urban language to local way of speaking [*govor*], capitalism introduces linguistic facts into the peasantry's consciousness, forcing them to notice, recognise and evaluate these facts. It [capitalism] transforms unconscious language, language-in-it-self into language-for-itself. Destroying feudal fixity, the traditionalism of peasant linguistic intercourse, through the class stratification of the village and the complex counterposition of the city to the village, capitalism forces the peasantry to choose between its own, old, local and the new urban, 'national' [language]. On this soil arises a struggle, and one of its weapons is mockery, linguistic parody of the speech of the backward or the innovators. (Iakubinskii 1930b, p.58–62)[8]

Bakhtin severed the historical argument from its institutional moorings and incorporated it into an account of literary history with different origins and historical coordinates. Like Iakubinskii, Bakhtin links the rise of parodic genres to the breakdown of linguistic isolation, but he transposes the formulation, shifting it from the penetration of capitalist relations into the backward Russian countryside and to an account of the literature of late antiquity. The framework into which Bakhtin inserted the Leningrad linguists' ideas had already been established by Aleksandr Veselovskii and Georg Misch. Veselovskii had described the rise of the novel as the product of the interaction of cultures, while Misch had described the 'discovery of individuality' in autobiography during Hellenic expansion as a 'sudden consequence of the extension of the field of view to previously unknown peoples, with different ways of living'.[9] The achievement of linguistic self-consciousness was thus generalised and then linked to literary practice in conditions of *mnogoiazychie*. The result is that 'in the process of literary creation inter-illumination with an alien language illuminates precisely the "world-view" side of one's own (and the alien) language, its inner form, the axiological-accentuated system inherent in it' (Bakhtin 1975 [1940], p. 472; 1981 [1940], p. 62).

From *Raznoiazychie* to *Raznorechie*

For Iakubinskii it is the advent of capitalism that brings about the reordering of linguistic relations. Where the peasantry comprised a collection of geographically dispersed and socially isolated communities, the urban proletariat constitutes a collective of social groups that arise from the division of labour. The linguistic specificities of such social groups are now subsets of an overarching proletarian standard:

> These intra-class groupings do not contradict the working class's objective interests as long as the specialised professional vocabulary is used within the narrow sphere of a given form of production and does not permeate the whole language of the worker, does not completely detach him, in linguistic relations, from the worker of another professional group. (Iakubinskii 1931a, p. 24)

The linguistic relations between professional linguistic groups in capitalist society are therefore sharply distinguished from those between the professional groups of feudalism, where 'secluded' groups developed their own mutually incomprehensible languages. The professional stratification of language within the proletariat is thus quite different from the '*raznoiazychie*' that the proletariat inherits from the peasantry. This latter contradicts the objective interests of the working class and must be 'liquidated' in the formation of an independent proletarian language (Iakubinskii 1931a, p. 24–25).

In its transformation from a 'class in itself' to a 'class for itself', the proletariat must develop its own language in contradistinction to the language of the bourgeoisie. The manifestation of this distinction is not, and here Iakubinskii shows considerable distance from Marr, in the proletariat's pronunciation, grammar or vocabulary, but in the proletariat's 'discursive method'. This is 'the mode of usage of the material of the common-national language', the 'treatment [*obrashchenie*]' of this material, 'the mode of selection from it of facts necessary for concrete purposes', the 'attitude toward these facts and their evaluation'. This 'proletarian discursive method' is formed spontaneously during the proletariat's struggle with the bourgeoisie 'in the order of everyday conversational intercourse and is organised by the most advanced linguistic workers, the ideologues of the proletariat (writers and orators) in the various genres of oral and written public discourse'. This method is at first mainly formed in the 'political, philosophical and scientific genres of public discourse', but after the proletariat's seizure of political power the process acquires a 'mass character' and spreads to 'all discursive genres' (Iakubinskii 1931a, p. 32–33).

The social stratification of language is now understood as stratification at the level of discourse and it is argued that workers become conscious of this stratification in and through the democratisation of discursive genres by a political leadership. Here we have a similar position to Bakhtin's idea that the democratisation of culture is synonymous with its 'novelisation'. The political leader is replaced by the novelist. Rather than 'political, philosophical and scientific genres of public discourse,' proving the locus for democratisation, it is in and through the novel that adopts this role. Just as Bakhtin detaches the concrete historical narrative from its institutional coordinates and absorbed into an ideal narrative, so he severs literature from its institutional moorings and subsumes politics into ethics and aesthetics.

Iakubinskii's series of articles end with a characterisation of the current state of 'linguistic politics'. He argues that all unnecessarily technical vocabulary associated with 'bourgeois specialists' must be shunned in favour of a truly 'popular-scientific language' [*nauchno-populiarnyi iazyk*] (Iakubinskii 1931c). Under the dictatorship of the proletariat the common-national language must be 'common in its tendency towards all the genres of discourse'. It will be 'more democratic the more it is accessible to the masses, and the less it is differentiated according to genre' overcoming the enormous differentiations of the 'assimilation of actuality in discursive genres' introduced by capitalism (Iakubinskii 1931c, p. 74). The development of a common-national language, and thus the overcoming of '*raznoiazychie*', can reach fruition. This is because capitalism's contradiction between town and countryside can be overcome and the subordination of previously oppressed classes can cease. Since the proletariat is a universal class, it aims to destroy the class structure once and for all, and so the national language can now become 'common to all classes of society' (Iakubinskii 1931c, p. 71).

Bakhtin's Relationship to Soviet Linguistics

A comparison of DiN and Iakubinskii's texts reveals that Bakhtin's discussion of *raznorechie* and *raznoiazychie* as different manifestations of stratification of language bears a thematic resemblance to Iakubinskii's views. Iakubinskii's theoretical ideas concerning social differentiation of language were shared, for instance, by Viktor Zhirmunskii whose view on the formation of national languages 'in fundamentals coincide with Iakubinskii's propositions in 1930' (Zhirmunskii 1936, p. 3). Thus, the general direction that Bakhtin's research took in the early 1930s is in concordance with the sociological approach of the Leningrad school. Consequently, the claims concerning Bakhtin's originality and the uniqueness of his conception of language, as discussed in DiN, are exaggerated and stem from the neglect of the study of the contemporary intellectual context of Soviet language studies. Bakhtin who criticised such contemporary literary scholars as Viktor Vinogradov, Gustav Shpet, Viktor Zhirmunskii and Boris Eikhenbaum for their views on the stylistics of the novel clearly did not try to oppose himself to the sociological approach of the Leningrad School. In fact, this would have been rather odd given the facts of Bakhtin's biography. At the time of writing DiN Bakhtin lived in internal exile which meant that he was not in a position to publicly criticise the views held by the representatives of the 'official' linguistic scholarship.

It is crucial to recognise that in the 1930s Bakhtin was not a linguist, but a theorist of the novel and his focus of attention was determined accordingly. For him, the novel embodies an image of society, but this is a verbal image of the verbal structure of society. The novel is 'a microcosm of *raznorechie*' (Bakhtin 1975 [1934–35], p. 411; 1981 [1940], p. 222). Leningrad linguists provided Bakhtin with a coherent model of the socio-linguistic relations that are both a precondition of the novel as a meta-genre and an object of its artistic imaging. Bakhtin essentially abstracted from the new account of the recent history of the Russian language, treating it as a general account of European linguistic history from antiquity to the Renaissance. Such a strategy fits in with the Marrist contention that all languages undergo a 'single glottogonic process', passing through the same stages of development, but not necessarily at the same tempo.[10] It also reminds one of the Bakhtin Circle's early adherence to the idea of the impending 'Third Renaissance' which would begin in Russia and sweep through Europe (Nikolaev 1997). This abstract use of historical categories, along with Bakhtin's own philosophical idealism, leads to a definite ambivalence over whether the novel is a historically specific phenomenon or an eternal principle.

Bakhtin's originality in these essays lies not in his description of discursive diversity of a national language but in his characterisation of how the novelist exploits that diversity. Thus, 'the novel begins to make use of all languages, manners, genres, it compels all the lived-out and decrepit, all socially and ideologically alien and distant worlds to speak about themselves in their own language and their own style'. The novelist plays a crucial role in the democratisation of linguistic relations by providing an image of the struggle between discourses that occurs within the 'various genres of oral and written discourse'. The nature of this engagement in the novel is, however, not simply polemical but, rather, artistic and creative. The author's and hero's words fuse together and are transformed into an artistic image within which an unresolved 'mutual interaction between worlds, points of view, accents' is captured (Bakhtin 1975 [1934–35], pp. 220–21; 1981 [1934–35], p. 409). If the *mnogoiazychie* of the period of Hellenic expansion was a precondition for the flowering of parodic genres, with language use becoming a conscious act, the *raznorechie* of the Renaissance, the point of transition between feudalism and capitalism, provides the conditions for a flowering of parodic genres at a higher level. At this point it is no longer only languages as such that become self-conscious, but also socio-specific discourses. The parodic genre par excellence is the novel. It is not only language as such, but '*raznorechie* in itself that 'becomes in the novel and thanks to the novel, *raznorechie* for itself'. Novels of the most advanced kind 'rise from the depths of *raznorechie* to the highest spheres of the literary language and overwhelm it' (Bakhtin 1975 [1934–35], p. 211; 1981 [1934–35], p. 400).

Where Iakubinskii saw the final democratisation of linguistic relations to lie in the future, Bakhtin appears to endorse the present time as fully 'novelised'. Where for Iakubinskii the 1917 revolution provided the final precondition for true linguistic democracy, Bakhtin located this back in the Renaissance:

> We live, write and talk in a world of free and democratised language: the old complex and multi-levelled hierarchies of words, forms, images, styles that permeated the whole system of the official language and linguistic consciousness was swept away by the linguistic revolutions of the Renaissance. (Bakhtin 1975[1940], p. 435; 1981 [1940] p. 71)

It is difficult to know how to take this passage, which was written at the height of the Stalin terror and the encodement of 'socialist realism' in narrative literature and elsewhere. One thing is certain, however. Such a judgement could be possible only if the institutions within which language and culture is articulated were bracketed out. This is the consequence of Bakhtin's neo-Kantian heritage, which compelled him to view culture as an ethical concern with all questions of determination from without consigned to the realm of the natural sciences.

An awareness of Iakubinskii's articles, which in many ways sum up the achievements of early Soviet sociolinguistics, may assist in restoring the factors that Bakhtin overlooked, but in order to move beyond such work one needs to overcome the significant problems that also continue to plague Iakubinskii's work. In his preface to Iakubinskii's posthumously published *History of Old Russian Language* (Istoriia drevnerusskogo iazyka, 1953), the prominent Soviet linguist and academician Viktor Vinogradov (1953, p. 17) argued that starting from the mid-1920s Iakubinskii's works on Russian language and its generic variety 'clearly begin to display the signs of vulgar sociologism and vulgar materialism'. It is noteworthy that Vinogradov's assessment was written in the aftermath of Stalin's denunciation of Marrism and he may have been paying lip-service to the 'Stalinist turn' in Soviet linguistics. Yet the assessment of Iakubinskii's views by Vinogradov, who became the Director of the Institute of Linguistics of the Academy of Sciences of USSR in 1950, seems quite appropriate, for it is true that Iakubinskii readily accepted major aspects of Marr's theory of language including the idea of the class-character of language in addition to which he even shared Marr's idea of stadial development of language and thought and adopted latter's paleontological semantics (see Iakubinskii 1927). While

Iakubinskii's linguistic training under the tutelage of Baudouin de Courtenay mitigated the most problematic aspects of Marr's heritage, he was not able fully to overcome them.

While it is undeniable that in his series of articles Iakubinskii is not free from 'vulgar sociologism', the attempt to correlate discursive variation with the institutional structure of society is not, in principle, a mistake. The problem is that Iakubinskii appears simply to equate language with both class and ideology and presents the ideological and linguistic differentiation as causally determined by the class-structure of a society:

> The different class psychology and ideology in class society unfailingly defines the languages of different classes as different languages because language is not only a technical means for the expression and communication of thoughts and feelings, but, above all, a fact of psychology and ideology. (Iakubinskii 1930b, p. 62)

Iakubinskii assumes that class ideologies and class-languages are inseparable. For him, the pre-existing class-structure of a society imposes a particular class-language on the members of the same social class who consequently share a particular ideological point of view and speak the same class-language. Bakhtin, in turn, rejects this kind of determinism and insists that idiolects are not imposed on individuals by social structures but based on the appropriation of others' words or alien discourses and making them one's own words. While Bakhtin sees *raznoiazychie* as an eternal principle, Iakubinskii holds that in a classless society there would eventually exist a single unified 'discursive method' instead of a variety of competing discursive methods suggesting an unappealing scenario in which a non-exploitative society would be marked by unanimity. Writing at the very moment that the USSR became a totalitarian regime in the exact sense, it is not difficult to see why this argument appeared plausible at the time. It would not be long, however, before it became apparent that 'the universality of public discourse remains just as much a myth… as liberty, equality and fraternity and so many other good things' (Iakubinskii 1930a, p. 91–92) in the Stalinist world too.

References

Alpatov, V.M. (2004) *Istoriia odnogo mifa. Marr i marrizm* (Moscow: URSS).

Bakhtin, M.M. (1975 [1934–5]) 'Slovo v romane', in *Voprosy literatury i estetiki* (Moscow: Khudozhestvennaia literatura), pp. 72–233.

Bakhtin, M.M. (1975 [1940]) 'Iz predystorii romannogo slova', in *Voprosy literatury i estetiki* (Moscow: Khudozhestvennaia literatura), pp. 408–446.

Bakhtin, M.M. (1981 [1934–5]) 'Discourse in the Novel', In *The Dialogic Imagination* (Austin: University of Texas Press), pp. 259–422.

Bakhtin, M.M. (1981 [1940]) 'From the Prehistory of Novelistic Discourse', In *The Dialogic Imagination* (Austin: University of Texas Press), pp. 41–83.

Bakhtin, M.M. (1986 [1951–53]) 'The Problem of Speech Genres', *Speech Genres and Other Late Essays*, trans. Vern W. McGee, (Austin, University of Texas Press), pp. 60–102.

Bakhtin, M.M. (1996 [1951–53]) 'Problema rechevykh zhanrov', *Sobranie sochinenii* t.5. Moscow: Russkie slovari, pp. 159–206.

Bakhtin, M.M. (2000 [1929]) 'Problemy tvorchestva Dostoevskogo', in *Sobranie sochinenii* t.2. Moscow: Russkie slovari, pp. 5–175.

Bakhtin, M.M. (2002 [1963]) 'Problemy poetiki Dostoevskogo', in *Sobranie sochinenii* t.6. Moscow: Russkie slovari, pp. 5–300.

Boduen de Kurtene, I.A. (Baudouin de Courtenay, J.N.) (1963 [1870]) 'Nekotorye obshchie zamechaniia o iazykovedenii i iazyke' in *Izbrannye trudy po ohshchemu iazykoznaniiu* (Moscow: Izd. Akademii nauk SSSR), pp. 47–77.

Boduen de Kurtene, I.A. (Baudouin de Courtenay, J.N.) (1963 [1904]), 'Iazyk i iazyki' in *Izbrannye trudy po obshchemu iazykoznaniiu* (Moscow: Izdatel'stvo Akademii nauk SSSR), pp. 67–95.

Brandist, C. (1999) 'Bakhtin's Grand Narrative: The Significance of the Renaissance', *Dialogism* 3, pp.11–30.

Bukharin, N. (1926 [1921]) *Historical Materialism: A System of Sociology* (London: Allen & Unwin).

Desnitskaia, A.V. (2001) 'Na putiiakh k sozdaniiu istoriko-tipologicheskoi teorii eposa: stranitsy nauchnoi biografii V.M. Zhirmunskogo' in D.S. Likhachev (ed.) *Iazyk, literatura, epos (k 100-letiiu so dnia rozhdeniia akademika V.M. Zhirmunskogo* (St. Petersburg: Nauka), pp. 377–401.

Dobrenko, E. (2002) *The Making of the Soviet Writer: Social and Aesthetic Origins of Soviet Literary Culture* (Stanford: Stanford University Press).

Hirschkop, K. (1999) *Mikhail Bakhtin: An Aesthetic for Democracy* (Oxford: Oxford University Press).

Howell, D.P. (1992) *The Development of Soviet Folkloristics* (New York and London: Garland).

Iakubinskii, L.P. (1927) 'K paleontologii nazvanii dlia "poloviny"', *Iazykovednye problemy po chislitel'nym* 1, pp. 191–201.

Iakubinskii, L.P. (1930a) 'Klassovyi sostav sovremennogo russkogo iazyka: iazyk krest'ianstva. Stat'ia chetvertaia', *Literaturnaia ucheba* 4, pp. 80–92.

Iakubinskii, L.P. (1930b) 'Klassovyi sostav sovremennogo russkogo iazyka: iazyk krest'ianstva. Stat'ia chetvertaia', *Literaturnaia ucheba* 6, pp. 51–66.

Iakubinskii, L.P. (1931a) 'Klassovyi sostav sovremennogo russkogo iazyka: iazyk proletariata. Stat'ia piataia', *Literaturnaia ucheba* 7, pp. 22–33.

Iakubinskii, L.P., (1931b) 'Russkii iazyk v epokhu diktatury proletariata' *Literaturnaia ucheba* 9, pp. 66–76.

Iakubinskii, L.P. (1931c) 'O nauchno-populiarnom iazyke', *Literaturnaia ucheba* 1, pp.49–64.

Ivanov, A.M. and L.P. Iakubinskii (1932) *Ocherki po iazyku dlia rabotnikov literatury i dlia samoobrazovaniia* (Moscow and Leningrad: Gosudarstvennoe izdatel'stvo khudozhestvennoi literatury).

Karinskii, N.M. (1903) 'O bronnitskikh govorakh', *Izvestiia ORIAS*, Part 2, vol.3, pp. 94–122.

Lähteenmäki, M. (2006) Da crítica de Saussure por Voloshinov e Iakubinski. In C.A. Faraco, C. Tezza, G. de Castro (eds) *Vinte ensaios sobre Mikhail Bakhtin*. (Petrópolis: Editora Vozes), pp. 190–207.

Medvedev, P.N. (1993 [1928]) *Formal'nyi metod v literaturovedenii* (Moscow: Labirint).

Medvedev, P.N./M.M. Bakhtin (1978) *The Formal Method in Literary Scholarship*, trans. Albert J.Wehrle, (Baltimore: Johns Hopkins University Press).

Misch, G. (1950) *A History of Autobiography in Antiquity* in 2 vols., trans E.W. Dickes; (London: Routledge & Kegan Paul).

Nikolaev, N.I. (1997) 'Sud'ba idei tret'ego vozrozhdeniia', *MOYSEION: Professoru Aleksandru Iosifovichu Zaitsevu ko dniu semidesiatiletiia*, (St. Petersburg), pp. 343–50.

Shakhmatov, A.A. (1915) *Ocherk drevneishego perioda istorii russkogo iazyka* (Petrograd: Imperatorskaia akademia nauk).

Shcherba, L.V. (1958 [1915]) 'Nekotorye vyvody iz moikh dialektologicheskikh luzhitskikh nabliudenii' in *Izbrannye raboty po iazykoznaniiu i fonetike* (Leningrad: Izdatel'stvo Leningradskogo universiteta), pp. 35–9.

Shcherba, L.V. (1957) 'Sovremennyi russkii literaturnyi iazyk', *Izbrannye raboty po russkomu iazyku* (Moscow: Uchebno-pedagogicheskoe izdanie), pp.113–130.

Tamarchenko, N. (1998) 'M.M. Bakhtin i A.N. Veselovskii (Metodologiia istoricheskoi poetiki)', *Dialog Karnaval Khronotop* 4, pp. 33–44.

Thomas, L. (1957) *The Linguistic Theories of N. Ja. Marr* (University of California Press, Berkeley and Los Angeles).

Tihanov, G. (2000) *The Master and the Slave: Lukács, Bakhtin, and the Ideas of Their Time* (Oxford: Clarendon Press).

Veselovskii, A.N. (1939) 'Grecheskii roman' in *Izbrannye stat'i* (Leningrad: Khudozhestvennaia literatura), pp. 23–69.

Veselovskii, A.N. (1940) *Istoricheskaia poetika* (Leningrad: Khudozhestvennaia literatura).

Vinogradov, V.V. (1953) 'Prof. L.P. Iakubinskii kak lingvist i ego "Istoriia drevnerusskogo iazyka"', in L.P. Iakubinskii, *Istoriia drevnerusskogo iazyka* (Moscow: Gosudarstvennoe uchebno-pedagogicheskoe izdatel'stvo ministersva prosveshcheniia RSFSR). pp. 3–40.

Zhirmunskii, V.M. (1936) 'Sravnitel'noe literaturovedenie i problema literaturnykh vliianii', *Izvestiia academii nauk SSSR, otdelenie obshchestvennykh nauk* 3, pp. 383–403.

Chapter 6

LANGUAGE AS A BATTLEFIELD – THE RHETORIC OF CLASS STRUGGLE IN LINGUISTIC DEBATES OF THE FIRST FIVE-YEAR PLAN PERIOD: THE CASE OF E.D. POLIVANOV vs. G.K. DANILOV

Kapitolina Fedorova

Introduction

For Soviet linguistics, the period often referred to as the 'Cultural Revolution' (1929–32) was the time of heated debates around social issues stimulated both by practical needs and by theoretical questions that were emerging in the new social reality. It is typical when speaking about this period to distinguish two extreme positions – the 'old', 'pure' Indo-European linguistics and 'new', 'social', supposedly 'Marxian' linguistics of Nikolai Marr and his disciples. It was this binary opposition that determined the scientific paradigm of the time in the minds of its contemporaries. As V. Karpiuk put it in his 1931 article 'Linguistic Theory and Language Practice': 'There are two main schools in modern linguistics: the so called Indo-European linguistics and traditional oriental studies which is almost the same thing, and the Japhetic theory of N. Ia. Marr' (Karpiuk 1931, p. 204).

The actual situation was much more complicated, however. *Marrism* was not the only 'social' opposition to 'bourgeois' linguistics – the label stuck to the traditional comparative linguistics of the period. It is true that Marr's 'New theory of language' was in a strong position to win the battle and become 'the only true language theory' for the next two decades. But at the turn of the decade the situation in the 'new' linguistics was far from homogeneous. Different scientific groups and associations, and outstanding individuals fought against each other. For most of the contending parties this struggle was a battle fought on two (or more) fronts – against the traditional approach to language and against other pretenders to the throne of the 'new linguistics'. These military metaphors – battle, struggle, fronts – are very important because they are an important part of the epoch's lexicon. Very revealing, for example, is the name *iazykovoi front* ('Language front'), also known as *Iazykfront*, adopted by a young linguists' group in 1930. So there was a front, and a battle was to be fought. But what was the battle for?

Of course all these passionate debates were not just about the extermination of 'idealistic' Indo-European linguistics, which was already in retreat at the time. Furthermore, traditional linguists did not constitute a united group actively defending itself, although their opponents referred to them as a *lager'* ('camp'). In a sense, setting up 'bourgeois' linguistics as a bugbear to be attacked was instrumental in a more serious and larger battle. Sergei Nikiforov writes in his review of the journal *Russian Language in Soviet School*: "Ia. Loia in his article 'For Marxist Linguistics' (No. 5 of 1930) correctly outlines the main goals for Marxist linguists at the moment; among them is the need to fight on two fronts, both against idealism and against mechanism" (Nikiforov 1931, p. 63).

By 'mechanicism' (*mekhanitsizm*) Nikiforov was referring to Marr's theory of language.[1] If 'old' linguistics was commonly criticized from the ideological point of view for being idealistic and bourgeois, Marrism could not be reprimanded ideologically – it was a doctrine that was widely held to be Marxist. Rather, it was Marr's methods that needed to be revised by those who were competing with him in the interests of 'true Marxism'. If we look closer, it was the questions 'Who is the real Marxist?' and 'What is Marxist linguistics?' that would become the most contentious issues in Soviet linguistics of the early 1930s. Language, therefore, was turned into a theatre of war in this battle for the soul of Marxism. It was not only language theory or policy that was exploited during the fight; the language used by the various contending parties was itself very revealing.

These texts may be analyzed as an extremely revealing picture of social variation and 'class struggle' in the Russian language of the Cultural Revolution, and the different linguistic strategies adopted in the discussion show the orientations of the adversaries no less than the content of their arguments. The episode with which the current article is concerned constitutes a particularly vivid example of what Sheila Fitzpatrick, in her seminal article of 1978 termed the motif of 'Cultural Revolution as Class War' (Fitzpatrick 1992 [1978]).[2] To illustrate this thesis I will concentrate the polemics between Evgenii Polivanov, elaborating his own 'Marxist linguistics', and his critic from the 'Language Front' group Georgii Danilov.

Polivanov vs. Danilov: Biographies and Positions[3]

While they differed radically in their attitudes towards social issues and methodology in linguistics, Evgenii Polivanov and Georgii Danilov shared much in their biographies – including their becoming the tragic victims of Stalin's repressions in the late 1930s. Both were active Communist party members (Polivanov from 1917, Danilov from 1920) and both fought in the Civil War. Each used his linguistic education to solve real-world problems: Polivanov is best known for his work on developing alphabets for various, chiefly Central Asian, languages, while Danilov set up Russian language courses for 'national cadres' and popularized African languages. Each in turn attacked the rising authority of Marr's 'New Theory of Language' but lost their battles and were ousted from their posts. Each was compelled to spend his last years working in the provinces, with Danilov even having to work as a teacher in colonies for juvenile delinquents. Danilov was arrested in April 1937 and executed in July of the same year (Ashnin and Alpatov 1994, p. 118–120). Polivanov was arrested just a month later and shot within six months (Ashnin and Alpatov 1997, pp. 125, 137). It is clear that they had much in common, and even shared some scientific interests, including 'exotic' languages and relations between social class and linguistic behavior. Nevertheless, this did not prevent them from becoming opponents, or even, in Danilov's terminology, 'class enemies'. There are more subtle differences in their life trajectories that are responsible for their respective developments.

Born in Smolensk in 1891 (Leont´ev 1983, p. 6), Polivanov was only five years older then Danilov but it seems that these five years were of crucial importance. Polivanov graduated from St. Petersburg University in 1912 and almost immediately began to teach at its Department of Oriental Studies. He spent the period between 1914 and 1916 in Japan conducting extensive field work. Thus, by 1917 he was already established both institutionally and academically, his general approach to linguistics being formed under the strong influence of one of the most significant linguists of the time, Jan Baudouin de Courtenay. Danilov enrolled at Moscow University in 1916, but was almost immediately drafted into the Imperial Army and spent two years at the front during World War One. His education therefore remained incomplete, although he formally graduated from the University in 1918. Polivanov was, thus, much better educated in linguistic methodology, but, as it seems, he was also more conspicuously talented – it is relatively well known that the Formalist literary critic Viktor Shklovskii described him as an 'ordinary genius' (Koroleva 2003, p. 230). Some of Polivanov's sociolinguistic ideas on class and age group variation in language, on the problem of language prestige, and on the process of linguistic change and so on, anticipated those that became generally recognized in the 1960s when sociolinguistics emerged as an independent discipline. While a separate article could easily be written on this subject, what interests us here is not the comparative quality of Polivanov's and Danilov's work but positions they took in their polemics on social issues in linguistics.

Polivanov criticized Marr not from the point of view of 'pure' linguistics (although the former's opponents sought to accuse him of being an adept of 'bourgeois Indo-European linguistics'). Rather, Polivanov presented his 'real Marxist approach to language' in opposition to Marr's vulgar Marxism. The title of his book *Za marksistskoe iazykoznanie* ('For Marxist Linguistics') was clearly a slogan, but he regarded Marxism first and foremost as a scientific method. Instead of a ready-to-use solution, Marxism was seen as a way to address a problem. Danilov and many other 'young linguists' approached Marxism dogmatically, assuming it self-evident that 'Marx's doctrine is all-powerful since it is true'. There was a powerful consensus among most linguistic circles at the time that Marxism was unquestionably true and that it was necessary to create a specifically 'Marxist linguistics'. The question they asked was what was 'real Marxism in linguistics' and who could be called a 'true Marxist linguist'.

Polivanov's position seems to us a logically coherent and sensible approach. He defended Indo-European linguistics as a science working with real linguistic facts rather than speculating on their ideological interpretation. At the same time he clearly believed that traditional linguistics unduly evaded the social aspects of language usage. He therefore suggested setting up a new branch of linguistics, which he termed social or sociological linguistics, that would investigate the relationship between language and social issues (Polivanov 1968, pp. 182–183). According to Polivanov (1968, pp. 206–121), different social classes tend to speak differently, especially in the realm of lexis, but there are no absolute borders either in social space or in historical time. A language is conservative by its very nature, which is why its grammar cannot change in just a few years even during such a social upheaval as a revolution. Furthermore, 'old' prestige speech norms can preserve themselves even when acquired by new speakers: the new 'proletarian' elite began to use the standard literary language of the previous epoch, thus inaugurating the process of more or less gradual language changes (Polivanov 1968, pp. 213–215; see also Alpatov 2003, pp. 186–188). It was this statement by Polivanov that provoked the most furious reaction from his opponents, Georgii Danilov among them:

Общелитературный язык нашей эпохи, по Поливанову, - это какой-то надклассовый язык, в который проникают элементы языка фабрично-заводских рабочих, крестьянского языка, блатного жаргона. <...> Остается один вывод: наш литературный язык в своей основе есть язык господствующих ранее классов – буржуазии и помещиков. Что это, как не явная пораженческая, перенесенная в область языкознания троцкистская позиция, отрицающая возможность для пролетариата в период его диктатуры построить свою пролетарскую культуру и свой пролетарский язык в национальных формах? (Danilov 1931b, p. 164)

('The common literary language of our epoch is, in Polivanov's opinion, a sort of a supra-class language permeated with some elements of the language of the factory worker and the peasant, and of thieves' jargon. <...> Thus, there can be only one conclusion: our literary language is, basically, the language of the ex-ruling classes – the bourgeoisie and the landowning classes. What is this, if not the obviously defeatist position imported into linguistics from Trotskyism which denies that during the period of its dictatorship the proletariat can build its own proletarian culture and its own proletarian language in national forms?')[4]

Accusing Polivanov of adopting an 'anti-proletarian' position, Danilov uses such evaluative epithets as 'porazhencheskii' (defeatist) and 'trotskistskii' (Trotskyist). This explicit negative evaluation and appeal to political authority rather than scholarly value is quite typical for the critique of the period. More interesting, however, is that these accusations pale in significance compared to some other accusations Danilov directs against Polivanov:

Как представитель буржуазного языкознания Е. Поливанов неминуемо должен грешить и в области национального вопроса. Недаром мы встречаем у него явно великодержавнические мотивы об «общерусском стандарте» (после Октября) как «языке советской культуры». (Danilov 1931b, p. 163)

('As a representative of bourgeois linguistics, E. Polivanov inevitably should sin in the field of the national question. No wonder that we find motives of great-power chauvinism in his work when he speaks of the "common Russian standard language" (after October) as "the language of the Soviet culture"')

A little later in the text Danilov writes: «Встречаем у него и нотки местного национализма» ('We can also find traces of local nationalism here') (Danilov 1931b, p. 163). It is apparently somehow possible for someone to be a Russophile and a Russophobe at the same time. Furthermore, in a different part of Polivanov's book Danilov finds a 'clear conception of subjective idealism dressed up with a good amount of mechanicism' («... ясная концепция субъективного идеализма, подправленного значительной порцией механицизма») (Danilov 1931b, p. 163.). This formula becomes particularly interesting when we recall that in the rhetoric employed by *Iazykfront* 'subjective idealism' was a characteristic of the Indo-European linguistics, whereas 'mechanicism' was related to Marrism (see the quotation from Nikiforov, above). It is clear that what is in question is not Polivanov's actual scientific or political position, rather all these *ism*-s are merely instruments in polemics.

As much as Polivanov's position is clear and scientifically reasoned, Danilov's argument is opaque and difficult to understand. Methodological differences between them come to the foreground here. Polivanov understands Marxism and materialism as involving a commitment to primacy of reality: scientific facts for him precede any interpretation. Danilov adopts the opposite approach: it is interpretation rather than fact that matters. Criticizing his own work of 1929 on Ukrainian workers' speech (Danilov 1929) Danilov wrote in his penitential article 'My mistakes':

Конечно, те факты, которые я приводил в своей статье по этому вопросу, не являются выдумкой. Рабочие, которых мне пришлось обследовать, действительно в важнейших случаях коммуникации (на производстве, в общественной жизни) пользовались русским языком. <...> Таким образом, мое изложение нисколько не противоречило фактам, но эти факты, эти явления были не существенны, не необходимы, а преходящи. Украинский пролетариат должен быть преодолеть и уже в значительной мере преодолел эти явления. В своем исследовании я осталcя, таким образом, на поверхности явлений, не вскрыв самой сущности этих явлений и свойственных им закономерностей. (Danilov 1931a, p. 9)

('Of course the facts I adduced in my article on the question were not fictions. The workers I had examined did use the Russian language in the most important communicative situations (in work, in social life). <...> Hence, my statement in no way contradicted the facts, but these facts, these phenomena were not essential, not necessary but transient. The Ukrainian proletariat had to overcome, and have, to a certain extent, overcome these phenomena. In my study, therefore, I remained on the surface of the phenomena, and did not reveal the very essence of these phenomena and the regularities peculiar for them')

Everything in this quotation is remarkable. The facts could be disregarded if they come into conflict with the 'right' class interpretation. Furthermore, they should be overcome. It seems that Polivanov and Danilov speak different languages: Polivanov uses the language and the logic of scientific argumentation, whereas Danilov exploits the jargon of class struggle. At the end of his article he directly calls his opponent a 'class enemy' (anyone working for the class enemy is a class enemy himself), and even issues a threat:

Но индоевропейскую невинность автор действительно сберег во всей неприкосновенности, добросовестно выполнив заказ классового врага. Тем хуже для Поливанова!! (Danilov 1931b, p. 165)

('But the author did preserve his Indo-European virginity, having conscientiously fulfilled class enemy's order. So much the worse for Polivanov!')

We now move on to a more detailed investigation of the way language is used by these opponents in this fight for Marxism. In what follows I refer to Polivanov's article 'Historical linguistics and language policy' (Polivanov 1931) and Danilov's review of Polivanov's book *For Marxist Linguistics* (Danilov 1931b).

Polivanov vs. Danilov: Language as an Instrument in Polemics

Differing so radically in their respective ideological and methodological orientations, Polivanov and Danilov also differ in their usage of the language when trying to counter their opponent's argument. Polivanov's rhetorical position can be characterised as one of intellectual superiority. His main objective is to show his opponent's failure as a scholar, and he does not hesitate to use very sharp expressions:

Становится немного смешно, правда, излагать это обвинение, которое, разумеется, ничего кроме смеха не могло возбудить у современных западно-европейских представителей компаративной лингвистики. Но что поделать? Раз такие более чем наивные обвинения высказываются и хором повторяются, их приходится цитировать и пересказывать. (Polivanov 1931, pp. 14–15)

('It is rather ridiculous to give an account of this accusation which could only make any representative of contemporary West-European comparative linguistics laugh. But it can't be helped. If these more than naïve accusations are expressed and repeated in chorus they have to be quoted and retold')

For Polivanov, everything contradicting scientifically recognized facts is ridiculous, naïve, and senseless:

Мне действительно приходилось встречаться именно с такой формулировкой протеста против индоевропеистики[5] – несмотря на то, что для всякого мало-мальски осведомленного в классификации научных дисциплин, эта формулировка звучит как совершенная бессмыслица. (Polivanov 1931, p. 16)

('I did indeed come across this very wording of protest against Indo-European linguistics, although for everyone conversant in the slightest degree with the classification of scientific disciplines this wording sounds as complete nonsense')

The use of words such as "ridiculous" or "nonsense" directly reveals Polivanov's condescending attitude towards critics of comparative linguistics who did indeed usually have a rather vague idea of its methods. Polivanov is absolutely convinced he is right, since scientific competence is on his side. His polemic is redolent with expressions such as *razumeetsia* ('obviously'), *estestvenno* ('naturally'), *nesomnenno* ('undoubtedly'), and the like. In addition, Polivanov often uses very vivid and ironic comparisons to appeal to the reason of his readers. Thus, he says that to reproach Indo-European linguistics for ignoring non-European languages is the same as to accuse ichthyology of not studying birds, or of even avoiding choral singing! (Polivanov 1931, pp. 16, 18). He compares linguistic rules with formulas in mathematics or chemistry and other facts of natural sciences such as biology or anatomy. He writes:

> Если бы кто-либо стал сомневаться в истинности фактов, собранных в анатомии человека, я полагаю, лучший способ разрешить эти сомнения был бы именно в том, чтобы самому заняться анатомией человека. То же, конечно, и в отношении исторических (в широком смысле) дисциплин, как, напр., сравнительной анатомии или, хотя бы, палеонтологии. То же и для лингвистики в целом, и для исторической лингвистики. (Polivanov 1931, p. 30).

('If someone begins to doubt the facts established by human anatomy I think the best way to destroy these suspicions for such person would be to begin to study anatomy himself. The same is true, of course, for historical (in broad sense) disciplines such as, e.g., comparative anatomy or let's say paleontology. The same is true both for general linguistics and for historical linguistics')

The word 'facts' which Polivanov uses repeatedly is crucial. For him a fact is the best argument; if something is established as a fact it can not be denied or ignored. Polivanov believes in facts to an almost fanatical extent. No wonder this word plays a large part in his lexicon. In his article from 7535 word usage 30 fall to the share of *fact*. It does not seem much, but if we compare the resulting frequency of this lexeme in Polivanov's language with its average frequency in modern data (as per *Chastotnyi slovar'*, the Russian frequency word-book) the former turns out to be 33 times more frequent (see Table 6.1).

While the subject matter of Polivanov's article no doubt accounts for some of this, the figures still stand for themselves. Thus, for Polivanov the fact is always more important than ideology and he assumes that others share this belief in facts. This leads him not only to appeal to facts as an argument in discussion but to take the liberty of making statements that sound absolutely shocking for his time. Among others he asserts that imperialistic colonial policy brought about the boom in linguistic studies of different non-European

Table 6.1. **Comparative Frequency for the Word** *Fact*

Frequency for 1 Million Word Usage	
Modern data	Polivanov's article
120.22	3981.42

languages (Polivanov 1931, pp. 19–20). He also cites A. Meillet: 'If bourgeois science consists in seeing the facts as they are, I am ready to take upon myself the accusation of being bourgeois' (Polivanov 1931, p. 15). This primacy of facts on ideology becomes clear in the following quotation:

Допустим, пускай, что Бопп был бы самым что ни на есть антиимпериалистическим и пролетарски настроенным интернационалистом и коммунистом (в 1816 г.), и в таком случае он тоже бы не включил в созданную им систему индоевропейской сравнительной грамматики чувашского или татарского языков, - просто потому, что им там не отведено места самой историей этих языков. (Polivanov 1931, pp. 16–17)

('Let's assume that Bopp was the most anti-imperialistic and pro-proletariat internationalist and communist (in 1816). But even then he would not have included Chuvash or Tatar grammar in his Indo-European comparative grammar system – just because it is not permitted by the history of these languages')

Danilov in his turn uses a fundamentally different system of argumentation. Thus, the same word *facts* he uses ironically when quoting Polivanov: 'the indisputable, in the author's opinion, facts' («бесспорные, по мнению автора, факты») (Danilov 1931b, p. 162). This is consistent with his position in his abovementioned article 'My Mistakes'.

In general, one might say that quotation marks play quite a big role in Danilov's language. First, there are a considerable number of quotations from Polivanov in his article, which is not surprising, of course, since it is the review of Polivanov's work. Yet almost all these quotations do not just inform the reader of Polivanov's ideas; they are used to disparage those ideas.

Quotation marks also regularly appear as a sign of irony:

"В этих цитатах что ни строка, то **'блестящее откровение'**". (Danilov 1931b, p. 164)

("Every line in these quotations is a **'brilliant revelation'**").

"Еще откровеннее профессор **'раскрывает'** себя на стр. 43 своего **'исторического'** труда, следуя уже непосредственно Бодуэну и Есперсену» (Danilov 1931b, p. 163)

("Even more openly the professor **'reveals'** himself on the page 43 of his **'historical'** work, directly following Baudouin and Jespersen")

«Поливанов, как и его западноевропейские коллеги-'**социологи**', исключительное значение придает языковому описательству» (Danilov 1931b, p. 165)

("Polivanov similar to his West-European **'sociologist'** colleagues treats language description as having an extraordinary importance")

Actually, both functions (quoting and ironic) are often combined when short extracts from Polivanov's are used for ironic purpose:

"Вступая же на путь объяснений, лингвист, по его мнению, перестает быть собственно лингвистом и занимается '**обывательскими рассуждениями**' (стр. 165)". (Danilov 1931b, p. 165)

("Starting down on the path of explanations, a linguist, as it seems to him, ceases to be a proper linguist and is busying himself **'philistine reasoning'** (p. 165)");

"... непогрешимый и '**самый плодотворный**' (стр. 10), с точки зрения Поливанова, сравнительно-исторический метод" (Danilov 1931b, p. 162)

("...the infallible and **'the most productive'** (p. 10), in Polivanov's opinion, is the comparative-historical method...").

Danilov is also sure he is right but his correctness is based not on intellectual superiority and scientific facts as in Polivanov's case, but on his knowledge of the 'correct ideology'. For him Polivanov is a cunning class enemy trying to pretend and mask himself:

"Проф. Поливанову неведомо – или от притворяется, что ему неведомо, - что..." (Danilov 1931b, p. 162) ("Prof. Polivanov does not know – or he **pretends** he does not know that...");

«Но Поливанов, как мы видели, не прочь прикинуться марксистом» (Danilov 1931b, p. 164)

("But Polivanov, as we have seen, does not mind to **feign** being a Marxist").

Speaking of Polivanov's statement that there are some persons in linguistics with whom he could speak a common language, Danilov among them; evidently due to his research on Ukrainian workers' speech, Danilov angrily declares (Danilov 1931b, p. 163):

"Для Данилова, например, да и не только для него, взаимное понимание с Поливановым абсолютно неустановимо и их разногласия касаются именно основного. Профессор не желает этого видеть. Но... **не нарочная ли это слепота?**"

("For Danilov, for example, and not for him alone, mutual understanding with Polivanov is absolutely impossible; their disagreement concerns the very basic things. The professor would not see it. But… **it is intentional blindness, isn't it**?")

From this perception of his opponent as someone pretending to be someone else comes the basic metaphor of Danilov's article – a *mask covering the enemy's true face*.

"Математикой Поливанов **прикрывает** бесплодность буржуазной" (Danilov 1931b, p. 162) ("Polivanov uses mathematics to **cover** the infertility of the bourgeois science");

"Профессор не прочь загримироваться под ортодоксального " (Danilov 1931b, p. 162) ("The professor does not mind to **make oneself up** as an orthodox Marxist");

"Поливанов 'отметает грубо-наивную ссылку на империализм и буржуазный характер индогерманистики' (стр. 23) и тем самым **открывает свое лицо** как агента буржуазии в советской науке" (Danilov 1931b, p. 163)

("Polivanov 'sweeps aside the rude and naïve references to the imperialistic and bourgeois character of Indogermanistics' (p. 23) and so **uncovers his face** as a bourgeois agent in the Soviet science")

"Поливанов грубо клевещет на молодежь <…> , хотя тут же, **заметая следы**, говорит…" (Danilov 1931b, p. 163)

("Polivanov slanders the youth <…> but right here, trying to **cover his tracks** he says…").

As a 'true' Marxist for Danilov it is not difficult to 'uncover' the enemy although some of his colleagues were deceived by this mask:

"Не стоит большого труда распознать в этих рассуждениях **неприкрытый механицизм**" (Danilov 1931b, p. 164)

("It is not difficult **to recognize uncovered mechanicism** in this argumentation");

"В других местах своей книги Поливанов уже прямо **выбалтывает** эти мысли" (Danilov 1931b, p. 164)

("In other parts of his book Polivanov **blabbed out** these thoughts openly");

"Поливанов, оставаясь индоевропеистом до мозга костей, продолжает фактически дело фортунатовской школы, но более тонкими и хитрыми средствами. **Маска** буржуазного агента в науке с него **не была сорвана** своевременно ни руководством РАНИОН, ни критикой" (Danilov 1931b, p. 165)

("Remaining an Indo-European linguist to the very marrow of his bones, Polivanov in fact continued the line of the Fortunatov school but with more subtle and skilful means. Neither RANION leaders nor critics **tore the mask off** this bourgeois agent in science at the right moment").

Finally, at the end of his article, when the whole conglomeration of contradictory accusations, discussed in the previous section, are over, Danilov passes his final verdict on Polivanov's ideas using again the same 'mask' metaphor:

"В книге «За марксистское языкознание» Поливанов выступил, хотя и **под маской,** но настолько прозрачной, что она вовсе **не скрыла его лица** "   (Danilov 1931b, p. 165)

("In his book 'For Marxist linguistics' Polivanov acted under **the mask,** but this mask is so transparent it **was not able to cover his real face**").

Thus, while Polivanov tries to prove his opponents are incompetent as scientists, Danilov affirms that Polivanov is ideologically hostile to the proletariat because of his bourgeois origin and support of bourgeois science, and so all his ideas are injurious by definition. The similarity of their social origins is not raised at all, of course. Nevertheless there remains something common in Polivanov's and Danilov's language usage which marks these texts as belonging to the same period in Soviet history. The first thing striking modern reader is an openness and directness in expressing opinions that is untypical for contemporary scholarly language. Polivanov is superciliously ironic ("Послушные, но совершенно несвещующие любители хорового пения" (Polivanov 1931, p. 15) ('Docile but absolutely ignorant fans of choral singing'), while Danilov is aggressively rude ("Книга, безусловно, вредна...", (Danilov 1931b, p. 162) ('The book is injurious without doubt...'); but both present their evaluations directly. The second common feature of these authors is 'colloquialism' of their language: there are many cases of words like *deskat', ne proch', ne pri chem, vysasyvat' iz pal'tsa, svalivat',* and similar in both texts.

But do they speak the same language in a broader sense? Is it possible to find any differences in Polivanov's and Danilov's texts which can be regarded as sociolinguistic indicators marking their authors as representatives of different social elite groups? I have attempted to answer these questions by using quantitative analysis of their respective texts.

Polivanov vs. Danilov: Language as a Sociolinguistic Indicator

For a quantitative analysis I took: 1) the whole of Danilov's text (1337 words); the sentences consisting mainly of quotations from Polivanov's work were excluded; and 2) a fragment of Polivanov's text of the similar length (1348 words) from the beginning of his article. For these texts several indexes[6] were considered, as summarized in Table 6.2. I will comment on those which differ significantly (all except *Analyticity* and *Adjectives quantity*).

Such indexes as *Verb quantity*, *Noun quantity*, *Pronoun quantity*, and *Conjunction quantity* are calculated as a ratio of respective parts of speech usages to the number of words in a given text. What can be said about the differences between Danilov's and Polivanov's language in relation to these indexes? It is evident that Polivanov prefers verbs (including participles and adverbial participles), pronouns and conjunctions, whereas Danilov shows a distinct preference for nouns. In general, nouns express lexical meaning, and the fact that Danilov uses them 44% more often allows us to conclude that he tends to prefer lexical to grammatical means, including conjunctions and pronouns.

The *Lexical diversity* index represents the ratio of different lexemes used in the text to the whole number of word usages. It allows us to assess the extent to which the text is constructed by repetition of the same lexemes. The markedly low value of this index for Polivanov can be explained if we remember that he uses more pronouns and conjunctions, i.e. grammaticalized elements that tend to be repeated regularly.

An equally interesting result is produced by comparing Polivanov's and Danilov's respective *negation indexes* – a ratio of 'negative' words (negative particles, pronouns and words with the prefix *ne-*) to the whole number of words in the text. It turns out that Danilov's text is almost four times more 'negative' than that of Polivanov. This distinctly negative character of Danilov's language should be related to his aggressive and critical position.

Table 6.2. The Results of Quantitative Analysis of Polivanov's and Danilov's Texts

Index	Polivanov	Danilov
Analyticity	0.28	0.28
Verbs quantity	0.11	0.08
Nouns quantity	0.25	0.36
Adjectives quantity	0.16	0.18
Pronouns quantity	0.17	0.08
Conjunction quantity	0.18	0.11
Lexical diversity	0.54	0.61
Negation	0.008	0.03
Length of sentence	35.47	17.36
Syntax complexity	2.63	1.54
Subordination	0.06	0.03

Two next indexes – *length of sentence* (the ratio of word number to the number of sentences) and *syntax complexity* (the ratio of the number of clauses to the number of sentences in the text) – are related to the syntactic organization of the texts. Here the differences between the two 'languages' under comparison become particularly striking: Polivanov's sentences are twice as long (the longest reaching some 94 words) and almost twice as complex in construction.

Finally, *subordination* constitutes an additional index for calculating the ratio of subordinate conjunctions to the number of words. It is evident that although the difference between the texts in this regard is partly due to the fact that Polivanov uses more conjunctions as a whole, the share of subordinate conjunctions in Polivanov's text is 33% whereas in Danilov's it is only 27%.

Summing up, it is possible to say that Polivanov's language is much more 'grammatical', i.e. he uses more linguistic elements with grammaticalized meaning (e.g. pronouns and conjunctions). Danilov in his turn prefers lexical means of expression. Moreover, Polivanov's language is noticeably more complex syntactically: the sentences are longer, and there are more complex and compound sentences and subordinate clauses in his text than in that of Danilov. Polivanov's language can, therefore, be considered an indicator of his belonging to higher and especially more highly educated social group.

At the same time, on the lexical level, Polivanov's language is rather simple or, more precisely, it seems rather simple: there are many instances of colloquialisms and everyday words in his texts. Danilov does speak a simple language replete with clichés, while Polivanov *tries* to speak the simple code of the period but finds it impossible to abandon his 'complex', 'grammatical' and 'out-of-time' language. In the same way he is unable or unwilling to neglect the logic of scientific fact for the sake of ideology. As Danilov said: '*So much the worse for Polivanov!*'

Conclusion

In my article I have tried to analyze the state of Soviet linguistics in the early 1930s by concentrating on a small sample of the evidence of the period. It was particularly important to demonstrate that it was the time of serious struggle for the right to proclaim a new science of language and to call it Marxist. This fight for Marxism was interpreted by many of its participants as a class struggle – the question of social class was at the centre of the polemics that served at the same time as an instrument of this struggle. Moreover, the language of the period itself can be seen as a battlefield: there were different languages that were, it seems, not always mutually intelligible.

The 'old', 'educated', and 'logical' language of Evgenii Polivanov and 'young', 'aggressive', and 'ideological' language of Georgii Danilov are particularly illustrative examples of this 'class struggle' in the Russian language in the field of linguistics.

References

Alpatov, V.M. (2003) 'Kniga E.D. Polivanova "Za marksistskoe iazykoznanie"', in E. D. Polivanov, *Za marksistskoe iazykoznanie*, (second edition) (Smolensk: SGPU), pp. 184–208.

Ashnin, F.D. and Alpatov, V.M. (1994) 'Georgii Konstantinovich Danilov – odin iz pervykh sovetskikh afrikanistov', *Vostok*, no. 2, pp.115–21.

Ashnin, F.D. and Alpatov, V.M. (1997) 'Iz sledstvennogo dela E.D. Polivanova', *Vostok*, no. 5, pp.124–42.

Bakhurst, D., (1991) *Consciousness and Revolution in Soviet Philosophy: From the Bolsheviks to Evald Ilyenkov* (Cambridge: Cambridge University Press).

Danilov, G.K., (1931a) 'Moi oshibki', *Revoliutsiia i iazyk*, no. 1, pp. 9–10.

Danilov, G.K., (1931b) 'E. Polivanov. *Za marksistskoe iazykoznanie. Sbornik populiarnykh lingvisticheskikh statei*, M: Federatsiia, 1931' (review), *Russkii iazyk v sovetskoi shkole*, no. 6–7, pp. 162–5.

David-Fox, M., (1999) 'What is Cultural Revolution?', *Russian Review* no. 58(2), pp. 181–201.

Fitzpatrick, S., (1974) 'Cultural Revolution in Russia 1928–1932', *Journal of Contemporary History*, vol. 9, no. 1, pp. 33–52.

Fitzpatrick, S., (1992 [1978]) 'Cultural Revolution as Class War', in S. Fitzpatrick, *The Cultural Front: Power and Culture in Revolutionary Russia* (Ithaca and London: Cornell University Press), pp. 115–48.

Iakhot, I. (1981) *Podavlenie filosofii v SSSR (20–30 gody)*, (New York: Chalidze).

Joravsky, D. (1961) *Soviet Marxism and Natural Science 1917–1932* (London: Routledge & Kegan Paul).

Karpiuk, V., (1931) 'Lingvisticheskaia teoriia i iazykovaia praktika', *Kul'tura i pis'mennost' Vostoka*, no. 7–8, pp. 204–209.

Koroleva, I.A., (2003) 'Imia E. D. Polivanova na Smolenshchine', in E.D. Polivanov, *Za marksistskoe iazykoznanie* (Smolensk: SGPU) pp. 230–236.

Ksenofontov, V.I. (1975) *Leninskie idei v sovetskiĭ filosofskoĭ nauke 20-kh godov (Diskussiia dialektikov s mekhanistami)*, (Leningrad: Izd. Leningradskogo Universiteta).

Lartsev, V. (1988) *Evgenii Dmitrievich Polivanov: stranitsy zhizni i deiatel'nosti*, (Moscow: Glavnaia redaktsiia vostochnoi literatury).

Leont'ev, A.A. (1983) *Evgenii Dmitrievich Polivanov i ego vklad v obshchee iazykoznanie*, (Moscow: Nauka).

Nikiforov, S., (1931) 'Teoriia iazykoznaniia v zhurnale "Russkii iazyk v sovetskoi shkole"', *Revoliutsiia i iazyk*, no. 1, pp. 63–6.

Polivanov, E.D., (1931) 'Istoricheskoe iazykoznanie i iazykovaia politika', in Polivanov, E.D. *Za marksistskoe iazykoznanie* (Moscow: Federatsiia), pp. 10–35.

Polivanov, E.D., (1968) *Stat'i po obshchemu iazykoznaniiu*, (Moscow: Glavnaia redaktsiia vostochnoi literatury).

Sharov, S. (2002) *Chastotnyi slovar' russkogo iazyka*, http://www.artint.ru/projects/frqlist.asp (last accessed 12.04.09).

Somerville, J., (1946) 'Basic trends in Soviet Philosophy', *The Philosophical Review*, vol. 55, no. 3, pp. 250–263.

Zhuravlev, A.F., (1988) 'Opyt kvantitativno-tipologicheskogo issledovaniia raznovidnostei ustnoi rechi', in Dmitrii Shmelev and Elena Zemskaia (eds), *Raznovidnosti gorodskoi ustnoi rechi* (Moscow: Nauka), pp. 84–151.

Chapter 7

THE TENACITY OF FORMS: LANGUAGE, NATION, STALIN

Michael G. Smith

... the beginner who has learnt a new language always translates it back into his mother tongue, but he has assimilated the spirit of the new language and can produce freely in it only when he moves in it without remembering the old and forgets in it his ancestral tongue.

Karl Marx, "The Eighteenth Brumaire"

Introduction

To understand the national question in Soviet history ultimately means to know the scholarship that informed it. Among the most important of the scholars, perhaps surprisingly, was I.V. Dzhugashvili, also known by his underground name as Koba Stalin. His first major article on the subject, "Social Democracy and the National Question" (1913), was not just a crafty polemic against the Austrian Marxists, as most scholars have proposed. Written for the party academic journal, *Enlightenment (Prosveshchenie)*, it was also a well-read piece on the subject of nations and nationalism. One of the last major publications before his death, "Marxism and the Problems of Linguistics" (1950), recapitulated the themes. Originally published in *Pravda* in serial parts, it was a polemic to be sure, but framed within the rather dry analysis of linguistics. In between came a host of speeches, articles, pamphlets and discussions on language and national issues. Some were more academic than others. All were political. All confronted, to one degree or another, language as a constituent "form" of the nation. Or, as Karl Marx intimated in the quote above, language as a privileged field within which we humans move and act and think. We can no more escape language than we can history. We can know them and master them, but only by learning and making them anew. They are our inheritance, they are our legacy, and all the spaces in between.

This concept of "form" remains something of a mystery. Stalin and his contemporaries used it with a frequency and self-evidence that belies its deeper meanings. More recently, scholars have recognized the Soviet Union as comprising a state of "ontological nationalities" (Slezkine 1994, p. 414), centered upon the "forms of nationhood" (Martin 2001, p. 5), exploring how "each of the Soviet socialist nations had taken form" (Hirsch 2005, p. 313). We need to parse these meanings of ontological "form" with more care. One possible key to unlocking its mysteries, its Stalinist senses, is Greek philosophy, namely the Platonic theories of Forms and the neo-Platonic dialectics that followed from them. Stalin studied these categories in the curriculum of his Tbilisi seminary, reading Plato in the original Greek. He returned to them in his essay on Linguistics of 1950: both as style, in the shape of a classical Greek dialogue; and as substance, through his exposition of the significance of language "forms." His language and national forms in history, I propose, mirrored Plato's Forms in metaphysics, or at least their reproductions in the neo-Platonism that ruled so much of learning in his part of the world at the turn of the century. Both Plato's and Stalin's forms were essential and existential, giving uniform structure to visible reality, making aesthetic order out of life's chaos. Both were multiple and equal, variations of an ideal type common to all humanity. They were both fonts of scientific knowledge and practical action, gauges of historical change both natural and historical.[1] Immutable and absolute Stalin's national forms were not. The dialectician equivocated here, as perhaps Plato himself did in the end. But the forms certainly were tenacious in time and space. Individual nations might come and go, but some form of the nation would always remain, especially through its language forms. None of these correspondences suggest provenance. They are simply points of reference. Plato's theories and Greek intellectual traditions were a model, practical metaphors, a classical education upon which Stalin framed some part of his thinking, a key to his intellectual biography along with what he later read of Hegel and Darwin, Marx and Lenin.[2]

Schooled in the ways of the ancients, Stalin was still a modern man. He came of intellectual age, in the 1913 work especially, at the dramatic intersection of the established age of nationalism and the coming age of socialism. One of his most lasting contributions to Marxist political theory, one with a significant international impact, was to make sense of nationalism in Marxist terms, for all colonial peoples everywhere, from South America to South Asia (Hobsbawm 1991, pp. 2, 136; Hutchinson and Smith 1994, p. 15). In 1913, Stalin was a minor Bolshevik, besieged by the age of nationalism all around him (in Baku and St. Petersburg, Vienna and Cracow), by a flood of literature and by the powerful complex of Austro-Marxist opinion on the nationality question. He wrote the

1913 article in multi-ethnic, cosmopolitan Vienna, at the home of Alexander Troyanovsky, editor of *Enlightenment*, this over the course of several busy weeks, relying on the translating help of his host's extended family and the tutorials of one Nikolai Bukharin (Stalin read German poorly).[3] All influences were upon him. By 1934, he was undisputed master of the Communist party and Soviet state, projecting his definitions, through *Marxism and the National and Colonial Problem*, far and wide to the world. The edition, in Russian or English, French or Chinese, always began with his 1913 article on the national question, now renamed for Marxism, rechristened as "theory." All influences now seemed to project from him. This was quite a transformation in just over twenty years. The world, in fact, was beginning to read Marx backwards from Stalin (Bloom 1941, p. 204).

I raise the Stalin card not to personalize or dramatize the cult in history, but to recognize that he was in many respects both most unique and most typical of party leaders. One of the ironies of the historiography is that Stalin remains the last of the great old Bolsheviks to be rehabilitated, not in any moral or political sense of course, but as a historical figure who enjoyed remarkable staying power and popular success. We are only now beginning to read comprehensive and authoritative intellectual biographies about him, some sixty years after his death (van Ree 2002; Davies and Harris 2005; Service 2005). What were the conditions and character traits for his success? Two recent studies reveal the irony, with a hint of shame, that Stalin still has much that is genuine to teach us, particularly about the power of his language theories and national policies (Dorn 2000, pp. 227–228; Avineri 1992, p. 299).

Stalin was such a unique figure early in his career because, as a Bolshevik of Georgian ethnicity with both pro-national "nativizing" and pro-Russian russifying sympathies, he was strategically placed to draft the party's first and lasting manifesto on the question, the 1913 article; to follow V.I Lenin's leads on the rights of nations to equality and self-determination, on the strategic importance of the anti-colonial and national liberation movement;[4] to direct the Commissariat of Nationality Affairs between 1917 and 1924; and to secure the grand compromise that was the federal system, the "union" of national republics and regions in 1922. With these and his other posts and experiences, he was uniquely positioned to succeed Lenin as de-facto head of both party and state. Yet Stalin also became, later in his career, quite typical of the vast majority of party members who understood the priority demand and central role of the Russian language in a modernizing economy. After 1935, his regime imposed new all-union Cyrillic scripts for the non-Russians, decreed terminological russification and obligatory teaching of Russian in the schools, yet always in the context of official multi-lingualism, codified in the federal, multi-national constitution of 1936.

There is a remarkable consistency to Stalin's language and national pronouncements through all of these years. The consistency was a function of the very "elasticity," as he called it, of his theories and policies (Stalin 1942 [1934], p. 79). Stalin the dialectician and politician was a master of the political center, the middle way, in good part because of his career path, which wove through multiple points of self-reference. He was always the man in between: as a Georgian between the advanced nation of Russia and the backward peoples of Asia; as a native Georgian speaker struggling with his second language of choice, Russian; as a world statesman between the advanced capitalist west and the backward communist east. As Alfred Reiber has suggested, "the politics of personal identity became the foundations of a Stalinist ideology and a homologue for the Soviet state system" (Reiber 2001, p. 1653). Stalin's appreciation for the elasticity of language communities, for the tenacity of their linguistic forms, helped him to steer this course, to implement his strategies, to join practice with theory.

Language and Nation

The 1913 article on the national question defined nations (*natsiia*) as "communities of culture." These communities were comprised of discrete forms: "language, territory, economic life and psychological makeup." No one element alone was definitive. Only all of them together constituted the community of culture called the nation. It was quite a formidable entity, a fascia of reinforced bonds. Nations were not primordial and immutable, but contingent historical realities, with beginnings and ends: their beginnings being the assimilation of peoples into compact groups of shared culture; the ends being their eventual assimilation into "streams of superior culture." Parts joined into wholes; wholes joined with other wholes. Nations were circles, self-sustaining and mutually intersecting communities; circles which expanded or contracted as they developed along lines of historical change, along a dialectical path from multiplicity to uniformity, Stalin's linear "streams," or what he also called the "higher rungs" of developed nations (Stalin 1942 [1934], p. 56). None of his positions in the essay were terribly original, as leading scholars have noted with some surprise. Here he drew insights from Karl Kautskii and V.I. Lenin; there from the very Austro-Marxists he was charged to attack.[5] Nations simply were, for this consummate politician, complex realities demanding recognition and cooptation.

Stalin's political task in the article was to confront the debates within the Austrian Socialist Party, as reflected in the protocols of the party's Brünn Congress (1899) and in the writings of two leading theoreticians, Karl Renner and Otto Bauer. Both gave proper due to language and national values through history. Renner offered a critique of the objective, indeed oppressive bonds between state power, territorial borders, and language conformity within the modern nation; arguing instead for a novel sense of nationhood in the subjective, "inward" dimensions of individual choice, based on linguistic equality and a freer multi-lingualism (Renner 2000 [1899], pp, 21, 26, 43). Bauer, too, negotiated the boundaries between the nation as something inherited and something chosen, especially in territory and language; like Renner he located the nation not in language as such but in its speakers and the "interaction" between them, a field for mutual equality and respect (Bauer 2005 [1907], pp. 112, 224). Renner and Bauer sought ultimately to detach the nation from the state, national culture from state politics. Their call for extraterritorial national-cultural autonomy, centered on the "personality principle," transformed nations into free associations of free individuals, with an accent on diffusion and decentralization, as well as on protection for national minorities. As Renner proposed, language should be left, like religion, to the devices of small, autonomous parish communities of national culture. Socialism meant overcoming the complex of characteristics and customs that we inherit as members of a traditional ethnic community (*Gemeinschaft*). Socialism meant acquiring the universal values of selfhood and reason that we share as participants in a modern civic society (*Gesellschaft*).[6]

In marked contrast, Stalin and Lenin drew the nation all the more closer to the state, sought to harness its powers for proletarian purposes. Their principle of ethnoterritorial national-cultural autonomy set national cultures within the bounds of prescribed territories and languages, the physical and mental spaces of self-reference and definition. Here was the basis of the "inter-national" relations at the heart of the modern world, the complex of national and multi-national states long existing and still yet to be, within which proletarian parties had developed and would long develop even into the socialist era. Stalin and Lenin had several good reasons to critique and undermine the platforms of extraterritorial national-cultural autonomy. Its "inter-class" psychic ties, joining bourgeoisie and proletariat alike, betrayed the Marxist theoretical heritage, endangered the unity of the working class and its party. Their arguments against Renner and Bauer were also means of undermining the proponents of extraterritorial national-cultural autonomy in the Russian empire, namely the Jewish Bund and Georgian Social Democrats, Bolshevik rivals both. Much of Stalin's essay targeted the Bund, attacking the Jews of Russia as a broken nation pursuing the false claims of extraterritorial national-cultural autonomy. They lacked the constituent forms of language and territory. They were most vulnerable to "assimilation." Their very "future" as a national entity was "open to doubt" (Stalin 1942 [1934], pp. 40–42, 46). They also shared, with the Muslims of Russia, the false and dangerous bonds of religious heritage, ritual, and belief. These were "harmful" characteristics of the nation (as opposed to its "useful attributes"), "patently noxious" and "pernicious institutions" (Stalin 1942 (1934), pp. 46, 47, 59).

Here Stalin was addressing, in one tactical sweep, Renner's precise analogy between religion and language and the broader issues of Russia's diaspora peoples. To detach language, like religion, from the territorial and linguistic conformity of the modern nation-state, allowing them freedom and mobility and privilege within civil society, meant to empower the Jews and Muslims of the empire. To empower the Jews meant to concede national-cultural autonomy to the Bund. To empower the Muslims with extraterritorial national-cultural autonomy meant to promote a pan-Islamism and pan-Turkism under the Volga Tatar standard, Russia's premier dispersed Turkic nationality. Stalin's advocacy of territorial autonomy, in this regard, besides his debts to Georgian national literature, owed something to his experiences in Baku (between 1905 and 1907), where he came to his first insights about the intricacies of the language and national questions. As Tadeusz Swietochowski has argued, there is a remarkable correspondence between Stalin's definitions of the nation in 1913 and the positions of the Azerbaijani nationalists among Transcaucasus Muslims and Turks, whose literary and linguistic debates peaked in 1913 around the identification of the "nation" (*millät*) with the "native language." These positions were later inscribed in the platforms of the Caucasian (Azeri) Muslim bloc and its most charismatic leader, Mammad Amin Räsulzadä, during the local and all-Russian Muslim congresses of 1917. "What is a nation," he asked, but "the bonds of the language and history ... of customs and tradition."[7] The Azeris wanted a national territory within which their native tongue and tradition might flourish; this against the predominantly Volga Tatar platform for representative national-cultural autonomy, meaning a cultural and religious pan-Turkism uniting the disparate Turkic speakers under one "Volga" standard (Rorlich 1986, pp. 128–129). The correspondence between Stalin's and Räsulzadä's views, between Bolshevik internationalism and Azerbaijani nationalism, were the first threads of a historical knot that tied emerging nations to territorial homelands in the future Soviet state, that targeted Tatar-sponsored pan-Turkism for suppression and defeat.

Stalin's concerns were not polemical or political alone. They approached a theoretical, even philosophical depth. Extraterritorial national-cultural autonomy presumed nations devoid of form, no nations at all. They were but a "union of individuals," scattered here and there, torn from the "compact mass" of the true nation, a mere "fiction deprived of territory," all psychology and no substance. They were "milk and water" nations, hardly visible to the eye or audible to the ear, dumbed down nations. Calling up imagery from his font of Greek mythology, he marked them as dismembered bodies, annihilated nations, torn and sheared to fit into the grotesque "Procrustes bed of an integral state" (Stalin 1942 (1934), pp. 29, 31, 33, 36, 64). Stalin's "inter-national" model instead stressed both a state of rest and a state of motion, what he called processes of "welding" and "dispersion" (Stalin 1942 (1934), pp. 36–37). Nations were meant to come together and to fall apart. Language and territory were both stable and moveable. Workers were inevitably members of fixed nations, speaking a common tongue and living in a common space. But they were also creators of new nations, subject to learning new languages thanks to the processes of movement and "migration" provoked by industrial capitalism. Language was but one of several constituent parts of the nation, to be sure. But for Stalin it was privileged. This view reflected the educated Western-European opinion of the day (Hobsbawm 1991, pp. 98–99). It reflected both Kautskii's and Lenin's appreciation for language as the crucial pillar of national community (Nimni 1991, pp. 91–92; Tucker 1973, p. 153). It was even consonant with an established tradition in Russian philosophy, from A.A. Potebnia to G.G. Shpet, that valued the semiotic over the psychological, that counted language as the system of meaningful signs that forms the basis of all human culture. "People surround themselves within a world of sounds in order to apprehend and cultivate the world of objects," wrote Shpet, in a quote from Wilhelm Humboldt. "At the very same moment that they elicit language from within themselves, so also they draw themselves back into it. In a sense, each language fills its own people [*narod*] within a kind of circle, which they can only depart by entering into another one" (Shpet 1927, pp. 16–17, 12–13).

Nation and State

Stalin's political formulas after the revolution, steeled in the heat of the civil wars and party debates, perfectly illustrate his skills with the tension, the "elasticity" between national rhetoric and Marxist ideology. We find printed and spoken affirmations of Leninist principles for national self-determination, anti-colonial struggle, and national liberation. We find such strategic, elastic constructs as the threats of "local/bourgeois nationalism" and "Great Power/Russian chauvinism" (1921); or the historical dialectic moving from capitalist and socialist nations to true communist proletarian internationalism. We find Stalin maneuvering between these tracks, relaying their negative or positive charges, in his promotion of territorial autonomy within the RSFSR and his campaign against Georgian nationalism (Smith 1999). His most ingenious formula, one he repeated time and again, defined Soviet nations as "socialist in content, national in form."[8] We scholars tend (as perhaps most rank and file party members did) to privilege "content" since it was socialist. Content meant economic development and psychological makeup, taking shape "in class composition and spiritual complexion and in social and political interests and aspirations," so Stalin confirmed in 1929.[9] Form meant territory, of course. Many of Stalin's writings from the first years of the revolution find him weighing and measuring the emerging RSFSR and USSR states: sizing up the spaces between "center" and "periphery;" counting Russians and "non-Russians" east and west; mapping the vast complex of similarities and differences between Russia's ethnic groups. His own favored plan for "autonomization" became, with some modifications, the very national hierarchy of union republics, autonomous republics, autonomous regions, and national territories that constituted Soviet state federalism (Hirsch 2005, pp. 42–45; Kaiser 1995, p. 105). Out of the chaos of civil war, true to his Platonic worldview, Stalin salvaged some semblance of uniformity and plurality, of the natural and national orders, some legitimacy and hierarchy for the young Soviet state.

Form meant, first and foremost, language, a constant in Stalin's writings on the national question. It was central among the "varied forms" of national experience, of the real and lived "signs" (*priznaki*), "traits" (*cherty*), and "particularities" (*osobennosti*) of national life, something people always "loved and understood."[10] Time and again, national form meant national-language alphabets, primers, grammars, publications, and schools – what Stalin consistently called the inviolable right to the "mother tongue" (Reiber 2001, p. 1667). This appreciation for the native language was not the result of some high-minded altruism. It was a function of the hard-headed, practical politics (*politika*) of the Bolshevik party, which in turn demanded a rational policy (*politika*) of language reforms to elevate the "non-Russian" languages and cultures. As Commissar of Nationality Affairs, Stalin was one of the first patrons of these reform initiatives between 1917 and 1924, a crucial period when the political line, embodied in the platforms for nativization (*korenizatsiia*) of the party and state apparatuses, set the contours of policymaking. Stalin's political overtures gave sanction and purpose to the major language reforms of the era, including the first educational imperatives to teach the native and Russian languages according to the tenets of pedagogical bilingualism; and the first state initiatives to codify and standardize languages, directed by some of Russia's premier structural linguists, like E.D. Polivanov and N.F. Iakovlev.[11]

Latinization of alphabets, of all the initial language reforms, best embodied the duality between language "politics" and "policy," the valency of *politika*.[12] Stalin was its most significant patron, promoting Latinization of the Arabic and eastern alphabets – first in the Central Committee in 1922, later through the Baku Turkological Congress of 1926. His most loyal allies – Anastas Mikoian in the North Caucasus, Sergei Kirov in Azerbaijan, and Lazar Kaganovich in Turkestan – implemented the campaign, part political attack on the clerical Muslim establishment and tradition, part policy reform to help nativize local languages based on more rational, phonetic scripts. Latinization was also especially effective in tightening that historical knot, reaching back to 1913, between Bolshevik internationalism and Turkic separatism. Based upon the Azerbaijani model of localism and territorial autonomy, Latinization proved most effective in denying the Volga Tatar movement for a reform of the Arabic script, championed by the linguist, Galimjan Ibragimov, awkwardly aligned with Mirsaid Sultan Galiev, party rebel and pan-Turkist. Stalin and his circle deployed the Azerbaijani model, essentially a form of divide and rule, against the Volga Tatar vision of extraterritorial national-cultural autonomy. The Bolsheviks did not allow Pan-Turkism to compete with pan-Russianism. Only the Russian language enjoyed the privilege of being everything, of encompassing all (*vse*), of defining that which was all-Russian and all-Union.

Stalin's posts and policies lent him a certain authority and expertise with language. It was the one "form" he knew and pretended to know well, both in space and through time. His speeches and off-hand comments often found him comparing Belorussian to Russian, Abkhazian and Adjar to Georgian, or Tatar to Bashkir. His writings were consistently drawn to the ends of language time, to a Marxian "eschatology" of language development (See Sandomirskaia 2006, p. 283). He promoted the consensus ideological line of the mid-to-late 1920s, that languages were developing from multiplicity to uniformity, from differentiation to assimilation. To this extent, his views aligned well enough, for the time being, with Nikolai Bukharin's popular and influential *Historical Materialism* (1921), an exposition on the ever developing and perfecting forms of human life, including language, which was ultimately dependant on the economic base, moving from the many to the one (Bukharin 1925 [1921], pp. 103, 203–208, 229, 311). Stalin's definitions matched well, too, with N.Ia. Marr's "new theory of language," which postulated the class nature of language, following developments in the economic base, locked into the trajectory of assimilation, toward the ultimate end of a single world language (Stelletskii 1935; Slezkine 1996, p. 843; Alpatov 1991). Yet Stalin admitted "little faith" in its immediate implications. Or as he wrote in both his private and his public communications between 1925 and 1934, later reaffirmed in his 1950 essay: the "period of the victory of socialism in one country" would mostly see multiplicity and differentiation in language development. Only the "period of the victory of socialism on a world scale" would see "the merging of nations and the formation of one common language."[13] He respected and valued, most of all, the present moment, his moment of "socialism in one country," of "socialism in content, national in form." He recognized, most of all, the "colossal power of stability possessed by nations," the "extraordinary stability and tremendous power of resistance" in their languages against any coercive change. In a most revealing phrase, Stalin demanded that Soviet socialist nations enjoy the right of "free development." This meant, so he emphasized in a flourish of repetition (a mark of his rhetorical and didactic style), a fusion of the social and the national always "in the native languages .... in the native languages ...in the native languages .... in the native languages .... in their native, national languages."[14]

A puzzle remains. What did "free development" ultimately mean? What would happen to national forms as they became infused with more and more socialist content? Would they remain nations, or would class content overwhelm them? A "reigning orthodoxy" in the scholarship, as Ronald G. Suny has termed it, holds that Stalin's nations counted most, that the USSR actually even invented new nations, that Soviet language and nationality policies created the foundations of a lasting "national awareness" among the non-Russian peoples, the basis for their national "identities" and "consciousness" (Suny 2001, p. 871). This literature weighs and values identity politics, the national psychology, above all: how people came to imagine and think of themselves as Ukrainians or Uzbeks. Not merely for the present, but for the past and future too, they became "primordial" nations: fixed and immovable, eternal and essential.[15] The orthodoxy reigns for good reason. Its scholars employ rare analytical and interpretive approaches, with a depth of archival sources and a range of cross-cultural and comparative perspectives. They highlight the great irony and paradox of the Soviet state. Originally devoted to class-based internationalism and world unity, it instead became the "odd empire" (Suny 1993), the "affirmative action empire" (Martin 2001), the "empire of nations" (Hirsch 2005), locked into its state architecture of calcifying nations. National form, so the argument holds, became filled with its own national content.[16] There is a fault line in this kind of scholarship, though. It is locked into the psychology of national "identity," something more mystical than real; or into the very paradox it addresses, the timeline of rise and fall, focused on the present tense alone, or more precisely – past imperfect.

We may need a freer grammar of Soviet history, a fuller appreciation of tenses. Because Stalin and his comrades always thought and wrote in terms of the future perfect tense, too – often on their minds, the dreamers. The USSR as a state of nations was to become, for them, a "nation" of nations, a new "community of culture" according to Stalin's 1913 definition, in time a new nation altogether.[17] Soviet policymakers, including Stalin, never seem to have uttered the phrase, "Soviet nation," in reference to the USSR as a whole. It would have been a violation of the norms of Soviet nationality policy, too much a fixation on the finality of the historical dialectic rather than its all important process. The closest they came was "Soviet people" (*Sovetskii narod*). Both phrases, at any rate, had theoretical legitimacy in Marx, who wrote in a most dramatic way, at the center of *The Communist Manifesto* (1848), about the proletarian class becoming "a vast association of the whole nation."[18] This image became a coin of the socialist realm, both west and east. For Edward Bellamy, it was the great "umbrella," nothing more than the progressive new architecture for the socialist "nation." Or, as socialist philosopher, Charles Vail, proposed, for socialism to be fulfilled, "Trusts must combine into one great trust, the Nation."[19] Bukharin toyed with the imagery of Marx's class-based "nation," too. Class became nation, in his words, by its real or potential capacity to rise to hegemony over the superstructure, to define and rule over the varieties of its ideological forms. This concept of Soviet *narod* also had express validation in G.G. Shpet's classic work, *Introduction to Ethnic Psychology*. Russia's premier philosopher of aesthetic and logical "forms," and always an astute commentator and elaborator upon Marx, Shpet looked to the future and theorized that, if traditional nations gave way to a new proletarian class, that very class, "transfusing between this nation and that," would basically have "created new, never before seen collectives," and history would have "given birth to new nations" (*narodilis' novye narody*).[20] The dialectic between content and form would not give way to the end of history and humanity, to no nations at all, but to a whole new form, altogether new nations.[21]

These approaches to a "Soviet nation" correspond well enough to the Marxist phenomenology of change, the logic of dialectical materialism, based ultimately upon Greek philosophy and so concisely expressed in the infamous *Short Course* of 1938 (Central Committee 1939, pp. 107, 112), one of the foundational texts of Stalinist dialectical materialism. Most historical forms became "fetters" over time, according to its strict Marxian logic, as new relations of production created and confronted new material forces of production. Bourgeois nationalism was just such a fettered ideological form, obstacle to positive historical change. Yet human beings were the subjects as well as the objects of revolutionary change. The revolution was, at its essence, all about the creation of new forms. In the case of the USSR, revolutionaries had overturned the fetters of bourgeois nationalism into the healthy forms of socialist nations. They had intervened into history's complex field of "transformations." After all, "the spontaneous process of development yields place to the conscious actions of men, peaceful development to violent upheaval, evolution to revolution" (Central Committee 1939, pp. 122, 130–131). Socialist nations were a function, in other words, of the material inheritances of natural and human history, of territory and ontology; and of the dialectical laws that informed them, now mastered by living people in the real world. "Matter is eternal and indestructible," testified one of the treatises on dialectical materialism from that banner year, 1938; "but it endlessly changes its forms, moves from one level of development to another." True materialism and scientific knowledge were "blood brothers" (Gurev 1938, p. 8). They were the keys to explaining the "laws of development of society," to transforming Socialism itself a transformative "science" (Central Committee 1939, pp. 114–115). Already prefigured here were Stalin's more strident claims to come, especially in the 1950 essay on Linguistics, about the practicality and universality of "objective scientific laws." What had been merely local, socialism in one country, was about to become more boldly global, a socialism for the world.

State and Language

Stalin's essay on Linguistics has, as a rule, been either shunned or ignored. It has always been so much easier for us to focus on the scandals surrounding T.D. Lysenko's eccentric theories on the inheritance of acquired characteristics. Five major books have been written on that controversy, the perfect case study of a sham Soviet "science." No books have been written on Stalin's Linguistics essay at all. True enough, intellectuals and philosophers across a wide political spectrum have always been willing to recognize and criticize its insights.[22] There are also several new works that expertly place the 1950 essay in the context of the elite scientific and ideological debates in Moscow in the post-war years: as an example of the "recantations and rituals" of "Stalinist science" (Krementsov 1997, p. 287); of the "games of Stalinist Democracy" (Kojevnikov 2000); and of the "politics of knowledge" (Pollack 2006). But we have achieved all of this at the expense of language politics and theories, which reveal to us a set of different facts and insights.

Stalin's essay was decisively political, an exercise in ideological control. By 1949, inspired by the claims and debates of the Lysenko camp, the followers of N.Ia. Marr's theories waged a campaign of their own to revive his teachings in higher and secondary education. Yet their campaign was destined to fail. The Marrists were a significant ideological force in Linguistic science and language reform through the 1930s. Their platforms matched close enough with the trajectory of party-state policies: against Latinization of alphabets; for the central role of the Russian language in the Soviet state; with the Leninist and Stalinist line on the long developmental path of languages (and nations) from multiplicity to uniformity (Smith 1998, pp. 81–102; Crisp 1990, p. 31). But they had also suffered a loss of status by 1938 (Slezkine 1996, p. 853). Although Marr's name still carried weight in Linguistics, in the public realm (biographies of Stalin or leading newspapers and magazines) his name rarely if ever appeared along with the great coryphaeus' of Soviet science: Mendeleev, Timiriazev, Pavlov, Tsiolkovskii, Michurin. Marr was, apparently, not Russian enough. Stalin's essay denied him final entrance into the pantheon, raising his own name instead. (Stalin was no more Russian than Marr, of course; but he was the model Soviet man.)

By 1948, in the wake of the Russian victory in World War II, and the exaltation of the Russian nation and language as never before, Marrist linguistics also proved itself unequal to the task. Its dependence on word origins and semantics were no match for the new Soviet project in advanced russification, for the new demands to teach Russian grammar and syntax. Stalin's essay was, in this sense, most practical. One of his government's reasons for opening the debate, centered upon the essay, was to finally reform the teaching of Russian in all of the USSR's schools. Earlier decisions and decrees had failed. Both Russian and non-Russian students were failing Russian-language courses at alarming rates. The essay was a signal to stop the discord, the misspellings and grammatical mistakes and mispronunciations that all amounted to one great broken Russian.[23] If the USSR was an empire by 1950, with Russian as its overarching linguistic standard, it was but an empire of accents. The hundreds of thousands of people who read Stalin's essay, Russians with their own dialects from the provinces and non-Russians with their own native languages from the peripheries, would certainly have received it with their own and with Stalin's accents in mind. These language barriers were divisive. People had to begin to speak with more of one voice.

Stalin's essay on Linguistics was also sufficiently theoretical, really a study in socio-linguistics. It joined the seriously social with the cautiously semiotic, expressing a sophisticated appreciation for language as something both dynamic and stable. It recognized language's "almost constant" propensity to "change." Language was subject to the influences of both base and superstructure; but beholden to neither, independent, a social product of the long *durée*. In this regard, Stalin took indisputable aim at Bukharin's rather "Marrist" definition of language as belonging wholly to the superstructure, dependent upon the economic base, even reflected in this or that "class" language (Bukharin 1925 [1923], pp. 203–208). The accent of Stalin's work was on Linguistics: about "the existing language with its structure," about "the great stability of language and its colossal power of resistance," about how it "sets rules for word changes, not specific words but words in general without any specificity" (Stalin 1950, pp. 71–74). Stalin repeated this term, Linguistics, at least forty times, often in quick succession. We like to think, in the shadow of the Lysenko and Marr controversies, that Stalin compromised Linguistics. Perhaps it compromised him: Linguistics as the "science" of language, a fundamental part of Science more broadly, which like language (and technology) was an independent social force. Science, according to the reigning dialectical materialism, was both a means and an end. The Soviet state counted such interventions within it as Michurinism and Lysenkoism in Biology, Pavlovism in Psychology, and Stalinism in Economics (van Ree 2002, pp. 186, 269–277; Krementsov 1997, p. 289). But Marxism, as dialectical materialism, was also the ultimate science of natural, historical and social change. Marxism is a "science …. a science …. a science …. a science …. a science," so Stalin concluded the essay. The art of language politics and policy (*politika*) had now given way to the certain science of knowing (*nauka*). Bolshevik ontologies, the circular orders of languages and nations, had begun to merge with a new Stalinist "epistemology," (Sandomirskaia 2006, p. 291; Wetter 1958 [1952], pp. 489, 549), a linear concordance of universal laws.

Composed in 1950 at the end of his life, the essay on Linguistics was essentially a meditation upon time. It was a tract for the ages. For the first time, really, Stalin was writing not about languages but "Language," not about nationalities but the "Nation." The essay addressed a kind of culmination. Much had changed since 1913. In terms of the Russian or Ukrainian or Uzbek nations, several traits of nationhood had changed completely. Economics and psychology had changed, for sure, as the new realms of socialist content. Territory had changed for some more than for others. But only one trait had remained basically the same: language. This was really the overriding conclusion of the essay. Class-building, at least in terms of language, was a more modest enterprise than Stalin and his loyalists had thought. Terminologies and idioms were beholden to grammar. Socialist content was beholden to national form, what Stalin now called a language's "specific features," its grammar and grammatical "structure." He recognized that languages would not fuse in his lifetime, quite a concession for a man and a party that had made revolution, enacted collectivization and industrialization, engineered the purges, and won a world war. He could lay claim to being an "engineer of human souls," but not an engineer of language. He could lay claim to shaping nature by the inheritance of acquired characteristics, to staging revolutionary leaps in biology, to transforming Nature through canals and dams and gigantic works projects. But he succumbed to the long evolutionary power of languages, and by implication their nations, to resist change. This was the Saussurian position, if for the moment. The nation was a pure form. The nation was to humanity as grammar was to language. Like grammar, the nation was, as a free universal form, well nigh indestructible.

There is a temptation to define these ideological and philosophical positions as a mark of Stalinist totalitarianism, a closed society of select governing elites, of strict social rankings and ordained tasks, a temptation as worthy of H.G. Wells as of Karl Popper.[24] The essay on Linguistics seems to show Stalin at his Platonic worst, beholden to a rigid hierarchy of languages and nations, everything and everyone in their proper place, under the guidance of his own philosophy and kingship. As "author of the most dogmatic and most essentialist 'definition' of the nation," Pierre Bourdieu has inveighed, Stalin was really perpetrating "the regal intention to rule and direct," the "royal science of frontiers and limits."[25] This may be the judgment of what Ronald Suny has called the "orthodox," "primordialist" school, as well: that the USSR became an empire of fixed, essential parts, a web of intractable identities. These are all worthy and valuable points of view. But changing our perspective, our conceptual grounds, through the lens of language, seems to change the material too, brings the model of a dialectical "nation of nations" into closer and clearer view. This model helps us to see how the Soviet state, as a "nation" coming to be, was not finally static and stagnant, but always moveable and changeable. The means and ends of language change, as discussed in Stalin's theories, did not speak of nations amalgamating through sudden tectonic shifts or revolutionary leaps, wholes joining with other wholes. The merging of nations was to happen, rather, more gradually and intermittently, as different parts of different wholes came together to form altogether new wholes, altogether new nations. As Gustav Wetter has written, the "final victory of communism," thanks to this tenacity of language and national forms, was even "thereby postponed to the Greek calends" (Wetter 1958 [1952], p. 224).

Stalin's model in his 1913 article was of simple physical spaces and linguistic parts, urban islands of economic development, in places like Baku, where people became more Russian (and from hindsight more Soviet). By 1950, the model was more complex, one of great territorial "zones," as he called them, a Soviet Union of many languages (a horizontal multilingualism) dissected by recognized national languages and the common standard of Russian (a vertical bilingualism). This was a model after Marx's own insights and Stalin's own life experiences, one in which a vast country of language learners always remembered the native language, but "assimilated the spirit of the new language" (Russian) only by forgetting "in it" (if only intermittently) their "ancestral tongue," just as Stalin did. Language was a physical space, too, a circle that individuals and peoples inhabited. Those circles shifted and intersected, just as their speakers did. But people always inhabited only one circle at a time. The USSR was perhaps becoming, oddly enough, something like Renner's and Bauer's model of national-cultural autonomy: a country of diverse languages and nations, governed by birth and choice, multi-national and multi-cultural. Bauer was wrong for the Austro-Hungarian and Russian empires both, for past and present. But he was right for the future. Because the USSR was simply fulfilling Bauer's own call for truly free socialist nations, for the "realization of the national community of culture in its pure form" (Bauer 2000, p. 411). The USSR was becoming a modern civil society (*Gesellschaft*) all its own. This was none other than Marx's utopian model of the "nation" in *The Communist Manifesto*: "an association, in which the free development of each is the condition for the free development of all." At least by design, Stalin's USSR was just such a sum of many parts, freely developing across its national spaces. The global imperatives of the Cold War era demanded nothing less, with Soviet influence having conquered half of Europe and spreading into all of Asia. Places like China and Indonesia, India and Pakistan, were the very sites where Stalin's works on the national question were now printed in mass editions, the very places where the communist question still remained a national question.

Conclusion

However repugnant the man and his regime, Stalin's notions about language and nation addressed a set of compelling truths, truths to which he vainly aligned his own political persona, as the great "internal form" of Soviet society (Sandomirskaia 2006, pp. 265–277). Nations are really nothing if not existential, if not lived, lived through language: spoken, written, printed, and read through language. It is our most reliable gauge of self-reference and definition, for ourselves and for others. True, for us "post-moderns" today, language is as much a knot of derivations and contradictions and ambiguities as nation (or race or class or gender, for that matter). These terms are all conceptual grounds for the codification and for the contestation of meanings, past and present. But there is an honesty about language that rivals other categories and objects of analysis. Because we always have language first. We can hide within it. We can equivocate and prevaricate to members of our own speech communities. But we cannot hide behind it. We cannot pretend to be members of a different speech community unless we already in some way are, unless we already "can produce freely in it" and "move in it without remembering the old." Bowing to his early schooling in Platonic theory, bound to the dictates of Marxist theory, Stalin reminded his readers then, reminds us even now, that language and nation are the circles within which we will always move, the anthropological conditions of our lives. He transformed the tenacity of forms into the permanence of form. Forms will come and go. Form never will.

References

Agnelli, A. (1969) *Questione nazionale e socialismo* (Bologna: Il Mulino).

Alpatov, V.M. (2000) *150 iazykov i politika, 1917–2000. Sotsiolingvisticheskie problemy SSSR i postsovetskogo prostranstva* (Moscow: RAN).

Alpatov, V.M. (1991) *Istoriia odnogo mifa. Marr i marrizm* (Moscow: Nauka).

Althusser, L. (1969 [1965]) *For Marx*, trans. B. Brewster (London: Penguin Press).

Althusser, L. and Balibar, E. (1997 [1968]) *Reading Capital*, trans. B. Brewster (London: Verso).

Avineri, S. (1992) 'Marxism and Nationalism', in J. Reinharz and G. L. Mosse (eds), *The Impact of Western Nationalisms* (London: SAGE), pp. 283–303.

Baldauf, I. (1993) *Schriftreform und Schriftwechsel bei den muslimischen Russland- und Sowjettürken (1850–1937)* (Budapest: Akademiai Kiado).

Bauer, O. (2000 [1907]) *The Question of Nationalities and Social Democracy*, ed. E. Nimni, trans. J. O'Donnell (Minneapolis: University of Minnesota Press).

Bellamy, E. (1960 [1888]) *Looking Backward, 2000–1887* (New York: New American Library).

Blank, S. (1988) 'The Origins of Soviet Language Policy, 1917–1921', *Russian History / Histoire Russe*, vol. 15, no. 1, pp. 71–92.

Blitstein, P. (1999) 'Stalin's Nations. Soviet Nationality Policy between Planning and Primordialism, 1936–1953', PhD dissertation (Berkeley: University of California).

Bloom, S.F. (1941) *The World of Nations: A Study of the National Implications in the Work of Karl Marx* (New York).

Bukharin, N. (1925 [1921]) *Historical Materialism. A System of Sociology* (New York: International Publishers).

Bourdieu, P. (1991) *Language and Symbolic Power*, trans. G. Raymond and M. Adamson (Cambridge: Harvard University Press).

Carrere d'Encausse, H. (1992) *The Great Challenge: Nationalities and the Bolshevik State*, trans. N. Festinger (New York: Holmes and Meier).

Central Committee of the CPSU (b) (1939 [1938]) *History of the Communist Party of the Soviet Union (Bolsheviks). Short Course* (New York: International Publishers).

Clay, D. (2000) *Platonic Questions* (University Park: Pennsylvania State University Press).

Connor, W. (1984) *The National Question in Marxist-Leninist Theory and Strategy* (Princeton: Princeton University Press).

Crisp, S. (1990) 'Soviet Language Planning since 1917–1953', in M. Kirkwood (ed.) *Language Planning in the Soviet Union* (New York: St. Martin's Press), pp. 23–45.

Dancy, R.M. (2004) *Plato's Introduction of Forms* (New York: Cambridge University Press).

Davies, S. and Harris, J. (eds) (2005) *Stalin. A New History* (Cambridge: Cambridge University Press).

Della Volpe, G. (1978) *Critique of Taste* (London: NLB).

Dorn, H. (2000) 'Science, Marx, and History: Are There Still Research Frontiers?', *Perspectives on Science*, vol. 8, no. 3, pp. 223–254.

Dupre, L. (1983) *Marx's Social Critique of Culture* (New Haven: Yale University Press).

Frings, A. (2007) *Sowjetische Schriftpolitik zwischen 1917 und 1941* (Stuttgart: Franz Steiner Verlag).

Gellner, E. (1983) *Nations and Nationalism* (Ithaca: Cornell University Press).

Grabowski, F. (2008) *Plato. Metaphysics and the Forms* (London: Continuum).

Gurev, G.A. (1938) *Nauka i religiia o vselennoi* (Moscow: Molodaia Gvardiia).

Hirsch, F. (2005) *Empire of Nations. Ethnographic Knowledge and the Making of the Soviet Union* (Ithaca: Cornell University Press).

Hobsbawn, E.J. (1991) *Nations and Nationalism since 1780* (Cambridge: Cambridge University Press).

Hutchison, J. and Smith, A.D. (eds) (1994) *Nationalism* (Oxford: Oxford University Press).

Joravsky, D. (1970) *The Lysenko Affair* (Chicago: University of Chicago Press).

Kaiser, R. (1994) *The Geography of Nationalism* (Princeton: Princeton University Press).

Kemp, W.A. (1999) *Nationalism and Communism in Eastern Europe and the Soviet Union* (New York: St. Martin's).

Kojevnikov, A. (2000). 'Games of Stalinist Democracy. Ideological Discussions in Soviet Sciences, 1947–1952', in S. Fitzpatrick (ed.), *Stalinism. New Directions* (London: Routledge), pp. 142–175.

Krementsov, N. (1997) *Stalinist Science* (Princeton: Princeton University Press).

Levy, B.-H. (1980 [1977]) *Barbarism with a Human Face*, trans. G. Holoch (New York: Harper Colophon).

Martin, T. (2001) *Affirmative Action Empire* (Ithaca: Cornell University Press).

Martin, T. (2000). 'Modernization or Neo-Traditionalism? Ascribed Nationality and Soviet Primordialism', in S. Fitzpatrick (ed.), *Stalinism. New Directions* (London: Routledge), pp. 348–367.

Molotov, V.M. (1993) *Molotov Remembers* (Chicago: Ivan Dee).

Montefiore, S.S. (2007) *Young Stalin* (New York: Alfred A. Knopf).

Nimni, E. (1991) *Marxism and Nationalism: Theoretical Origins of a Political Crisis* (London: Pluto Press).

Pipes, R. (1964) *The Formation of the Soviet Union* (Cambridge: Harvard University Press).

Pollack, E. (2006) *Stalin and the Soviet Science Wars* (Princeton: Princeton University Press).

Popper, K. (1962 [1945]) *The Open Society and its Enemies*, vols. 1 and 2 (London: Routledge and Kegan Paul).

Reiber, A. (2001). 'Stalin. Man of the Borderlands', *American Historical Review*, vol. 106, no. 51 (December), pp. 1651–1691.

Renner, K. (2005 [1899]) 'State and Nation', in E. Nimni (ed.), *National Cultural Autonomy and its Contemporary Critics* (London: Routledge), pp. 15–47.

Rorlich, A.-A. (1986) *The Volga Tatars. A Profile in National Resistance* (Stanford: Stanford University Press).

Sandomirskaia, I. (2006). 'Iazyk-Stalin: *Marksizm i voprosy iazykoznaniia* kak lingvisticheskii povorot vo vselennoi SSSR', in Ingunn Lunde and Tine Roesen (eds), *Landslide of the Norm. Language Culture in Post-Soviet Russia* (Bergen: University of Bergen), pp. 263–291.

Service, R. (2005) *Stalin. A Biography* (Cambridge, MASS.: Harvard University Press).

Shpet, G.G. (1927) *Vnutrenniaia forma slova* (Moscow: GAKhN).

Shpet, G.G. (1989 [1927]) *Vvedenie v etnicheskuiu psikhologiiu*, in E.V. Pasternak (ed.), *Sochineniia* (Moscow: Pravda).

Slezkine, Y. (1994). 'The USSR as a Communal Apartment, or How a Socialist State Promoted Ethnic Particularism', *Slavic Review* vol. 52, no. 2 (Summer 1994), pp. 414–452.

Slezkine, Y. (1996). 'N.Ia. Marr and the National Origins of Soviet Ethnogenetics', *Slavic Review*, vol. 55, no. 4 (Winter), pp. 826–862.

Smith, J. (1999) *The Bolsheviks and the National Question, 1917–1923* (Basingstoke: Macmillan).

Smith, M.G. (1998) *Language and Power in the Creation of the USSR* (Berlin: Mouton de Gruyter).

Stalin, J.V. (1942 [1934]) *Marxism and the National Question* (New York: International Publishers).

Stalin, J.V. (1954) *Works* (Moscow: Foreign Languages Publishing House).

Stalin, J. (1950) 'On Marxism in Linguistics', in *The Soviet Linguistic Controversy*, trans. J. V. Murra et al (New York: King's Crown).

Stelletskii, V.I. (1935). 'Klassiki Marksizma o iazyke', *Literaturnaia ucheba*, no. 6, pp. 3–20.

Suny, R.G. (2001). 'Constructing Primordialism: Old Histories for New Nations', *The Journal of Modern History*, vol. 73 (December 2001), pp. 862–896.

Suny, R.G. (1993) *The Revenge of the Past. Nationalism, Revolution, and the Collapse of the Soviet Union* (Stanford: Stanford University Press).

Swietochowski, T. (1985) *Russian Azerbaijan, 1905–1920* (New York: Cambridge University Press).

Talmon, J.L. (1981) *The Myth of the Nation and the Vision of Revolution* (Berkeley: University of California Press).

Tucker, R.C. (1973) *Stalin as Revolutionary. A Study in History and Personality, 1879–1929* (New York: Norton).

Vail, C.H. (1899) *Principles of Scientific Socialism* (New York: Commonwealth).

van Ree, E. (1994) 'Stalin and the National Question', *Revolutionary Russia*, vol. 7, no. 2 (December), pp. 214–238.

van Ree, E. (2002) *The Political Thought of Joseph Stalin* (London: Routledge).

van Ree, E. (2007) 'Heroes and Merchants. Stalin's Understanding of National Character,' *Kritika*, vol. 8, no. 1, pp. 41–65.

Wells, H.G. (2005 [1933]) *The Shape of Things to Come* (London: Penguin).

Wetter, G.A. (1958 [1952]) *Dialectical Materialism. A Historical and Systematic Survey of Philosophy in the Soviet Union*, trans. P. Heath (New York: Frederick A. Praeger).

Chapter 8

THE WORD AS CULTURE: GRIGORII VINOKUR'S APPLIED LANGUAGE SCIENCE

Vladislava Reznik

A brilliant linguist, Grigorii O. Vinokur (1896–1947) stands out from the famous 1920s constellation of Russian/Soviet linguistic and literary scholars as a theoretician of applied linguistics and the proponent of language culture (*kul'tura*), a specifically utilitarian language science, which laid the foundation for Soviet scholarship in the social and cultural history of language, and theory of language usage, including but not confined to stylistics. Whilst in a broader sense Vinokur used the term 'language culture' to refer to verbal practices of a society,[1] more specifically it also presents one of the many models of sociological linguistics, developed and employed by Soviet theorists and language practitioners in the immensely language-conscious period of the 1920s and early 1930s. Also referred to as 'linguistic technology', Vinokur's language culture in its second, narrower, meaning offers perhaps one of the most consistent attempts at a methodological delineation of the newly emerging branches of social and human sciences in Soviet scholarship. Against the advance of the so called vulgar sociologism in literary criticism and linguistics, Vinokur sought to delimit the boundaries of linguistics, poetics and sociology with the help of a scientifically sound method which, for him, had been outlined in Ferdinand de Saussure's *Cours de linguistique générale* [Course in General Linguistics] (1916). What is, however, less obvious, but certainly no less important, is that Vinokur undertook the unique task of reviving philology as a distinct field of knowledge and a methodological system in his outwardly Saussurean – and what is expected by extension to be a rigidly linguistic – approach. This article examines Vinokur's works of the 1920s that are concerned with the issue of 'language culture' and follows their progress as marked by the scholar's intellectual path and institutional agendas. It looks at the articles which appeared between 1923 and

1925 in the journals *LEF* and *Pechat' i revoliutsiia* and were later collected in Vinokur's famous book *kul'tura iazyka. Ocherki lingvisticheskoi tekhnologii* [Linguistic Culture. Essays on Linguistic Technology], published twice in 1925 and 1929. In reference to these articles Viktor Shklovskii wrote that 'they had left a significant trace in world linguistics' and 'had ploughed a furrow in the virgin soil' (Shklovskii 1961, p. 173). The changes, made by Vinokur in each of the subsequent editions, reflect his gradual synthesis of Saussureanism with phenomenological thought, which the scholar himself regarded as a revival of a philological tradition.[2]

Defining Poetics

Vinokur belonged to the younger generation of Moscow scholars, and was trained as a Slavist and a comparative linguist at Moscow University. His active involvement with the Moscow Dialectological Commission and the Moscow Linguistic Circle determined his evolution as a scholar, thanks in the first place to the Circle's sociological concerns. It is in the MLC period that Vinokur's attention was directed towards the social aspects of language and he became a committed propagandist of sociological linguistics. The famous 'Saussure meeting' of the MLC which took place on 5 March 1923, was devoted to the discussion of Saussure's *Course*, and began with an introductory talk by Vinokur, in which he summarized Saussure's doctrine and emphasized its importance for Russian linguistics. The discussion was mainly centred on Saussure's rigid separation of linguistic synchrony and diachrony, and his insistence on the primacy of the static language system and its synchronic analysis. This, for Vinokur at least, is the most valuable aspect of Saussure's doctrine, which 'turns upside down the essence of linguistic problems' (Vinokur 1923a, p. 104). Vinokur's biographer, Raliia Tseitlin, believes that his talk at the meeting not only became the basis for his 1923 article 'Kul'tura iazyka' but, generally speaking, marked the beginning of Saussurean history in Russia (Tseitlin 1965, p. 16–17). Recognized as one of the most enthused followers of the new theoretical framework, Vinokur was among those Russian scholars who looked for possible ways of reconciling the intrinsic controversies of Saussure's theory and set out to do so by designing his own brand of a sociological synchronic linguistics. This process, while certainly determined by Vinokur's intellectual programme, was also influenced by the general drive for the sociologization of Soviet humanities and by Vinokur's institutional affiliations of the time.

Between 1923 and 1925 Vinokur worked as a journalist and contributed to the activities of *LEF*, leading the work of its press section and extensively publishing in the eponymous journal. One of *LEF*'s programmatic goals was to bring together the formal and the sociological methods. Consistent with this was a topical methodological problem of the time, the correlation between linguistics and sociology, which was frequently discussed on the journal's pages. Vinokur contributed to the debate with his article 'Poetika, lingvistika, sotsiologiia' [Poetics, Linguistics, Sociology], in which he sought to establish a methodological ground for distinguishing between poetics, linguistics and sociology on the basis of Saussure's conception. More specifically, Vinokur's article is concerned with the problem of elucidating the subject of poetics as a philological discipline and establishing its methodological *specificum* in the light of Saussure's dichotomy *langue* and *parole* (*iazyk* and *govorenie* in Vinokur's terminology). In an attempt to reconcile Saussurean and Humboldtian paradigms, Vinokur refines Saussure's strict antinomy by focusing on the distinction between language in general and style, which is clearly perceived in terms of Karl Vossler's contrastive pair 'syntax vs. stylistics'.[3] Vinokur's emphasis on Saussure's understanding of *langue* as a societal norm and *parole* as an individual execution of the norm,[4] leads to a conclusion that the speaker constantly deviates from the societal norm in the process of speaking in order to find a better expression for a thought. Crucially, Vinokur introduces and underscores the significance of the wilful element in the process of speaking: speaking is a wilful superstructure over the system of language signs that has been *a priori* imposed on the speaker (Vinokur 1923b, p. 108). Thus, the essence of *parole* lies in teleological creative use and individual interpretation of the given normative system of language (*langue*) in the process of speaking. Therefore, if linguistics is understood as a discipline dealing exclusively with the normative system of language, Vinokur proposes stylistics as a specific discipline devoted to the examination of *parole*. It is defined as the discipline that studies individual speaking in relation to its goal, and analyzes the phenomena of language from the standpoint of their purposeful use by the speakers (Vinokur 1923b, p. 108). Stylistics is thus envisaged as a *linguistique de la parole*, an offspring and a counterpart of linguistics *per se*, the *linguistique de la langue* of the Saussurean paradigm.

Poetics, argues Vinokur, is an inseparable part of stylistics; its aim being to study the word as the material of a 'purposefully constructed structure', created on the basis and within the limits of the given linguistic system. In his argument Vinokur follows Viktor Zhirmunskii's thesis that poetics should be based on linguistics (Zhirmunskii 1921). It is useful to point out here a significant evolution of the scholar's thought on poetics in the early 1920s, which reflects his departure from the radical futurist platform. In the 1920 article 'Chem dolzhna byt´ nauchnaia poetika' [What Scientific Poetics Ought to Be Like], Vinokur sought to construct a theory of poetic language (*poeticheskii iazyk*) in the light of the early OPOIaZ thesis on the principal difference between poetic and practical language. Vinokur brought out functional difference as a chief criterion of a forceful distinction between poetic and practical everyday language. In the works of 1923, however, one can observe a significant change in Vinokur's theorizing, consistent with the MLC's distinct position on the issue of the poetic language. While trying to define an object of inquiry for poetics, Vinokur insists on the new concept of poetic speech and poetic speaking (*poeticheskaia rech'*, *poeticheskoe govorenie*), as a purposeful process, in which the speaker consciously 'overcomes' the superimposed system of language. Rejecting his earlier thesis of poetic language as a separate linguistic system, Vinokur argues that the poetic word is subject to the same laws as the word in general: 'it is the same practical word, only served, so to speak, under "a different sauce"' (Vinokur 1923b, p. 109).

But what is this special dressing that distinguishes a poetic phenomenon from other stylistic phenomena? Vinokur's answer to this question demonstrates the strong influence of phenomenological thought, which the scholar imbibed through one of the most influential Russian philosophers of the time and a frequent guest at MLC meetings, Gustav Shpet. In phenomenological terms language is understood antinomically as a system of signs endowed with social collective value, on the one hand, and, on the other, as a 'thing' (*veshch'*), a product of wilful creativity, the organizing principle of human culture and all forms of socio-cultural experience. Correspondingly, Vinokur defines poetic art as the creative process, in which the word is treated not only as a sign, but as a thing, whose constituent elements provide the material for every new poetic work. Moreover, in his polemic against the proponents of the irrational language (*zaumnyi iazyk*), Vinokur asserts that the meaning (*smysl*) of the word is no less important than its formal elements; that in the poetic work the meaning should be equally taken as a thing and as its constructive material, becoming as such one of the links of the whole poetic construction. Ultimately, the poetic work is characterized by the breakdown of the structure of the sign into its elements, which are then constructed anew, but in a shifted, displaced way, different from their usual systemic correlation. The newly created poetic construction facilitates the elucidation of the core linguistic value of its constituent parts (Vinokur 1923b, p. 109). In this way, each constituent element of the structure of the sign may become semanticized, whilst the word acquires the potential of denoting itself.

It is worth noting here how Vinokur's emphasis on the inner structure of the sign, inspired by Husserl's and Shpet's investigations on the inner form of the word, succeeded in overcoming what was often seen as one of the most serious flaws of Saussure's theory, namely, the 'excessive schematism' of his definition of the linguistic sign, which ignores the structure of its inner forms (Shor 1926; Shapir 1990). At one point Vinokur himself explicitly formulated his discontent with 'the main shortcoming' of the new doctrine: Saussure looks at language as a *system*, the organization of its external grammatical elements, whilst it is necessary to examine its *structure*, shifting the focus from the external towards the internal essence of language (Vinokur 1925, p. 2).

With this in mind, it becomes obvious how the notion of structure, the inner form of the linguistic sign, forms a central concept of Vinokur's analysis of the poetic language and, indeed, his whole methodological delineation of poetics and stylistics. Vinokur even succeeds in providing a non-teleological, structural definition of the purpose (*tsel'*), as the main characteristic of stylistic phenomena (Shapir 1990, p. 276). He argues that the concept of purpose is not to be understood in a psychological sense, that is, as an actual intention of the speaker (orator or poet), but as the 'structural task' (*strukturnoe zadanie*) of each particular stylistic utterance. It is the structure itself of the given utterance that 'uncovers its stylistic task, which determines the utterance as a whole'. The stylistic task of the utterance becomes evident through the correlation, juxtaposition and composition of its structural elements (Vinokur 1923b, p. 108). From this standpoint, Vinokur establishes the specificity of the poetic work in terms of its peculiar stylistic task: the stylistic task of a poetic work presupposes treating the word as a thing, rather than simply a form, subjecting it to a regrouping and re-semanticization of its structural elements.

Apart from the structural task, constituting its unique stylistic purpose, the poetic work is differentiated from other types of stylistic utterances by its specific poetic function. This is a second methodological characteristic that allows us to delimit poetic phenomena in the generic realm of stylistic phenomena. Vinokur describes the poetic function as that of displaying the structural elements of the word, or 'as telling us about the word with the help of the word itself'.

On the basis of these characteristics, Vinokur formulates the subject of poetics as a discipline within the boundaries of stylistics, concerned with the phenomena of speaking, and determined both by a poetic purpose and a poetic function, which are understood in terms of their attitude to the word as a thing, an object. However, delimiting the *specificum* of poetics as part of stylistics and, hence, *linguistique de la parole*, Vinokur is keen to uphold the contention that only linguistics can provide foundation for a poetic analysis, and to demonstrate that its subject, poetic facts, are by no means entirely a-social phenomena. Born in the process of speaking as part of the wilful and purposeful overcoming of the superimposed language norm, stylistic phenomena are certainly phenomena of the individual, a-social character. On the other hand, however, stylistics in general and poetics, in particular, regard these facts as the elements of a specific system, which is created above the normative system of language and acquires social, albeit limited, value and meaning. With this in mind, Vinokur argues, the subject of poetics can be further presented as the system of the acts of poetic speaking, while one of the principal tasks of poetics becomes to explain 'how individual speaking turns into an element of the new "normative" system' (Vinokur 1923b, p. 111). In other words, in Vinokur's theory poetic creativity is not only viewed as the violation of the normative system of language, but as the creation of a new system of poetic norms, which embodies the social value of poetry as a form of verbal art. In a certain sense, this conclusion may be seen as almost a refutation of the earlier-formulated concept of poetic speech, as a superstructure over the given system of language, and a return to Vinokur's 1920 idea of the existence of poetic language as a specific system of newly established language norms. This earlier theory of poetic language was in fact developed in Vinokur's later works of the 1940s (Shapir 1990, p. 273, 279).

In the final part of the article, Vinokur turns directly to the debatable issue of establishing the methodological boundaries between linguistics and sociology, which in the context of the 1920s was becoming an increasingly politicized topic. In his opinion, linguistics and poetics are descriptive disciplines, whilst sociology should be called upon to explain linguistic and poetic facts. Elsewhere Vinokur insists: 'genuine linguistics does not "explain" but analyzes language, simply because it is not able to explain anything in language by itself. [...] The causes that create language and its history lie clearly not within language itself, but outside of it, and consequently linguistics is not able to explain those by its own means' (cf. Shapir 1990, p. 279). The explanatory sociological context can be introduced, however, only after an immanent linguistic analysis of the linguistic and poetic phenomena *per se* has taken place. At a time, when sociological and vulgar sociological analysis of linguistic and literary phenomena was becoming increasingly popular and influential in Soviet humanities, Vinokur's appeal to sociological explanations of real facts instead of 'fictitious, fantastic abstractions' was a highly polemical, well-aimed shot. Unfortunately, Vinokur's 'discrimination of interests' between linguistics and sociology did not find support among the sociologists in the first place, as is clear from the reviews of his 1925 book *Kul'tura iazyka*.

Utilitarian Language Science

Vinokur's second programmatic article of 1923 'Kul'tura iazyka' was published in *Pechat' i revoliutsiia* and eloquently subtitled as 'the tasks of contemporary linguistics'. In the light of the prevailing 'spirit of the time', glorifying the image of the machine, construction, conscious human intervention into nature, Vinokur saw the main task for Soviet linguists as the creation of the so-called linguistic technology: a utilitarian, socially useful language science, which, in Vinokur's opinion, should be aimed at the '*programmed organization of that sphere of cultural life which constitutes its subject*' (Vinokur 1923a, p. 105).[5] A possibility of constructing such an applied science of language was opened up by Saussure's theory, which allowed Saussure to formulate the static method of linguistic research through the establishment of the principle of the social primacy of language. It is this discovery that means 'tremendous perspectives' for linguistic science, specifically in terms of 'the socially useful, utilitarian application of linguistic experience' (Vinokur 1923a, p. 104).

But what precisely is implied under the programmed organization of language and its socially beneficial, utilitarian application? Broadly, it is the formulation of functional stylistics as a linguistic discipline that could be called upon to organize and govern all spheres of public speech production, from poetry to propaganda leaflets, and from revolutionary leaders to speaking masses. Regarding language as one of the most important factors of human culture, Vinokur asserts that specific linguistic needs exist in a society alongside other cultural needs. The process of speaking, as any social process, is carried out under various social conditions, and it is only natural that, depending on its specific current conditions, the speaker seeks to organize this process in the most rational way. What follows can be easily characterized as one of the earliest explications of the subject of 'functional stylistics': writing an office document or a scientific treatise, speaking to a friend or a person of higher authority, the speakers must always 'manipulate with their linguistic skills in order to achieve the most complete, active-purposeful application of the possibilities stored in our speech' (Vinokur 1923, p. 105). This statement leads to Vinokur's central contention that the process of speaking must be *constructed*. As an object of cultural overcoming (*kul'turnoe preodolenie*), it should not be left entirely in the power of the speaker's individual will, but must be *stylistically organized from outside*. In opposition to the traditional view of language as a natural organism, impervious to conscious influence from outside (which was shared by Saussure himself), Vinokur argues that if a society can define its attitude to objective social processes and attempt to affect their course through organized social policy, then by the same token, a society should develop a wilful attitude to language questions and exert its organizing influence on language processes through a conscious language policy. More precisely, the societal involvement in language can be defined as 'the problem of *language culture*' (*kul'tura iazyka*), which implies a rational organization of language, including both the regulation of linguistic processes and direct influence on language structure (Vinokur 1923a, p. 106). In view of this, Vinokur considers the provision of a scientifically-grounded linguistic basis for language policy as one of the imminent tasks of Soviet linguistics. More specifically, he argues that the first stage in the creation of language culture would involve a search for those constituent elements in the system of language, which could provide a foundation for its more rational organization. Vinokur was convinced that the solution of this problem would finally dispense with the established conception of language as a natural force and lead to the transformation of language 'from the means of instinctive use into the fully apprehended material of cultural construction' (Vinokur 1923a, p. 106). Based on this 'constructive', utilitarian view of language, linguistics becomes *sui generis technology*, an applied science and a scientific platform for societal language construction, aimed at elaborating its methods and procedures. Characteristic is Vinokur's vision of the linguist-technologist who, equipped with Saussure's theory and methodology, learns to distinguish between the nuts and bolts of the language machine and to assemble and dismantle it when necessary. Thus, in Vinokur's imagination, the linguist of the future becomes an engineer of social culture, and linguistics – an applied utilitarian science at the disposal of society.

Aimed at language itself and focused on the elaboration of a scientific methodology for rational language usage, Vinokur's concept of 'language policy' was by no means identical to the official one, understood by Soviet authorities as a central component of the nationality policy and designed to ensure linguistic self-determination of Soviet ethnic minorities. For Vinokur, this was social policy in the sphere of language, but did not touch language itself, and, consequently, did not qualify as linguistic policy proper.

An extended formulation of Vinokur's own views on language policy is found in another of his *LEF* articles, 'O revoliutsionnoi frazeologii (Odin iz voprosov iazykovoi politiki)' [On Revolutionary Phraseology (One of the Questions of Language Policy)]. In refutation of the traditional concept of the intangibility of language, Vinokur asserts the possibility of language policy as the 'conscious, organizing influence of society on language'. This, however, is not to be understood in the light of the official language policy of the Soviet state, which, according to Vinokur, is not aimed at its real and unique object – language – but at the speakers who use it. Conversely, an adequate language policy should imply a scientific, rigorous intervention of social will into the structure and development of language itself (Vinokur 1923c, p. 106). In order to illustrate how a workable language policy should be targeted at language itself, Vinokur sets out to examine the issue of revolutionary phraseology. He understands phraseology as a stylistic phenomenon and distinguishes between various phraseologies by their social origin (such as the phraseology of an individual or a class) and by the social function they perform (scientific phraseology, political phraseology, etc.). From this standpoint, revolutionary phraseology can be seen as social in origin and political in function. Its main components are specific Marxist political and economic terms, as well as ready-made slogans and maxims. Vinokur describes how revolutionary phraseology, which was at first familiar only to a limited circle of Russian underground revolutionaries, turned into the common language of the masses and a powerful social force during the Revolution. With time, however, its fiery slogans and mottoes had transformed into worn-out clichés and void formulas, whose meaning had been lost and whose outer form stopped being accessible to conscious perception. Providing a number of examples of well-known trite revolutionary clichés, Vinokur ironically remarks that 'behind such high-flown words there is no real thought, no real feeling' (Vinokur 1923c, p. 112–13). He compares such revolutionary phraseology to a devalued currency, whose circulation, in Vinokur's words, brings about a great social danger – the danger of developing a meaningless, stereotyped, standardized type of thinking.

Vinokur's linguistic taste and eye for social tendencies are remarkable: his fear of revolutionary clichés and his protest against their wide-spread usage amounts to nothing less than a warning of the rise of Soviet Newspeak, the propaganda language of the state, whose meaningless formulas were honed and used to prevent its citizens from independent thinking. Giving a foresight characteristic of this future Russian language of ideological indoctrination, Vinokur is trying to alert the speaking masses of the dangerous tendency of clichéd phraseology to impede their logical thinking, hiding the real essence of things and their relationships behind a petrified nomenclature (Vinokur 1923c, p. 115). In his critique, Vinokur resorts to the support of one of the most powerful Bolsheviks of the time – Lev Trotskii's dismay at the stale phraseology of the revolutionary slogans and posters, which have apparently lost their power to speak to the people and inspire them. On the other hand, Trotskii, for Vinokur, is a brilliant orator, outstanding in his creative conscious approach to language, which results in the production of a true revolutionary phraseology, carefully selected and constructed in order to achieve the maximum impact on the reader/listener. The scholar argues that such wilful, meticulous stylistic work should be carried out systematically by linguists-technologists and should be among the first tasks addressed by the state language policy: 'What we need is a broad, planned, rational, I would say, industrial approach to the problem' (Vinokur 1923c, p. 117). A revival and qualitative renewal of revolutionary phraseology can be achieved learning from poetry, as the highest form of language culture and a source of novel and inspiring linguistic material.[6] Finally, Vinokur asserts that such a purely linguistic, scientifically-guided language policy can be successful only when it is supervised and carried out by qualified linguists according to the principles of linguistic technology, a utilitarian static science of language. A striking feature of Vinokur's treatment of Saussure is therefore his use of its fundamental precepts, such as the social primacy of language and its synchronic analysis, as the basis for the construction of a linguistic science of social utility, aimed, above all, at a conscious, guided influence on language by the speaking collective, the possibility of which was utterly rejected by the author of the *Course*. In this way, Vinokur tried to resolve at least one of the perceived intrinsic antinomies of Saussurean theory: the social character of language and, at the same time, its immunity to social influence. He believed that since the theory of language as a social fact and not an individual utterance had already become firmly established in scientific thought, then it was inevitable that scientific attention should be shifted towards the problem of the social influence on language, on the problem of language policy (Vinokur 1923d, p. 207).

One should remember here that Vinokur's reading of Saussure's sociology of language was largely influenced by the phenomenological thought in its Husserlian and Shpetian versions. A phenomenological perspective delivered Saussure's theory from its excessive abstraction and allowed Vinokur to establish language as a cornerstone of human cultural and social experience. As such, and as the main subject and object of cultural production, language should be subjected to a careful organization from outside, aimed at its best possible functioning and application. This process, for Vinokur, amounted to a reassessment of philology, which in the 1925 version of *Kul'tura iazyka* emerges as a productive synthesis of linguistics and phenomenology.

On the Path to Philology

Throughout his career Vinokur described himself as philologist. Between 1943 and 1946 he realized his long-term dream: teaching at Moscow University an introductory course in philological scholarship, with a particular focus on what was a central methodological problem and a subject of reflection in Vinokur's entire scholarly life – the delineation of linguistics and philology.[7] It may be argued that Vinokur's gradual move towards his trademark philological approach to language occurred in 1924, when he started to collaborate closely with Shpet's *Gosudarstvennaia akademiia khudozhestvennykh nauk (GAKhN)* [State Academy of Artistic Sciences] and subjected his previously more distinct sociological concerns to a phenomenological adjustment.

In a letter to Roman Jakobson of August 1925, Vinokur affirmed: 'My path is towards philology in the genuine sense of this term.' (Gindin, Ivanova 1996, p. 66) This was Vinokur's response to Jakobson's criticism of the recently published *Kul'tura iazyka*, which his erstwhile MLC colleague accepted only in those points 'where Vinokur remained a linguist' (Gindin, Ivanova 1996, p. 65). Jakobson's critique was aimed precisely at what might have seemed Vinokur's philological 'deviation' from linguistics, but constituted a fundamental step in his philosophical and methodological position as compared to his 1923 articles. In the foreword to the book Vinokur provides an explanation for this, arguing that the current crisis of scientific linguistics is bound to result in a rapprochement between linguistics and philology, which understands the word as culture in its specific expression. Such an understanding allows linguistics to formulate language questions from a cultural synchronic point of view, as problems of cultural *byt*. It is, therefore, on the basis of philology that an applied linguistics becomes possible (Vinokur 1925, p. 5).

In advocating such a symbiosis, Vinokur relied on his teacher Viktor Porzhezinskii's differentiation between linguistics and philology, as found in his 1916 textbook *Introduction to Linguistics* (Gindin, Ivanova 1996, p. 66). According to Porzhezinskii, linguistics is concerned with language in general and with universal laws of language development, which can be observed in any individual language. Philology, on the contrary, is distinguished by its specific focus on an individual language as 'an element of the general culture of a given nation' (Porzhezinskii 1916, p. 10). Clearly, this was the direction of Vinokur's own research and a programme for his proposed 'linguistic technology', which he saw as a synthesis of the achievements of Saussure's synchronic linguistics and a philological perspective. While the former provided the ground for a *linguistique de la parole*, the latter allowed the creation on its basis of the discipline of stylistics, dealing with the 'questions of social verbal behaviour' (Vinokur 1925, p. 5).

In the 1925 edition of *Kul'tura iazyka*, Vinokur had provided a broader and a more comprehensive definition of stylistics as *linguistique de la parole*. The subject of stylistics is a tool of cultural communication. Stylistics regards the system of language (*langue*) as the material, which is used and interpreted by the speaking individual, or as the normative tradition within which individual linguistic creativity is realized (Vinokur 1925, p. 20). Stylistics should teach the art of *parole* in the broadest sense of this term, the art of individual use of the traditional language norm in different social conditions. It is a purposeful, rational and conscious attitude towards the language system, which determines the choice of linguistic elements from the system with regard to the concrete social circumstances and the aim of every individual act of speaking. From this point of view, numerous functional sub-systems, or styles, can be distinguished within a single language. Extending his own analysis of styles from the everyday language of the masses to newspaper style, including the role of print form and size, and to poetic and literary language, Vinokur sets his fellow-linguists the task of formulating stylistic laws for various types of written texts – official documents, private correspondence, advertisements and others. This would also be beneficial for raising the level of mass linguistic culture, allowing linguistic technologists to teach general skills of rational language usage, on one hand, and the specific application of concrete styles, on the other. From this point of view, stylistics becomes a central instrument of the social and cultural construction in Soviet society (Vinokur 1925, p. 26–8). In addition, on a different level, it also emerges as the methodological platform for Vinokur's declared rapprochement between linguistics and philology.

The second, reworked, edition of *Kul'tura iazyka* (1929) confirms this assumption. Together with the book's subtitle, Vinokur removed its direct reference to the notion of linguistic technology. Similarly, the old 'Introduction', whose origins go back to the 1923 article, had its previous subtitle 'On the Possibility of Applied Linguistics' changed to 'Practical Stylistics as a Problem'. And together with a new article, it was included into the first part of the book, under the characteristic name 'Linguistics and Stylistics'. It is possible that Vinokur's exclusion of the constructivist metaphor was partly due to the eclipse of Formalism; but it is also obvious that by 1929 he had arrived at an important milestone on his path to philology. In 1923 a phenomenological perspective allowed Vinokur to delineate the boundaries of linguistics and sociology. Later, he went on to reconcile linguistics and philology by formulating the subject and the methodology of stylistics as a discipline, concerned with the cultural aspect of verbal practice. Finally, in the 1929 edition of *Kul'tura iazyka* linguistic stylistics is unequivocally presented as the scholarship that provides the framework for such reconciliation, being what Vinokur will later call 'a philological problem of linguistics par excellence' (Vinokur 1959, p. 226).

References

Gindin, S.I., Ivanova, E.A., (1996) 'Epizod epistoliarnoi polemiki G.O. Vinokura i R.O. Iakobsona', *Izvestiia AN. Seriia literatury i iazyka*, vol. 55, no. 6, pp. 60–74.

Gindin, S.I., (2000) 'Ot istorii k tekstu i ot nauki k iskusstvu: G.O. Vinokur v razdum'iakh nad predmetom i statusom filologii'. In G.O. Vinokur, *Vvedenie v izuchenie filologicheskikh nauk* (Moscow: Labirint), pp. 122–59.

Gorham, M. (2003) *Speaking in Soviet Tongues: Language Culture and the Politics of Voice in Revolutionary Russia* (DeKalb: Northern Illinois University Press).

Porzhezinskii, V.K., (1916) *Vvedenie v iazykovedenie* (Moscow: tipo-lit.t-va I.N. Kushnerev i K°).

Shapir, M.I., (1990) 'Kommentarii', in G.O. Vinokur, *Filologicheskie issledovaniia. Lingvistika i poetika* (Moscow: Nauka), pp. 255–341.

Shklovskii, V.B., (1961) 'Zhili-byli', *Znamia*, no. 12.

Shor, R.O., (1926) *Iazyk i obshchestvo* (Moscow: Rabotnik prosveshcheniia).

Toddes, E.A. and Chudakova, M.O., (1981) 'Pervyi russkii perevod "Kursa obshchei lingvistiki" F. de Sossiura i deiatel'nost' Moskovskogo lingvisticheskogo kruzhka'. In *Fedorovskie chteniia* 1978 (Moscow: Nauka) pp. 229–49.

Vinokur, G.O., (1923a) 'Kul'tura iazyka (Zadachi sovremennogo iazykoznaniia)', *Pechat' i Revoliutsiia*, no. 5, pp. 100–11.

Vinokur, G.O., (1923b) 'Poetika, lingvistika, sotsiologiia (Metodologicheskaia spravka)', *LEF*, no. 3, pp. 104–13.

Vinokur, G.O., (1923c) 'O revoliutsionnoi frazeologii (Odin iz voprosov iazykovoi politiki)', *LEF*, no. 2, pp. 104–18.

Vinokur, G.O., (1923d) 'Futuristy – stroiteli iazyka', *LEF*, no. 1, pp. 204–13.

Vinokur, G.O., (1925) *Kul'tura iazyka. Ocherki lingvisticheskoi tekhnologii* (Moscow: Rabotnik prosveshcheniia).

Vinokur, G.O., (1929) *Kul'tura iazyka* (Moscow: Federatsiia).
Vinokur, G.O., (1959) 'O zadachakh istorii iazyka'. In *Izbrannye raboty po russkomu iazyku* (Moscow: Gos. Uchpedgiz), pp. 207–26.
Vinokur, G.O., (1967 [1943]), *Maiakovskii – novator iazyka* (Munich: Wilhelm Fink Verlag).
Vinokur, G.O., (2000), *Vvedenie v izuchenie filologicheskikh nauk* (Moscow: Labirint)
Zhirmunskii, V.M., (1921), 'Zadachi poetiki', *Nachala*, no. 1, pp. 51–81.

Chapter 9

LANGUAGE IDEOLOGY AND THE EVOLUTION OF *KUL' TURA IAZYKA* ('SPEECH CULTURE') IN SOVIET RUSSIA

Michael S. Gorham

Attitudes toward language carry import beyond what they tell us about dominant trends in a particular country's national linguistics. Whether they appear in the public press or more narrow trade journals, in philosophical discussions or classroom lesson plans, discourses on language quite often reflect concerns that go well beyond the realm of linguistics, however broadly defined. The study of "language ideologies" or "linguistic ideologies" attempts to capture this metalinguistic dimension by taking as a starting premise that implicit in our attitudes about language are basic assumptions about power and authority – about who has the ability to shape the language and ultimately ideas and realities of a society and whether or not that is even possible in the first place. Linguistic ideologies further illuminate the manner in which individuals, societies, and nations understand and talk about language: their attitudes toward appropriate forms it should take, about its function in society, and about its relationship to the speaking and writing public. Looking at language ideologies allows for the examination of "the ways in which beliefs about languages and habitual engagement in particular linguistic practices create or buttress the legitimacy of specific political arrangements" (Gal and Woolard 1995, pp. 130–132).

If on some level we recognize this ability of language to serve as a symbolic forum for broader discussions, for example, of statehood, citizenship, and the role of the individual citizen speakers and writers in articulating the central ideas of the state, then an examination of certain keywords of Soviet-era linguistics should provide insight into attitudes not only about language, but also about its role in shaping citizens, society, and the state. In the following pages I do just this using the notion of "speech culture," or *kul'tura rechi*, as my primary analytical lens. Particularly on the frontlines of Russian language methodology and instruction and in contrast to other, more well- researched keywords of the time (such as 'dialogicity' or '*skaz*'), speech culture came to enjoy enormous cultural and linguistic capital over the decades of Stalin's rule – despite its decidedly unproletarian, unrevolutionary and unmarxist orientation – capital that has lasted well into the post-communist era.

The Lost Legacy of Grigorii Vinokur

From the post-Stalin era to the present day, the study of "speech culture" has largely occupied itself with tracking, documenting, and proscribing speech practices of the Russian speaking and writing population. Practitioners pride themselves in their role as negotiators of norms and arbiters of proper usage. Comparisons of prefaces to speech-culture manuals from the 1950s and 1990s reveal little substantive difference – despite the enormous political and social transformations that had taken place over the decades dividing them. Speech culture, according to a 1956 textbook on the topic, is dedicated to the study of "those norms of the literary language, the stepping back from which leads to a worsening of speech" (Golovin 1956, pp. 3–4). Forty three years later the editors of a comparable textbook geared toward a university audience remark in their introduction that "One of the main tasks of speech culture is the protection (*okhrana*) of the literary language, its norms. It behooves us to note that such protection is a matter of national importance, in so much as the literary language is the very thing that, on the linguistic level, unites a nation" (Graudina and Shiriaev).

The continuity of this norm-oriented understanding of *kul'tura rechi* might not be so remarkable if not for its stark contrast to the original spirit of the term as introduced by its Russian progenitor, Grigorii Vinokur. Particularly in his earlier writings, the term had far more radical, even revolutionary implications. For the Vinokur of 1923 language was a "social fact" and "an object of cultural overcoming," language culture – a means of "overcoming language inertia." In his first published article on *kul'tura iazyka*, he wrote about language as something that was "constructed" and, in its stagnated state, a domain ripe for human overcoming and organization: "In so much as it is a social process, the speech process is realized in the widest variety of environments of social order. We build our language, be it written or oral, in dependence upon these environments. Our language must obviously be *constructed*. It is the object of cultural negotiation (*preodolenie*), requiring a certain *organization from the outside*." (Vinokur 1923, p. 105, emphasis original). While he does show some concern for nurturing basic linguistic competence that presumes pre-existing norms, Vinokur devotes far greater attention to metaphors of "technology" and "organization" that lead him ultimately to conclude that language can and should be "material for cultural construction" (Vinokur 1923, pp. 106, 110).

Implicit or explicit throughout the early writings of Vinokur is a language ideology that ascribes to speakers both the power and the responsibility to "construct" and "organize" their speech, to engage in a process of "cultural negotiation." Rather than viewing language as a pre-existing set of rules and norms that must be obeyed for speakers to earn the badge of proper speech culture, he focuses instead on linguistic self-consciousness and invention. Language is a technology that is rightly the object of human engineering, rather than an organic and essential precursor to human identity.

Lineage of Linguistic Engineering

The contrast between the linguistic ideology underlying Vinokur's original discussions of language and that implicit in the *kul'tura rechi* movement dominant throughout the final decades of Soviet Russia and persisting well beyond leads one to wonder what became of this more pro-active, or constructive strain of discourse on language. One certainly does see vestiges of it in the writings of some of the more frequently studied linguistics. Valentin Voloshinov's main criticism of Saussure and others is directed precisely at the basic assumption that language consists of objective, self-replicating norms and thus constitutes an objectively identifiable "system" that exists apart from individual and collective users. He argues that this is neither what language is, nor how it is perceived by users – that such a norm-oriented view of language is based on a philological tradition that places priority on dead, written texts. Language, he counters, cannot be isolated from its social and ideological context and it *is* not by ordinary users. We choose the words and phrases we do not out of some pressure from abstract norms, but rather in order to express ourselves in a concrete, dialogic context (Voloshinov 1993 [1929], pp. 71–90). Norms hold some sway, he argues, but "they exist only in relationship to the subjective consciousness of the members of a given collective": "For the individual speaker, linguistic form is important not as a stable signal that is always one in the same, but rather as a constantly changing and flexible sign" (Voloshinov 1993 [1929], pp. 72, 74).

Curiously enough, in terms of language ideology, Nikolai Marr shares common space with Voloshinov to the extent that each views language as a constructed or created product of society prone to significant "recreation" during times of "truly new social forms of life and *byt*" (Marr 1927, p. 19). In an article on writing and grammar reform Marr argues that "norms are outdated and reflect different class relations; the reason why teachers and scholars are reluctant to abandon them (and grammar) is because they recognize it would mean abdicating their power and authority in this area; need for complete 'speech revolution' using the 'new language material' " (Marr 1930, pp. 46–47). In a 1931 speech to Academy of Sciences, he makes frequent reference to "language creation" (*iazykotvorchestvo*) and "creativity of speech" (*tvorchestvo rechi*), declaring that "the monistic process of language creation has been established," and contrasting the primacy of spoken, colloquial language, to "obsolete (*otzhivshikh*) systems of speech" (Marr 1977 [1931], p. 32). Tellingly, in the same speech, Marr acknowledges that the practical application of his theories must be deferred to a time when they are better "understood and accepted," implying that they are not yet understood or accepted – a gap between theory and practice that was to persist through the 1930s and 1940s (Marr 1977 [1931], pp. 34–35).[1] A revival of Marrism in the late 1940s brings more attention to the school in educational circles, but the calls it issues for more integration of Marr's ideas into the curricula belie the fact that they are largely missing at this relatively late stage ("Protiv idealizma v iazykoznanii" 1949; "Soveshchanie, posviashchennoe tvorcheskomu naslediiu Akademika N. Ia. Marra" 1949). As late as 1949, one Marr sympathizer asks point blank on the pages of *Russian Language in the School*, "How are they understanding and teaching language in school? The deep teaching of N. Ia. Marr has not penetrated the schools due to the strength of resistance from formalists. Our textbooks in no way provide the correct understanding of language" (Petrova, 1949).

From a purely political standpoint, we are accustomed to viewing Marr and Voloshinov through quite different lenses. And yet, when examined more closely, they appear to share a common language ideology that views the individual speaker as to a greater or lesser extent the master over his or her language production. Curiously, all three ascribe the moniker of a Marxist linguistics to their ideas. Substantively, as Vladimir Alpatov has shown, all three claims are questionable, but the claims nevertheless remain striking by virtue of the relative lack of impact they had on the language practitioners – not only the more formal practitioners responsible for disseminating language models, be it through grammars, guides, dictionaries, curricular guidelines, or classroom instruction – but also the informal practitioners, the citizens engaged in everyday language production in Stalinist Russia (Alpatov 2000). If, indeed, this is the case, then, for all the attention they've received in the study of Soviet linguistics, the ideas of these powerful thinkers wound up having relatively little impact, in the end, on the institutions which arguably had the greatest ability to actually influence how both the state and its citizens both talked about and used language. As it turns out, the linguistic ideology that came to dominate linguistic practice of the Stalin era – despite the institutional domination of the students of Nikolai Marr – turned out to be one that made little pretence of its lack of Marxist affinities, and relied, instead, for its symbolic authority on the parallel discourses of culturedness, or *kul'turnost'*, and norms.

The Quiet Conservatism of the Practitioners

It is in the quiet conservatism of the practitioners – the mavens, the codifiers, and the pedagogues – where we witness the emergence of "speech culture," or *kul´tura rechi*, as a dominant linguistic ideology. While some discourse on norms could be found in the writings of Aleksei Shakhmatov, both he and most linguists at the turn of the twentieth century viewed the task of the linguist as one of describing "how people speak" not proscribing "how they should speak" (Shvartskopf 1970). Indeed, in this earlier period it was widely held that norms and language could not be managed or manipulated by society or linguists or individual speakers. Vasilii Chernyshev changed that with his publication of *The Correctness and Purity of Russian Speech* (*Pravil´nost´ i chistota russkoi rechi*) in 1911, a book he intended as a practical guide to what he referred to as the "frequently asked questions" of "how to speak better and more properly" (Chernyshev 1911, p. 3). Noting the frequency of "violations of unquestionable rules of speech in books, newspapers, letters, and conversation…," Chernyshev identifies four different source models for "literary language": "1) generally accepted contemporary usage; 2) the works of representative/model Russian writers; 3) the best grammars and grammar research on the literary Russian language"; and, finally, the language of the people (*narodnyi iazyk*)" (Chernyshev 1911, p. 3).

The Codifiers

Lev Shcherba was among the first linguists in Soviet times to employ a more norm-oriented discourse – perhaps due to the fact that he also worked in the "trenches" as a Petrograd school director and, later became involved in curricular design. In a 1931 essay "On the Threefold Aspect of Linguistic Phenomena and Experiment in Linguistics," Shcherba allows for the possibility of more "catastrophic" events bringing about significant change to language, but describes the process largely in terms of forces that go beyond the individual speaker. Instead, he ascribes the agency of norm change to more abstracted "language material" and recasts speakers as either passive objects of that change or absent altogether: "People usually say that change to a linguistic system occurs upon generational change. This is in part true, but the experience of our revolution has shown that a sharp change in the language material inevitably entails change to the speech norms even of the elderly. A mass of words and phrases that several years ago would have seen wild and unacceptable have now entered into everyday use" (Shcherba 1974 [1931], p. 29). Unlike many of his contemporaries, he directly invokes the notion of norms, albeit in a somewhat qualified manner: "I shall now touch upon another issue of so-called 'norms' in language. Our spoken language activity is in fact guilty of numerous deviations from the norm" (Shcherba 1974 [1931], p. 36). By 1939 Shcherba is less guarded in his normative orientation, arguing unequivocally that it is the "literary language," based on the literary classics, that serves as the source for linguistic "norms" (Shcherba (1957 [1939], pp. 113, 126). It also exhibits the sort of patriotic discourse on language that appears more frequently in metalinguistic commentary of the early 1940s, where metaphors of language as a tool, weapon, or technology take back stage to ones of a more organic or biological slant: "And truly the word 'native' (*rodnoi*) is a magical word and touches upon the most treasured side of our essence. With its intimate warmth it heats up everything it is placed next to as a modifier: 'native country', 'native home', 'birth mother', 'native language'" (Shcherba (1957 [1939], p. 113).

Dictionaries, almost by definition, presume the existence of norms and the need for codification, but in his preface to the *Interpretive Dictionary of the Russian Language*, Dmitrii Ushakov distinguishes his compendium apart from its predecessors precisely due to its "normative goal – of being a guide for the model literary language" (Ushakov 1935, pp. 1–2). In his own rendition of constructing publics, Ushakov claims that the events of 1917 have increased the need for a dictionary that is "intended for the common (*shirokii*) reader, indicates the norms of usage for words and is close to the here and now (*blizkii k sovremennosti*)." [3] The speaking and writing public, in his linguistic-ideological slant, consists not of newly empowered proletarian or popular innovators, but rather of needy recipients of established or codified models.

Sergei Obnorskii, as one of the initiators and the first director of the Academy of Sciences' Russian Language Institute (established in 1944), could claim a fair amount of authority when he weighed in on the issue of speech culture in a pair of articles written in the 1940s (Obnorskii 1960 [1944]; Obnorskii 1960 [1949]). In them, he clearly presents a model of language as an inherited legacy with "inexhaustible inner strength and beauty," but also susceptible to "spoiling," and thus in need of "preservation" and "purification." They also display, like the later Shcherba, a heightened sense of language as a source of national identity and patriotism, no doubt reflecting the war time climate: "The Russian language is a great language of the great Russian people. Language enters as an essential component into the notion of nation. It serves as one of the primary weapons of culture, a basic factor in the spiritual development of a nation, its works, its national self-consciousness" (Obnorskii 1960 [1949], p. 272). It is on the basis of these spiritual, creative, and national underpinnings that the normalization of the contemporary literary language should be established. The speaking and writing public should, moreover, "in its work on its own speech and in common activities in the area of speech culture take its departure from the literary language established by Pushkin" (Obnorskii 1960 [1949], p. 283).

More than any of the commentators on language culture quoted here, Obnorskii earns the moniker of a Soviet purist (in the linguistic sense of the term). In his narrative of Maxim Gorky's role in the development of Soviet linguistic culture, he offers a stunning display of Soviet newspeak that in a queer sort of way puts to question the by this time well-established Stalinist formula (in language as elsewhere) of "national in form, socialist in content." In the following passage, it's quite the opposite: Obnorskii employs head-splitting Soviet-ese (form) to tell the story of the nationalization of language. In doing so, he recruits an army of metaphors and implied language-speaker relationships underscoring language's status as an organic entity, a national heritage, a treasure, and a boundary marker of national and civic identity:

Такое положение не могло не привлечь общественного внимания к проблеме развития литературного языка. Известна дискуссия на эту тему начала 30-х годов, в которой руководящая роль принадлежала великому нашему деятелю и тонкому ценителю русского слова А. М. Горькому. На этой дискуссии было подчеркнуто, что русский литературный язык есть величайшее общественное достояние, что направление развития его далеко не безразлично для самой общественности. И действительно, итоги дискуссии были чрезвычайно важны для дальнейшего развития русского литературного языка.

Активно было начато оздоровление языка. Так, при быстрых темпах строительства в начальный период революционной поры в язык в громадном количестве стали проникать сокращенные слова разных типов образования. Но это не полнокровная, не дающая нормального обогащения языка лексика, это слова условного, временного назначения.

Понятно, что началось освобождение языка и от этих пластов лексики.

Подобным образом определились грани допустимой для литературного пользования лексикой диалектного происхождения, просторечной и т. д. Наш литературный язык постепенно, в результате неуклонных забот о нем, выравнялся [sic] (в своей общей линии) и принял прежнее устойчивое положение языка, преемственно развивающегося на основе прочных традиций. (Obnorskii 1960 [1949], pp. 284–285)

[Such a situation could not but have attracted public attention to the problem of the development of the literary language. The discussion of this theme in the beginning of the 1930s, in which our great public figure and keen evaluator of the Russian word, A. M. Gorky, played a leading role, is well known. In this discussion it was emphasized that the Russian literary language is the greatest of public achievements [and] that the direction of its development was by no means a matter of indifference for the public itself. And, in fact, the conclusions of the discussion were enormously important for the subsequent development of the Russian literary language.

The revitalization of the language was actively commenced. In the context of fast tempos for construction in the beginning period of revolutionary times, truncated words of various types of formation had begun to infiltrate the language in huge quantities. But this was not a full-blooded lexicon that contributed to the normal enrichment of the language; these were words of a conditional, temporary function.

It is clear that the liberation of the language from these layers of vocabulary had begun.

In such a manner the acceptable limits for the literary use of vocabulary of dialectal origin, colloquial vocabulary, etc., were determined. As a result of the unwavering concern for it, our literary language gradually came into alignment (in its general line) and assumed its formerly stable status of a language developing in its continuity on the basis of durable traditions.]

Even Grigorii Vinokur in his later writing (from the mid-1940s), though devoting less of his attention to *kul'tura rechi*, displays a shift in emphasis from the creative aspects of language production to the more organic role of literary language as a marker of national identity, or cue to membership: "To speak like [the founders of the Russian state and the classics of our literature and science] means to become a member of their cultural milieu, an equal participant in the Russian cultural-historical process, to earn the right to consider oneself as *belonging* (*schitat' sebia svoim*) in this spiritual atmosphere" (Vinokur 1967 [1945], p. 11).

He even raises the stakes by drawing the link between linguistic norms, on the one hand, and civic and ethical norms, on the other ("the observance of linguistic norms grows in meaning to the level of observing norms of civil and ethical content" [Vinokur 1967 (1945), p. 11]). The other constructive or creative dimension is there, only it now is the de-emphasized member of the partnership, something of an afterthought introduced by Vinokur only in the closing pages of the article ("The master of language use not only knows the norms of language well, but also influences and creates them himself" [Vinokur 1967 (1945), p. 13]) – and even then is burdened with various limitations and qualifications ("not all people are equally gifted in this regard" [Vinokur 1967 (1945), p. 10]).

Speech Culture and *Kul'turnost'*

Particularly due to their emphasis on "mastery" and the "masters of high literature," proponents of "speech culture" left themselves prone to accusations of being among the most "bourgeois practices and hierarchies" of the day. Although that may well have been so, it also happened to fall right in sync with growing concerns, beginning in the mid-1930s, over the more general need for *kul'turnost'*, or "culturedness." In his study of the topic, Vadim Volkov identifies 1935 as the point at which *kul'turnost'* eclipsed class-based models of behavior in an effort to bring about what he calls the "Stalinist civilizing process," characterizing *kul'turnost'* as an "inculcation of norms and types of discipline" (Volkov 1999, p. 15). Svetlana Boym makes a similar observation, interpreting *kul'turnost'* as a way of translating ideology into everyday life, a type of "civilizing process," and a means of justifying bourgeois practices and hierarchies (Boym 1994, pp. 104–105). If *kul'turnost'* in everyday life and behavior became the key means of instilling order and discipline, then so much the better for *kul'tura rechi*, given language's central role in giving shape to identity.

Language, of course, is particularly susceptible to the discourse of *kul'turnost'* given the common perception that it is somehow more essential or innate to our national and personal identity. B. M. Volin, a high-ranking education minister, illustrates this new interweaving of literacy, discipline, and culturedness in a 1935 speech dedicated to the continuing problem of illiteracy in Soviet schools, referring in passing, for instance, to "those directives which were given by the Central Committee on the issues of the school and about the struggle we are now initiating with regard to literacy, to discipline, to the culture of the schools," and hoping that they will be able to report back to the Central Committee that "the break has been completed, the school issue is progressing, literacy is strengthening, culture becoming ingrained, and discipline is being provided." What ostensibly is an article bemoaning the still-low levels of literacy in the country (itself a significant fact) eventually turns into a call for more cleanliness, "culture," and discipline in the schools, the basic argument being, "How is it possible to teach kids, raise them as literate, knowledgeable, cultured Soviet citizens if order and culture are absent from the schools themselves?" (Volin 1936, pp. 16–17).

Volin found plenty of support for this sentiment among Soviet school teachers, who had been asking this same question for decades and by the mid-1930s were fed up with relentless reforms from above and frustrated by deteriorating linguistic competence from below (Ewing 1994, pp. 143–48; Kotriakhov and Holmes 1993, pp. 62–64). Articles bearing titles such as "In the Battle for Pupils' Speech Culture" grew more common on the pages of trade journals and lamented that "it was clear that the worst situation of all existed in the teaching of the Russian language" ("V bor'be za kul'turu rechi uchashchikhsia" 1936, p. 31). Flying in the face of Marr's "New Teaching on Language," period pedagogues espoused a more pragmatic approach to language instruction in which grammar (which Marr proposed exiling from the classroom) was once again let in the door (Tekuchev 1937). With this sort of focus of attention, one can understand the shift in discourse on language from "creativity" to "normalization." The shift in discourse on language reflects a greater shift toward some modicum of basic standard "decency," in the broadest sense of the term, in a variety of spheres.

Linguist Stalin and the Purist Revival

Whatever awkwardness there was in the underlying bourgeois ideology of the "speech culture" movement it was relieved altogether by Joseph Stalin's foray into the realm of linguistics in his *Marxism and Issues in Linguistics* (Stalin 1950). Originally published as a part of an ongoing "discussion" on the pages of Pravda, these essays are all more or less intended to dethrone Marrism and its followers from Soviet linguistics. Didactic and repetitive in tone, they boil down to a few main points: 1) a refutation of Marr's claim that language is a superstructure which changes with every change of the base; 2) a rejection of the idea (held by Marr and others) that language is class-based; and 3) a debunking of Marr's theory of language evolution and change, known as *stadial'nost'*. Each refutation effectively creates a more conducive atmosphere for the flourishing of *kul'tura rechi*, as each in its own way asserts that there are certain traditions in the history of the language that are less mutable, and that, as a consequence, there are "standards" and "norms" that govern it. "Language," Stalin declares, "is the product of a whole series of eras, over the course of which it has been formed, enriched, developed, and polished.... Everywhere and at all stages of its development as a means of communication among people in a society, language has been one and the same for society, equally serving the members of society without regard to social status" (Stalin 1950, pp. 17–18, 25).

In addition to providing political cover for the speech culture movement, Stalin's treatises gave immediate and absolute legitimacy to the more purist attitude toward language teaching and production commonly espoused by the practitioners. All allusions of a revolutionary language culture – be it avant-garde or proletarian – quickly dissolved in the more immediate demands of a minimally articulate population. Special issues dedicated to various pedagogical issues "in the light of Stalin's teaching on language" spilled over with calls for cleaning up student speech: "Every teacher must rigorously monitor the oral speech of students, correct pupils' speech deficiencies in a timely manner, and aggressively press for an elevation in the culture of their speech" (Dobromyslov and Solov'ev 1951, p. 25). As the main poster child for norms, grammar instruction resumed a central role in language instruction, having "reestablished its rights" as one commentator put it. Grammatically conscious speech, as he explained it, "disciplined thought and regulated pupils' speech" (*distsiplinirovat' mysl' i uporiadochit' rech' shkol'nikov*) (Dobromyslov 1951, p. 2, 10). Metaphors of norms, linguistic vigilance, and regulation were accompanied by descriptions of language itself as a "national wealth" (*narodnoe dostoianie*) that must be "enriched" and "preserved from spoiling and pollution" (Barkhudarov 1951, p. 10).

Institutionalization of *Kul'tura rechi*

This shift to a norm-oriented ideology ultimately becomes institutionalized in the form of the "Institute of Linguistics," later the "Russian Language Institute," with the lexicographer Sergei Ozhegov as its head. Soon thereafter, under Ozhegov's editorship, the Institute began publishing *Issues in Speech Culture* (*Voprosy kul'tury rechi*), dedicated, according to the preface of the first volume, to "the normalization of literary languages in the area of lexicon, stylistics, grammar, pronunciation, and terminology" (*Voprosy kul'tury rechi* 1955, p. 3). In his opening essay on "Recent issues in speech culture," Ozhegov focused first and foremost on the issue of norms. In an attempt to underscore the scholarly status of *kul'tura rechi*, he takes care to put distance between it and what he calls "purism," by which he means unscholarly attempts (by Russian émigrés during the Revolution, for instance) to regulate language. At the same time, he invokes the folk linguistic practices of common users writing usage-related letters of inquiry and concern to central newspapers as evidence of the popular demand for specialized attention to speech culture (Ozhegov 1955, p. 15). And while he acknowledges that language is a dynamic force and therefore norms are constantly evolving, he stops short of recognizing the more creative understanding of speech culture posited by Vinokur as recently as 1945 and acknowledged by Istrina in 1948 – namely, speech activity that effectively challenges, recalibrates, and transforms the norms themselves.

* * * * * *

Any given theory about the form and function of language in social context presupposes a relatively discrete "public" with underlying rules of linguistic practice that bind that public into a coherent whole (Gal and Woolard 1995, p. 129). Inevitably, linguistic ideologies also engage in boundary drawing – identifying what sort of linguistic practices fall within the realm of the permissive, and which lie beyond the margins. In the emergence of *kul'tura rechi* as a dominant language ideology we see a shift in imagined speech community from socialist to national, and a shift in imagined speakers from linguistic builders, creators and engineers to norm-seekers desperate to belong, if only by association, to the national linguistic legacy of Lomonosov and Pushkin.

References

Alpatov, V. M. (1991) *Istoriia odnogo mifa. Marr i marriszm* (Moscow: Nauka).

Alpatov, V. M. (2000). 'What is Marxism in Linguisitics?', in Craig Brandist and Galin Tihanov (eds.), *Materializing Bakhtin: The Bakhtin Circle and Social Theory* (New York: St. Martin's Press), pp. 173–93.

Barkhudarov, S. G. (1951) 'Itogi i perspektivy perestroiki iazykovedcheskoi raboty v svete stalinskogo ucheniia o iazyke', *Russkii iazyk v shkole*, no. 5, pp. 1–11.

Boym, S. (1994) *Common Places: Mythologies of Everyday Life in Russia* (Cambridge, MA: Harvard University Press).

Chernyshev, V. I. (1911) *Pravil'nost' i chistota russkoi rechi. Opyt russkoi stilisticheskoi grammatiki* (St. Petersburg: Tipografiia Morskogo Ministerstva).

Dobromyslov, V. A. and N. V. Solov'ev (1951) 'Osnovnye zadachi prepodavaniia russkogo iazyka v shkole v svete ucheniia I. V. Stalina o iazyke', *Russkii iazyk v shkole* no. 1, pp. 15–25.

Dobromyslov, V. A. (1951) 'God raboty na osnove trudov I. V. Stalina po iazykoznaniiu', *Russkii iazyk v shkole*, no. 4, pp. 1–10.

Ewing, E. T. (1994) 'How Soviet Teachers Taught: Classroom Practices and Stalinist Pedagogy, 1931 to 1939,' *East/West Education*, vol. 15, no. 2, pp. 117–152.

Gal, S. and K. Woolard (1995) 'Constructing Languages and Publics: Authority and Representation,' *Pragmatics*, no. 5, pp. 129–138.

Golovin, B. N. (1956) *O kul'ture russkoi rechi. Nauchno-populiarnyi ocherk* (Vologda: Pedogogicheskii institute im. Molotova).

Graudina, L. K. and E. N. Shiriaev (eds.) (1999) *Kul'tura russkoi rechi. Uchebnik dlia vuzov* (Moscow: Izdatel'skaia gruppa NORMA-INFRA). Retrieved from: http://www.iu.ru/ biblio/archive/graudina%5Fshiryaev%5Fspiking%5Fculture/

Kotriakhov, N. V. and L. E. Holmes (1993) *Teoriia i praktika trudovoi shkoly v Rossii (1917–1932 gg.)* (Kirov: Kirovskii gosudarstvennyi pedagogicheskii institut im. V. I. Lenina).

Marr, N. Ia. (1927) *Iafeticheskaia teoriia. Programma obshchego kursa ucheniia ob iazyke* (Baku: AzGIZ).

Marr, N. Ia. (1930) 'K reforme pis'ma i grammatiki', *Russkii iazyk v sovetskoi shkole*, No. 4, pp. 44–48.

Marr, N. Ia. (1977 [1931]) 'Iazyk i myshlenie', in *Iazyk i myshlenie*, Russian Titles for the Specialist No. 107 (Prideaux Press: Letchworth, Herts, England).

Anonymous (1936) 'V bor'be za kul'turu rechi uchashchikhsia', *Russkii iazyk v sovetskoi shkole*, no. 1, pp. 31–40.

Anonymous (1949) 'Protiv idealizma v iazykoznanii', *Russkii iazyk v shkole*, no. 1, pp. 70–73.

Anonymous (1949) 'Soveshchanie, posviashchennoe tvorcheskomu naslediiu Akademika N. Ia. Marra', *Russkii iazyk v shkole*, no. 3, pp. 67–73.

Obnorskii, S. P. (1960 [1944]) 'Pravil'nosti i nepravil'nosti sovremennogo russkogo literaturnogo iazyka', in S. P. Obnorskii, *Izbrannye raboty po russkomu iazyku* (Moscow: Gosudarstvennoe uchebno-pedagogicheskoe izdatel'stvo Ministerstva Prosveshcheniia RSFSR), pp. 253–272.

Obnorskii, S. P. (1960 [1949]). 'Kul'tura russkogo iazyka', in S. P. Obnorskii, *Izbrannye raboty po russkomu iazyku* (Moscow: Gosudarstvennoe uchebno-pedagogicheskoe izdatel'stvo Ministerstva Prosveshcheniia RSFSR), pp. 272–293.

Ozhegov, S. I. (1955) 'Ocherednye voprosy kul'tury rechi,' *Voprosy kul'tury rechi*, vol 1, pp. 5–33.

Petrova, E. N. (1949) 'Nikolai Iakovlevich Marr i ego znachenie dlia sovetskoi shkoly', *Russkii iazyk v shkole*, no. 5, p. 32.

Shcherba, L. V. (1974 [1931]). 'O troiakom aspekte iazykovykh iavlenii i ob eksperimente v iazykoznanii', in *Iazykovaia sistema i rechevaia deiatel'nost?* (Leningrad: Izd. Nauka, Leningradskoe otdelenie), pp. 24–39.

Shcherba, L. V. (1957 [1939]) 'Sovremennyi russkii literaturnyi iazyk,' in L. V. Shcherba, *Izbrannye raboty po russkomu iazyku* (Moscow: Gosudarstvennoe uchebno-pedagogichskoe izdatel'stvo ministerstva prosveshcheniia RSFSR), pp. 19–26.

Shvartskopf, B.S. (1970). 'Ocherk razvitiia teoreticheskikh vzgliadov na normu v sovetskom iazykoznanii,' in V. G. Kostomarov and L. I. Skvortsov (eds.), *Aktual'nye problemy kul'tury rechi* (Moscow: Nauka), pp. 369–404.

Stalin, I., (1950) *Marksizm i voprosy iazykoznaniia* (Moscow: 3-ia tipografiia 'Krasnyi proletarii' Glavpoligrafizdata pri Sovete Ministrov SSSR).

Tekuchev, V. (1937) 'Na soveshchanii uchitelei-otlichnikov (Moskva),' *Russkii iazyk v shkole*, no. 1, pp. 120–23.

Ushakov, D. N. ed. (1935) *Tolkovyi slovar' russkogo iazyka* (Moscow: OGIZ, 1935), 1–2.

Vinokur, G. O. (1923) 'Kul'tura iazyka. (Zadachi sovremennogo iazykoznaniia)', *Pechat' i revoliutsiia*, no. 5, pp. 100–111.

Vinokur, G. O. (1967 [1945]) 'Iz besed o kul'ture rechi', *Russkaia rech'*, no. 3, pp. 10–14.

Volin, B. M. (1936) 'Bor'ba za gramotnost' – osnovnaia zadacha shkoly,' *Russkii iazyk v sovetskoi shkole*, no. 1, pp. 16–17.

Volkov, Vadim, (1999) 'The Concept of *Kul'turnost'*: Notes on the Stalinist civilizing process', in Sheila Fitzpatrick, ed., *Stalinism: New Directions* (London: Routledge).

Voloshinov, V. N. (1993 [1929]) *Marksizm i filosofiia iazyka: Osnovnye problemy sotsiologicheskogo metoda v nauke o iazyke* (Moscow: Labirint).

Chapter 10

PSYCHOLOGY, LINGUISTICS AND THE RISE OF APPLIED SOCIAL SCIENCE IN THE USSR: ISAAK SHPIL'REIN'S *LANGUAGE OF THE RED ARMY SOLDIER*

Craig Brandist

Studies of the influence of the Revolution on the language of the masses were common in the USSR in the 1920s, but what is unusual about the work on which this chapter focuses is that while it constitutes one of the most impressive pieces of empirical work about language of the period, it does not originate within the field of philology at all, but from within nascent applied psychology. *The Language of the Red Army Soldier* (*Iazyk krasnoarmeitsa*) by Isaak Shpil'rein (1891–1937) and a group of his research assistants from the Psychotechnics Section of the Moscow Institute of Experimental Psychology (Shpil'rein et al, 1928) was published in 1928, but was based on research carried out in 1924–5.[1] It was commissioned by the Agitation Department of the Political Administration of the military Soviet (*Politicheskoe Upravlenie Revoliutsionnogo Voennogo Soveta Respubliki*, PUR) and analyses the language of worker and peasant conscripts of the Moscow Garrison at various stages of their military careers during which many progressed from almost totally illiterate and untutored raw recruits through two years of intensive training in literacy, basic education, military and political instruction. In order to understand how such a work came to be written, it is important to recognise that in the 1920s, just as sociological linguistics in the USSR was extricating itself from the hold of the neo-grammarians and *Völkerpsychologie*, according to which language was understood as an aspect of the national-popular spirit or *Volksgeist* (Brandist 2006), so psychology was extricating itself from physiology and philosophical idealism. In each case, theoretical reformulation was driven by the proliferation of applications for the new disciplines, and by the 1920s this led to a widespread sense that both disciplines were in a state of crisis, with compartmentalism and methodological fragmentation everywhere.[2] In the case of linguistics the need to catalogue ways of speaking and codify a new, standard language, for recently formed nation states was felt across Europe, but nowhere more keenly than in the early USSR (Smith 1998; Martin 2001). In the case of psychology, the need to raise the productivity of industry in the face of economic and military competition, which culminated in World War One, and the need to deal with the pathologies of urbanising societies, presented new problems and drove theoretical innovation (Viteles 1923). Again the early USSR was a particularly acute case, and psychotechnics played a leading role in the development of Soviet psychological thought.

Lev Vygotsky (1896–1934) was one of those to recognise the methodological importance of applied psychology, viewing it as a crucial factor in bringing about the 'crisis in psychology' as well as providing a possibility for its resolution. For Vygotsky, the rise of applied science provided a link between psychology and social practice by its direct relationship to industrialisation and the development of mass communications. Social practice was for the first time held to be the criterion of the truthfulness of psychological theory, since psychological phenomena could be explained through fulfilment of tasks connected with predictions of development, the formation of psychological qualities and the direction of their changes. Researchers could reach agreement by generalising from empirical facts and analysing practical data and this would provide a basis for a new theoretical approach that could transcend the division between 'explanation' and 'understanding' that plagued psychology. Hitherto this division had not been transcended but had been taken to such a stage that the problem could no longer be ignored:

[T]he development of applied psychology... has led toward the restructuring of the whole methodology of science on the basis of the principle of practice, i.e., towards its transformation into a natural science. This principle bears down on psychology and is pushing it to split into two sciences... only the split and the selection of a single psychology will provide a way out of the crisis. The dialectical unity of methodology and practice, applied to psychology from two sides, is the fate and destiny of one psychology. A complete severance from practice and the contemplation of ideal essences is the destiny and fate of the other. A complete split and separation is their common destiny and fate. This rupture began, continues, and will be completed along the lines of *practice*. (Vygotsky 2004 [1926–7], pp. 145–6; 1997 [1926–7], p. 310)[3]

For Vygotsky, the task of Marxists working in psychology was to carry this development through to its conclusion, and to provide a new theoretical foundation for psychology that bourgeois science was incapable of supplying. Thus, the further development of applied psychology within a Soviet context was of significant historical importance for the development of the sciences on which they were based. As A.N. Leont'ev (1904–79) argued, for Vygotsky, psychotechnics, as a psychology of labour, 'was the first to proceed to the psychological analysis of the practical, labour activity of man, although it did not yet understand the full importance of these problems for scientific psychology... Marxist psychology must begin with a psychological analysis of the practical, labour activity of humans on the basis of Marxist positions' (Leont'ev 1997, p. 16). As the leader of the Soviet *psikhotekhnika* and a Marxist, Shpil'rein played a crucial role, and it was in his work that applied psychology was to converge with another field that reached an impressive level of development at the time: applied linguistics.

Psychotechnics

The term *Psychotechnik* was first introduced by the German psychologist William Stern (1871–1938) in his 1900 book *Über Psychologie der individuellen Differenzen. Ideen zu einer "Differentiellen Psychologie"* and then revised and elaborated in his 1911 book *Die differentielle Psychologie in ihren methodischen Grundlagen* (Stern 1900, 1911). It denoted that realm of applied psychology which is oriented towards the future, reforming social life and influencing social behaviour for the better. It was contrasted with '*Psychognostik*' or cultural psychology, which is oriented towards the past and is of an explanatory character. The work to which Psychotechnik was most oriented at the outset was the development of systematic, differential criteria for the selection of workers to perform certain tasks. To this end Stern proposed four elements of an empirical approach: 1) the study of the features or characteristics (*Merkmale*) of persons manifested in their behavioural variations; 2) the study of the correlations of two or more features with indications of labour efficiency; 3) psychographics, the plotting of an aggregate or totality of features characteristic of a given subject; 4) the comparison of psychographs. In Stern's own work these techniques are united into an idealist philosophical system called personalism, where the person is understood as a finite, structured totality of goals, a telos that is inaccessible to experiment and causal investigation and therefore open only to interpretation. Features are now understood as *symptoms*, and the task of the psychologist is to establish the aetiological connections between symptoms and those inner faculties (*Fähigkeiten*) or tendencies (*Tendenzen*) that are not immediately observable but which produce certain dispositions.[4]

Stern's empirical techniques were keenly adopted in Germany in the period after the First World War, especially when dealing with the need to place demobilised soldiers in civilian work. However, Stern's categories were often detached from their philosophical foundation in subsequent years, especially as his ideas came into contact with the style of utilitarian and business-oriented psychological investigation pioneered by the British polymath Francis Galton (1822–1911).[5] Galton's 'anthropometric method', which was based on testing in order to yield statistical information, was anything but personalistic, but rather characterised individuals solely 'by their deviation from the statistical norm established for the population with which they had been aggregated' (Danziger 1990, p.77). Galton's innovations received their most enthusiastic reception and development among psychologists in the United States, and in 1892 a senior colleague of Wilhelm Wundt (1832–1920), Hugo Münsterberg (1863–1916), moved from Leipzig to Harvard University, bringing with him a profound knowledge of contemporary German psychology.[6] Münsterberg combined the two approaches and sought to turn *Psychotechnik* into an empirically based applied science dealing with causal structures, oriented upon practical goals and promoting social progress and eugenics:

If we are to change the world, to reform and improve men, to teach or to cure them, to make them perform efficient labour or to organise them for common action, then we must treat man as a system of causes which will produce certain effects. We must be able to foresee what will happen and to determine how we can mould the mind. (quoted in Sutherland 1915, p. 306)

Münsterberg's prolific work had a considerable effect on the development of the field, and one of his books, *Psychology and Industrial Efficiency* (Münsterberg 1913), appeared in Russian translation as early as 1914 (Miunsterberg 1914), to be followed by his two-volume textbook *Grundzüge der Psychotechnik* (Münsterberg 1914) in 1922 (Miunsterberg 1922). Shpil'rein, a polyglot who has studied in Germany and was evidently well-versed in the English-language psychology of the time, was to draw on both Stern and Münsterberg in leading the development of Soviet *psikhotekhnika*.

Soviet *psikhotekhnika* developed as a result of the introduction of the techniques of scientific management, Taylorism, into Russia as a means of raising production under the pressure of imperial encirclement. The initial leader of the Taylorist movement was Aleksei Gastev (1882–1938), who directed the Central Institute of Labour where Shpil'rein began his work. Gastev argued that the scientific organisation of labour (*nauchnaia organizatsiia truda*, NOT) would lead to a 'mechanised collectivism', where personality, the 'individual face' would be replaced by 'uniform steps' and 'expressionless faces', devoid of emotion where measurement would be by a speed or pressure gauge rather than any human criterion (Gastev 1919, pp. 44–5).[7] Shpil'rein's philosophical education in Heidelberg, Leipzig and Berlin under the humanists Wundt and Hermann Cohen (1842–1914) had left him hostile to such mechanistic ideas and open to aspects of Stern's 'biologo-teleological monism' (Shpil'rein 1923, p. 209). In 1923 he founded the Psychotechnic Laboratory under the Ministry of Labour, where he was able to develop a more humanistic brand of NOT, focusing on the behaviour of human subjects in the labour process, and he joined the editorial board of the organ of the mass organisation of NOT, formed by Gastev's rival Platon Kerzhentsev (1881–1940), *Liga Vremia/Liga Not: Vremia*.[8] Like Trotsky, with whom he sat on the board, Shpil'rein opposed any attempt to 'transmute the theory of Marx into a universal master key and ignore all other spheres of learning', and saw no problem in adopting and adapting the categories and techniques developed by bourgeois psychologists (Trotsky 1973 [1925], p. 221).[9] He explicitly regarded *psikhoteknika* as a weapon that could equally serve the Whites or the Reds and regarded the most significant difference to lie in the 'social mission' (*sotsial'nyi zakaz*) of the researcher (Kol'tsova et al 1990, p. 115).[10] He was also quite prepared to openly criticise reductionist pretenders to the title of Marxist psychology such as Konstantin Kornilov's (1879–1957) 'reactology' which had a leading role at the Moscow Institute of Psychology. To Shpil'rein the failure of reactology was symptomatic of misguided attempts to treat psychology as a single, unified discipline in which the person is seen as something general rather than a member of a specific social group. Instead, psychological science needed to be seen as 'a chain of disciplines, the separate links of which lead from the biological sciences to the social [sciences]'. The *psikhoteknika* link is 'the closest of all to the social sciences, having direct dealings with man as a member of a collective, be it productive, military or whatever' (Shpil'rein 1930, p. 35).

In 1929 Shpil'rein argued that the 'social mission' of Soviet *psikhoteknika* was to employ differential psychology in areas topical for 'socialist construction'. This involved introducing the 'methods of class analysis' and developing 'a dynamic approach to finding dialectical oppositions even where there would appear to be socially homogenous groups and where the social significance of the phenomena being investigated by psychologists (courtroom, cinema, language) is beyond doubt' (Shpil'rein 1930, p. 11). Psychotechnic tests, such as those that had been developed by Münsterberg needed to be adapted to this end. Soviet psychotechnics must not only note the existence of 'age, class, sex and other such differences' but must study them, to determine:

which features *can be* understood as class-conditioned, what criteria there are to determine whether a difference is a stable feature or not, something *accidentally appearing or an indicator* of a type, what criteria there are that allow us to determine whether a *divergence* from the norm has become settled, what criteria we have to determine whether a phenomenon *is repeated*, in order to consider it *regular [zakonomernyi]*, to determine that it depends on *one* rather than *another* fact. (Shpil'rein 1930, pp. 35–36, original emphasis)

Two areas were highlighted for particular attention: the selection and preparation of workers and, of particular interest for the current article, the 'ideological and technical preparation of cadres'. The latter required 'the study of the laws of training and instruction, in particular the huge propaganda experience of our party and its methodological mastery; questions of social class and biological (national, sex, age) differences must provide the basis of Marxist differential psychology' (Shpil'rein 1930, p. 10).

The Red Army and Political Education

The Revolution of 1917 found itself under considerable military pressure from its inception, and this was only to intensify as the Civil War developed, fuelled by foreign intervention. Although the Bolsheviks had no plans to create a standing army, the low proportion of worker as opposed to peasant recruits and a relatively poor railway system in a huge territory had made the preferred, territorially based militia defence system impossible to organise (Smilga 1921, p. 16–17). A centralised military structure had arisen, and from the beginning of the Civil War the Bolsheviks had been compelled to re-appoint ex-tsarist officers and place them under the supervision of political commissars. Marx could have scarcely found a better illustration for his rhetorical question to Engels in a letter of July 1866: 'Is there any sphere in which our theory that the *organisation* of labour is determined *by the means of production* is more dazzlingly vindicated than in the industry for human slaughter?' (Marx 1987 [1866]).

Recruiting a predominantly peasant army meant that political work among rank and file soldiers became as important as supervision of ex-Tsarist officers, and a dedicated system to facilitate this arose. From the time of its formation, the Red Army was viewed as a vital instrument in the dissemination of enlightenment throughout a backward country and for this reason the Army was immediately committed to the eradication of illiteracy. PUR argued that a soldier who was illiterate when drafted but literate on demobilisation 'would never forget that the workers' and peasants' government had provided him with the most powerful weapon for the defence of his interests–enlightenment' (Quoted in Hagen 1990, p. 97). Literacy classes were made mandatory for soldiers along with classes in the rudiments of political knowledge, the two being united in the notion of 'political literacy' (*politgramota*).[11] One leader, formulating the principles in a report to he Ukrainian Commissariat of Enlightenment in 1919, argued that in order for the political consciousness of the soldier to be profound 'it must be based on a general-cultural foundation' and from this it followed that 'both political and cultural-enlightenment work must go hand in hand, reinforcing each other' (TsDAVOVUU 166/2/453/4). Considerable attention was given to formulating materials that were relevant and accessible to recruits and to developing techniques to encourage the active engagement of recruits in lessons. Instructions issued to teachers the same year stressed the need to 'widen the intellectual horizon of the soldier, to raise his curiosity and confidence':

> The teacher should lead discussions on questions of social science (*obshchestvovedenie*) natural science, history and literature. Having posed a problem, the teacher should only lead the thread of the discussion and explain the unfamiliar, allowing the soldiers to find the truth by means of the exchange of views, i.e raising their self-confidence. (TsDAVOVUU 166/2/453/30)

This was backed up by instructional theatrical performances, and the production of newspapers, to which soldiers often wrote with complaints and questions. Trotsky made it clear that the 'blind herd instinct' of the Tsarist army needed to be replaced by a new 'psychological cement by means of which we can create a new army, a real, conscious Soviet army, bound together by a discipline that has passed through the soldiers brains, and not just the discipline of the rod'. The aim was to form a peasant and worker-soldier who is 'aware of himself as a human personality, with a right to respect, but also feels that he is part of the working class of republican Russia and will be prepared unquestioningly to lay down his life for this republican Soviet Russia' (Trotsky 1979 [1923–25] vol. 1, pp. 419–20).

   In the early years of the Civil War the main task of political instructors was to develop a structure of 'rational relationships' that maximised coordination of action and firm discipline among its various components. When the War had ended, however, and the size of the army had been reduced dramatically, new recruits who arrived for a term of service entered 'a ready-made organization with an internal regime and definite traditions' (Trotsky 1923). The army increasingly became the focus of the most acute forms of bureaucratic centralism, political commissars subordinated Party collectives in response to the prolonged emergency and structures of authority had tended to ossify. As Trotsky was to remark in retrospect, '[t]he army is a copy of society, and suffers from all its diseases, usually at a higher temperature' (Trotsky 1970 [1936], p. 222).

Concern about the effectiveness of political education in the Red Army began to rise as soon as post-war demobilisation began, since discipline and a range of other problems were revealed. The staff of PUR was increasingly demoralised, not helped by 'incessant tinkering with the programs of political education' (Hagen 1990, p. 175).[12] Matters became even more serious when the army became an arena for the struggle against bureaucratisation, which Trotsky headed, in 1923 (see Vilkova 1996). In his series of articles in Pravda, later collected as the pamphlet *The New Course*, Trotsky mounted a blistering attack on the form of bureaucratisation that had come to characterise political education in the Red Army, and that he called 'conventionalism' [*kazenshchina*]:

When, due to habituated forms, people cease to think about content, smugly use conventional phrases without thinking about their sense, give customary orders without considering their rationality and, instead, are afraid of every new word, criticism, initiative, sign of independence, – this means that we are dealing with the most dangerous, moldy conventionalism. (Trotsky 1923)[13]

Trotsky warned that this problem led the 'revolutionary tradition' to be transmitted to new recruits as if it were a 'dead canon or official romance [*kazennaia romantika*]':

A tradition must not be learned by heart, it must not be taken as gospel, one must not simply believe the older generation 'on its word of honour'. No, a tradition must be won by profound inner work, independently, critically worked through and actively assimilated. (Trotsky 1923)

In December 1923, Trotsky's ally and head of PUR, Vladimir Antonov-Ovseenko (1883–1939) boldly sought to tackle the problem by sanctioning the introduction of party democracy in the army. In January 1924, however, he was removed by the Central Committee majority and replaced by Andrei Bubnov (1884–1938), whose first move was to revoke the order (Hagen 1990, pp. 200–01). As the cause of the Left Opposition went down to defeat, Bubnov led a thorough purge of PUR, where opposition support was considerable. This was particularly true of the Moscow Garrison, where Shpil'rein's research was conducted, since until June 1924 the Garrison was commanded by the prominent Left oppositionist, Nikolai Muralov (1877–1937). With the defeat of the 1923 opposition, an overhaul of the whole system of political education in the Garrison and an attempt to root out political support for the opposition was even more urgent.

Shpil'rein's study sampled the army in 1924–5, as it was on the eve of important reforms inaugurated by Mikhail Frunze (1885–1925) who took over from Trotsky as head of the army.[14] Even before Frunze's accession in the middle of 1924, it seems the Army had not formed the centre of Trotsky's attention since the Civil War ended in 1921. Instead, Trotsky's attention had shifted to economic problems and the need to overhaul techniques of propaganda in the new post-war environment, to promote 'culture in work, culture in life, in the conditions of life'. Central to this was the need to train the worker and peasant masses 'to work efficiently: accurately, punctually, economically' (Trotsky 1973 [1923], p. 16). Trotsky's involvement with *Liga Vremia* was an important part of this reorientation, and it was precisely now that Shpil'rein began to focus on the theoretical and practical tasks connected with agitational and propaganda work. The ideal context for this work was the Red Army where, at the beginning of 1924, Trotsky was still titular head, and where both formal literacy training and agitational and propaganda work was carried out according to a centralised programme. When PUR and then the Moscow Committee of the Party commissioned Shpil'rein, the opportunity was accepted with enthusiasm.

The Study

At the beginning of *Iazyk krasnoarmeitsa*, Shpil'rein and his research group defined the aim of the work 'to study the vocabulary of newspapers and political instructors, i.e. the instrument of their influencing work, and to study the Red Army Soldier as the object of this work, i.e. to establish precisely of which words Soldiers themselves have a command, and which of these words, he does not use in his active political work, but nevertheless understands' (Shpil'rein et al 1928, p. 5). The instrument used by political workers was, of course, language. But while Shpil'rein acknowledged the need to take account of the specificities of all instruments, he saw, in principle, no reason why language needs to be treated as fundamentally different from the other materials with which people work. Here Shpil'rein was very close to the Marxist linguist Evgenii Polivanov, who argued that speech is 'a process of labour (as well as having the most serious economic functions)' (Polivanov 1931, p. 44). However, where Polivanov developed a theoretical approach to the detriment of empirical research, Shpil'rein's approach was significantly less theorised but far more advanced in terms of data collection and analysis than almost all linguistic research of the period.

The social complexion of the recruits in 1924–25 remained predominantly peasant in character, and given that at that time around 40% of peasant children of school age remained outside the school system, its recruits were often devoid of any prior formal education (Rozhkov 2000, p. 77).[15] Three categories of soldiers were studied: 1) 500 soldiers demobilised in April 1924; 2) 1,100 new recruits tested within 3 weeks of their mobilisation and 3) two intermediary groups totalling 801 soldiers who had been mobilised six months and one year previously. Comparison of category 1 and 2 allowed an assessment of the intellectual development of recruits during their time in the Army, while comparison of the two groups within category 3 allowed an assessment of the effectiveness of political education within the six months that differentiated them. The following material was utilised in order to analyse the soldiers' language: a) two 1924 issues of the army newspaper *Krasnyi voin*; b) shorthand records of discussions between the political instructor and soldiers; c) the language of letters written from soldiers to the editors of *Krasnyi voin* and d) materials gathered from multiple-choice tests given to soldiers by the researchers.

Comparison of the **active** vocabulary of the groups revealed a significantly greater assimilation of nouns than other parts of speech over the period of service. This was especially evident in written language, which increasingly resembled the language of the newspapers. In the political sphere the researchers estimated that the soldiers used 6,200–6,500 words and that while the language of the soldiers and instructors differed rather little, the language of the newspapers was richer (Shpil'rein et al 1928, pp. 37–40). Analysis of the soldiers' letters revealed the following order of syntactical features, with the most frequently used first: predicate, object, adverbial clauses, subject, attribute and address. The high frequency of subjectless sentences accounted for the low frequency of subject. Main clauses accounted for 74.2% of clauses with the remainder being subordinate clauses. Oral speech was marked by simple, abrupt, often incomplete and complexly coordinated sentences, while written discourse tended towards more extended, complete and complexly subordinate sentences. Written discourse also revealed the following types of errors: phonetic (51%), by analogy (18%), spelling (16%), slips of the pen (13%), use of old orthography (2%).

The tests used for assessing the **passive** vocabulary of soldiers yielded the most interesting results. 400 words from the sphere of social and political discourse were offered, and soldiers were asked to choose an appropriate definition or synonym. In each case soldiers were presented with 4 options, in various orders: 1) a correct response or synonym; 2) the opposite of the true meaning, 3) a 'provocative' or misleading response, which invited selection according to phonetic similarities and 4) something unconnected or non-sensical. The correct option needed to be underlined. One clear example, which also works in English translation, would be question 18, 'who may be a veteran?'. The categories of responses offered were 1) 'an old man', 2) 'a doctor', 3) 'a child' and 4) 'a horse'. It seems fully 61% were misled by the 'provocative' connection between veteran and veterinarian and chose option 2) (Shpil'rein et al 1928, p. 82). The longer the soldiers had been in the army a greater number of correct responses and a surer understanding of concepts and history were recorded. The rise was from 57% of in 1924 to 70.9% in 1925. Researchers now moved to present one correct and three 'provocative' options, suggesting misunderstandings of the meaning, phonetic resemblances or previously observed errors. Where mistakes did arise, this sometimes arose from phonetic confusion, and sometimes from distortions of meaning, such as understanding *natsionalizatsiia* (nationalisation) as 'for the use of the poor'.

Reviewing the results, the researchers recommended instructors directly and systematically address the problem of how new words were being introduced to soldiers, and the need to ensure they are defined and explained adequately. Assimilation of new words depended, in part, on the current topicality of issues (Shpil'rein et al 1928, p. 114), but how they were understood also depended on the low but improving level of general, formal education among the young peasant recruits (Shpil'rein et al 1928, p. 116). Instructors therefore needed constantly to adjust their 'systematic', 'measured' and 'rationalised', 'influencing work' to the previous 'lexical experience' of the 'object of influence' (the soldier) (Shpil'rein et al 1928, pp. 116–7). Inadequate attention to the previous experience of the soldiers, the assumption that the authoritative discourse of instructors was clear to, and understood by, the soldiers led to important features being misunderstood: up to 75% of respondents misunderstood important borrowed or jargon terms such as *blokada* (blockade), *import* (import), *monopoliia* (monopoly) and *biurokrat* (bureaucrat). To avoid this distortion, new words needed more carefully to be assimilated into the soldiers' existing word stock. A whole complex of terms needed to be examined by the instructor to 'inoculate' [*privit*] the soldiers against characteristic distortions and allowing the newly assimilated term to find its appropriate place (Shpil'rein et al 1928, p. 117).

It is also worth noting that the problem Shpil'rein identified also extended to sensitive proper nouns. When Stalin's name was presented, it seems only 75% of first category soldiers recognised this correctly, and just 26% of second category recruits. This contrasts with 75–100% of soldiers correctly recognising Il'ich (Lenin), Frunze, Zinoviev, Kolchak and the author Demian Bednyi (Shpil'rein et al 1928, p. 99–112).

Professor S.M. Vasileiskii, reviewing the book in the main Soviet journal of *psikhotekhnika* in 1929 called the study 'first-class, fundamental research to which not only political enlightenment workers in the Red Army, but pedagogues and child-specialists (*pedologi*) more generally will often refer' (Vasileiskii 1929, p. 110). Early reports of the results of research aroused considerable interest and complimentary comments by, among others, the head of the Commissariat of Enlightenment's Political Education department, *Glavpolitprosvet*, N.K. Krupskaia

(1927, p. 16). The study also inspired other studies using the same methods within various branches of the army and its educational institutions (Shpil´rein et al 1928, pp. 121–27). Following Krupskaia's comments, the same methods were applied to schools of 'political literacy' in Kazan by M.A. Iurovskaia at the Kazan Institute of NOT. Though there was not a focus on linguistic development here, problems in political development were traced back to the prevalence of similar, 'superficial-mechanical', associations, carelessness when instructors used foreign or jargon words, and a general lack of appreciation among instructors of the need to attune instruction to the specific social environment and origins of the students. Characteristic mistakes that were 'fatal' to political development included the following definitions:

1) Fascism—kingdom; 2) blockade—declaration of independence; 3) chauvinism—supporters of war in the west; 4) imperialism—German legislative organ; 5) trades union (*trediunion*)—abroad; 6) specialist-baiting (*spetseedstvo*)—food prescribed by a doctor. (Iurovskaia 1928, p. 35)[16]

Shpil´rein's research, and the studies that it inaugurated, revealed the deteriorating effectiveness of the Party's political propaganda in conditions where its apparatus was crystallising into a bureaucratic ruling class with diminishing organic connections to the classes that had moved together in revolution. Diagrams illustrating the problem were presented to delegates at the 13th Party Congress in May 1924, and they no doubt contributed to the decision to adopt new approaches to agitation and propaganda (Noskova 1998, p. 336).[17] As we have seen, Shpil´rein's study also suggested ways in which this problem could be addressed, but appearing in the context of the Stalin's 'revolution from above', when the bureaucracy was finally asserting itself as a consciously independent force, this was much less likely to achieve a positive reception. The study essentially provided empirical evidence to support Trotsky's diagnosis of bureaucratism and conventionalism, and it even referred to Trotsky's work on this very issue (Shpil´rein et al 1928, p. 8). This, along with Shpil´rein's connections with Trotsky in *Liga Vremia* and his framing of the historical importance of *psikhotekhnika* in terms of Trotsky's theory of permanent revolution in his programmatic article of 1924 (Shpil´rein 1924, p. 21) left Shpil´rein vulnerable as the vestiges of Trotskyism were subject to liquidation in the early 1930s (Kurek 2004, pp. 93–97). Shpil´rein was arrested in 1935 and shot, while most of his collaborators on *Iazyk krasnoarmeetsa* spent years in the Gulag (Kol´tsova et al 1990, pp. 123–31; Begantsova 2007).

The Significance of the Study

Shpil´rein's study has since rarely been recognised as the trail-blazing research it really represented. It provides an extraordinarily well documented insight into the dynamics of social psychology of the Russian proletarian and peasant masses at a crucial moment in the history of the Revolution.

There are several reasons for looking at this today, not least in illuminating important aspects of Soviet literature in the 1920s. Much prose of the period focuses upon the fractured language of workers or peasants who have suddenly found themselves drawn into a world of literacy and formal education. The *skaz* narration of Isaak Babel's Cossacks or the contorted language of the characters in Andrei Platonov's stories and novels have attracted the attention of many scholars, who have turned to contemporary literary theories or philosophies to analyse the peculiarities of this form of literary language. Shpil'rein's study illuminates what actually lay behind the semi-comical distortions of Revolutionary rhetoric that we find among Platonov's alienated masses. It has often been recognised that such literary works are of significant sociological interest in illustrating the relationship between literate and oral culture and the shifting power relations in the period between the Revolution and the consolidation of the Stalin dictatorship. Shpil'rein's study reveals the nature of such linguistic phenomena prior to artistic appropriation and reworking, such research provides an important means of assessing the psychological and sociological aspects of such language and consequently enabling a more adequate assessment of the aesthetic appropriation of that language.

More significantly, however, the study also provides ample empirical and analytical material for the study of the relationship between what the leader of the Italian Communist Party, Antonio Gramsci (1891–1937), called 'normative' and 'immanent or spontaneous grammars' (Gramsci 1985, p. 181). Indeed, Shpil'rein's methodological procedures suggest an approach to language and politics similar to that we find theorised in Gramsci's work on hegemony. For Gramsci, as for Shpil'rein, linguistic and political power is inseparable, since language is 'a totality of determined notions and concepts and not just of words grammatically devoid of content' (Gramsci 1971, p. 323). Similarly, where for Shpil'rein formation of language and worldview takes place under the pressure of two types of influence: systematic (school, time in the army etc) and unsystematic (general conditions of life, undirected reading, occasional conversations) (Shpil'rein et al 1928, p. 116), for Gramsci, normative grammar is constituted both formally, through the influence of intellectuals, and informally, ('reciprocal monitoring, reciprocal teaching and reciprocal "censorship" expressed in such questions as "What do you mean to say?", "What do you mean?", "Make yourself clearer", etc., and in mimicry and teasing') (Gramsci 1985, pp. 180–81).[18] In each case language and worldview is never purely 'spontaneous' but always at least partially structured through participation in civil society and the operation of prestigious norms. This latter factor Shpil'rein discussed in an article on the patterns of personal name changes published a year after *Iazyk krasnoarmeetsa*, where he discussed the pressures on subordinate social groups to adopt the outward trappings, linguistic and otherwise, of more powerful social groups and the resistance individuals who do so face from the first social group, which regards them as renegades (Shpil'rein 1929). Once more, statistical analysis of cases notified through the press indicates the tendencies at work. Gramsci discussed this in relation to the radiation of linguistic and ideological features from more to less prestigious social groups on the basis of the theories of semantic change developed by, *inter alia*, Antoine Meillet (1866–1936) and Matteo Bartoli (1873–1946). This convergence is almost certainly explained by intersecting intellectual sources adapted according to the demands of the same political contexts.[19]

For both thinkers, it was 'rational to collaborate practically and willingly to welcome everything that may serve to create a common national language, the non-existence of which creates friction particularly in the popular masses among whom local particularisms and phenomena of a narrow and provincial mentality are more tenacious than is believed' (Gramsci 1985, p. 182). Yet in both cases the approach taken towards the drive to ideological and linguistic unity is significantly nuanced. The studies by Shpil'rein and his followers provide excellent illustrations of the different effects of what Mikhail Bakhtin (1895–1975) would later call authoritative and 'internally persuasive' discourse (Bakhtin 1975 [1934], pp. 154–60; 1981 [1934], pp. 342–6). The former is *imposed* on the prior linguistic consciousness from without, where it encounters a substratum of perspectives and pragmatic-linguistic usages. The result is a structural internal inconsistency within linguistic consciousness, a fractured worldview along the intersection between those elements passively accepted as authoritative and those that have arisen in 'unrationalised' social interaction. Where Bakhtin discussed these effects in terms of the psychology of the individual hero in the novels of Dostoevsky and others, Shpil'rein and Gramsci were interested in the effects on the consciousness of the masses. Bourgeois hegemony is founded upon and perpetuates the intellectual subordination of the masses, manifested in the unstable 'contradictory consciousness' of workers. This reduces them to 'moral and political passivity' and leaves them open to further subjugation (Gramsci 1971, pp. 333–34). Proletarian hegemony is, however, achieved through the active assimilation and organic integration of the words of 'organic intellectuals' into the only partially structured worldview of the masses. Worldview is enriched, structural cohesion is promoted and independent discursive activity is facilitated. In short we are dealing with two opposing *hegemonic principles*.

Shpil'rein's study caught the process of political education at the very point at which the future of the Soviet Union was being determined in the wake of the defeat of the German Revolution. This crucial development left the

Revolution isolated in a backward country, galvanising and consolidating the counter-revolutionary process that gave rise to Stalinism. A sharp choice between hegemonic principles faced the political leadership, between what Gramsci termed democratic centralism and bureaucratic centralism (Gramsci 1971, pp. 188–90), the linguistic dimensions of which Shpil´rein documented.

References

1) Archival

Tsentralnyi derzhavnyi arkhiv vishchykh organiv vlady ta upravlinnia Ukrainy (TsDAVOVUU) f.166 Narkompros Ukrainskoi SSR.

2) Published

Bailes, K.E. (1977) 'Alexei Gastev and the Soviet Controversy over Taylorism', *Soviet Studies*, 29(3), pp. 373–94.

Bakhtin, M.M. (1975 [1934]) 'Slovo v romane', in *Voprosy literatury i estetiki* (Moscow: Khudozhestvennaia literatura), pp. 72–233.

Bakhtin, M.M. (1981) 'Discourse in the Novel', in *The Dialogic Imagination* (Austin: University of Texas Press), pp. 259–422.

Begantsova, I.S. (2007) 'psikhotekhnika v kontekste sovetskoi ideologii', in E.B. Muzrukova and L.V. Chesnov (eds), *Nauka i tekhnika v pervye desiatiletiia sovetskoi vlasti: sotsiokul´turnoe izmerenie (1917–1940)*, (Moscow: Academia), pp. 159–79.

Benvenuti, F. (1988) *The Bolsheviks and the Red Army, 1918–1922* (Cambridge: Cambridge University Press).

Brandist, C. (2003) 'The Origins of Soviet Sociolinguistics', *Journal of Sociolinguistics* 7(2), pp. 213–231.

Brandist, C. (2006) 'The Rise of Soviet Sociolinguistics from the Ashes of *Völkerpsychologie*', *Journal of the History of the Behavioral Sciences*, XLII(3), pp. 261–77.

Brandist, C. (2007) 'Konstantin Siunnerberg (Erberg) i issledovanie i prepodavanie zhivogo slova i publichnoi rechi v Petrograde-Leningrade. 1918–1932 gg.', *Ezhegodnik Rukopisnogo otdela Pushkinskogo Doma na 2003–2004 gody* (St. Petersburg: Dmitrii Bulanin), pp. 58–82.

Brown, S. (1995) 'Communists and the Red Cavalry: The Political Education of the Konarmiia in the Russian Civil War, 1918–1920', *Slavonic and East European Review*, 73(1), pp. 82–99.

Bühler, K. (1927) *Die Krise der Psychologie* (Jena: G. Fischer).

Danziger, K. (1990) *Constructing the Subject: Historical Origins of Psychological Research* (Cambridge: Cambridge University Press).

Deutcher, I. (2003) *The Prophet Unarmed: Trotsky 1921–1929* (London: Verso).

Figes, O. (1990) 'The Red Army and Mass Mobilization during the Russian Civil War 1918–1920', *Past and Present*, 129, pp. 168–211.

Gastev, A. (1919) 'O tendentsiiakh proletarskoi kul´tury', *Proletarskaia kul´tura*, 9–10, pp. 36–45.

Gramsci, A. (1971) *Selections from the Prison Notebooks* (London: Lawrence and Wishart).

Gramsci, A. (1985) *Selections from the Cultural Writings* (London: Lawrence and Wishart).

Grigor´eva, I.V. (1998) 'Rossiiskie stranitsy biografii Antonio Gramshi (1922–1926 gg.) po dokumentam arkhiva Kominterna' in *Rossiia i Italiia*, 3: XX vek (Moscow: Nauka), pp. 96–123.

Hagen, M. von, (1990) *Soldiers in the Proletarian Dictatorship: The Red Army and the Soviet Socialist State, 1917–1930* (Ithaca and London: Cornell University Press).

Iurovskaia, M.A. (1928) 'Psikhotekhnicheskaia proverka znanii v shkole politgramoty', *Psikhofiziologiia truda i psikhotekhnika*, 1(2), pp. 29–40.

Ives, P. (2004) *Gramsci's Politics of Language: Engaging the Bakhtin Circle & the Frankfurt School* (Toronto: University of Toronto Press).

Killen, A. (2007) 'Weimar Psychotechnics Between Americanism and Fascism', *Osiris*, 22(1), pp. 48–71.

Kol'tsova, V.A., O.G. Noskova and Iu. N. Oleinik, (1990) 'I.N. Shpil'rein i sovetskaia psikhotekhnika', *Psikologicheskii zhurnal*, 2(2), pp. 111–33.

KPSS (1984) *KPSS v rezoliutsiiakh i resheniiakh s''ezdov konferentsii i plenumov Ts.K.*, t.3, 1922–25 (Moscow: Politicheskaia literatura).

Krupskaia, N.K. (1927) *Osnovy politprosvetraboty: Izuchenie mass i konkretnykh uslovii v kotorykh oni zhivut i rabotaiut* (Moscow and Leningrad: 'Doloi negramotnost'')

Kurek, N. (2004) *Istoriia likvidizatsii pedologii i psikhotekhniki* (St. Petersburg: Aleteiia).

Leont'ev, A.N. (1997) 'On Vygotsky's Creative Development', in *The Collected Works of L. S. Vygotsky*, vol. 3, ed. R. W. Reiber and J. Wollock, (New York and London: Plenum Press), pp. 9–32.

Lo Piparo, F. (1979) *Lingua intellectuali egemonia in Gramsci* (Bari: Laterza).

Martin, T. (2001) *The Affirmative Action Empire: Nations and Nationalism in the Soviet Union, 1923–1939* (Ithaca and London: Cornell University Press).

Marx, K. (1987[1866]) 'Marx to Engels, 17 July 1866', in Karl Marx and Friedrich Engels, *Collected Works*, Vol. 42 (London: Lawrence & Wishart), p. 289.

Münsterberg, H. (1913) *Psychologie und Wirtschaftsleben: ein Betrag zur angewandten Experimentalpsychologie* (Leipzig: Barth).

Münsterberg, H. (1914) *Grundzüge der Psychotechnik* (Leipzig: Barth).

Miunsterberg, G. (1914) *Psikhologiia i ekonomicheskaia zhizn'* (Moscow: Sovremennye problemy).

Miunsterberg, G. (1922) *Osnovy psikhotekhniki* (Moscow: Russkii knizhnik).

Munipov, V. M., and L. A. Radzikhovskii (1981) 'Psikhotekhnika v sisteme nauchnykh predstavlenii L. S. Vygotskogo', in V. V. Davidov (ed.), *Nauchnoe tvorchestvo L. S. Vygotskogo i sovremennaia psikhologiia* (Moscow: Akademiia pedagogicheskikh nauk SSSR), pp. 104–07.

Noskova, O. G. (1981) 'L. S. Vygotskii o roli psikhotekhniki v razvitii psikhologicheskoi nauki', in V. V. Davidov (ed.), *Nauchnoe tvorchestvo L. S. Vygotskogo i sovremennaia psikhologiia* (Moscow: Akademiia pedagogicheskikh nauk SSSR), pp. 115–16.

Noskova, O.G. (1998) *Istoriia psikhologii truda v Rossii 1917–1957gg.* (Moscow: Dissertation for the degree of Doctor of Psychology, MGU).

Polivanov, E.D. (1931) *Za marksistskoe iazykoznanie* (Moscow: Federatsiia).

Rabinbach, A. (1992) *The Human Motor: Energy, Fatigue, and the Origins of Modernity* (Berkeley: University of California Press).

Reber, A.S. (1985) *The Penguin Dictionary of Psychology* (Harmondsworth: Penguin).

Rosengarten, F. (1985) 'The Gramsci-Trotsky Question (1922–1932)', *Social Text* 11, pp. 65–95.

Rozhkov, A. Iu. (2000) '"V Moskve ia slyshal odno, zdes' vizhu drugoe..." Krasnoarmeets 20-kh godov: kartiny mira i sotsial'yi oblik', *Sotsiologicheskie issledovania*, 10, pp. 76–83.

Shcherba, L.V. (2007) 'Pamiati A. Meie', in *Iazykovaia sistema i rechevaia deiatel'nost'* (Moscow: URSS) pp. 405–12.

Shpil'rein, I.N. (1923) 'Personalizm Vil'iama Shterna v ego otnoshenii k psikhotekhnike', *Vestnik sotsialisticheskoi akademii*, 3, pp. 200–09.

Shpil'rein, I.N. (1924) 'Nauchnaia organizatsiia psikhotekhniki', *Vremia*, 4, pp. 19–24.

Shpril'rein, I.N., D.I. Reitynbarg, G.O. Netskii, (1928) *Iazyk Krasnoarmeitsa: Opyt issledovaniia slovaria krasnoarmeitsa moskovskogo garnizona* (Moscow and Leningrad: Gosizdat).

Shpil'rein, I.N. (1929) 'O peremene imen i familii (sotsial'no-psikhologicheskii etiud)', *Psikhotekhnika i psikhologiia truda*, 4, pp. 281–86.

Shpil'rein, I.N. (1930) *Psikhoteknika v rekonstruktivnyi period*, (Moscow: Izd. Komakademii).

Shor, R.O. (1926) 'Krizis sovremennoi lingvistiki', *Iaficheskii sbornik*, 5, pp. 32–71.

Smilga, I.T. (1921) *Ocherednye voprosy stroitel'stva Krasnoi armii* (Moscow: Gosizdat).

Smith, M.G. (1998) *Language and Power in the Creation of the USSR, 1917–1953* (Berlin: Mouton de Gruyter).

Sochor, Z.A. (1981) 'Soviet Taylorism Revisited', *Soviet Studies*, 33(2), pp. 246–64.

Stern, W. (1900) *Über Psychologie der individuellen Differenzen. Ideen zu einer "Differentiellen Psychologie."* (Leipzig: J.A. Barth).

Stern, W. (1911) *Die differentielle Psychologie in ihren methodischen Grundlagen* (Leipzig: Barth).

Stites, R. (1989) *Revolutionary Dreams: Utopian Vision and Experimental Life in the Russian Revolution* (Oxford: Oxford University Press).

Sutherland, A.H. (1915) 'Review of Hugo Münsterberg, *Grundzüge der Psychotechnik* (Leipzig: Barth, 1914)', *The American Journal of Psychology*, 26(2), pp. 306–08.

Trotsky, L.D. (1923) *Novyi kurs*, Online at http://www.marxists.org/russkij/trotsky/1924/newc.htm#st09 (accessed 31 Jan 2007).

Trotsky, L. (1970 [1936]) *The Revolution Betrayed: What is the Soviet Union and Where is it Going?* (New York: Pathfinder Press).

Trotsky, L.D. (1973 [1923]) 'Not by Politics Alone', in *Problems of Everyday Life* (New York: Monad Press), pp. 15–24.

Trotsky, L.D. (1973 [1925]) 'Dialectical Materialism and Science' in *Problems of Everyday Life* (New York: Monad Press), pp. 206–26.

Trotsky, L.D. (1973 [1926]) 'Culture and Socialism' in *Problems of Everyday Life* (New York: Monad Press), pp. 227–49.

Trotsky, L.D. (1979 [1923–25]) *How the Revolution Armed, Vol. 1: The Year 1918* (London: New Park Pubs.).

Vasileiskii, S.M. (1929) 'Iazyk krasnoarmeitsa', *Psikhotekhnika i psikhologiia truda*, 2, pp. 108–111.

Vilkova, V. (1996) *The Struggle for Power: Russia in 1923* (New York: Promethius Books).

Viteles, M.S. (1923) 'Psychology in Business in England, France and Germany', *Annals of the American Academy of Political and Social Science*, 110, pp. 207–20.

Vygotsky, L.S. (1997 [1926–27])'The Historical Meaning of the Crisis in Psychology: A Methodological Investigation', in R. W. Reiber and J. Wollock (eds) *The Collected Works of L. S. Vygotsky*, vol. 3 (New York and London: Plenum Press), pp. 233–343.

Vygotsky, L.S. (2004 [1926–7]) 'Istoricheskii smysl psikhologicheskogo krizisa', in *Psikhologiia razvitiia cheloveka* (Moscow: Smysl), pp. 41–190.

Appendix 1

INTRODUCTION TO JAPHETIDOLOGY: THESES

Ivan Meshchaninov

Translated and with an Introduction by Craig Brandist

Introduction to Meshchaninov

Very little work by the theorists of Japhetidology have appeared in English translation, and so the Anglophone reader has hitherto had to rely on second-hand accounts, many of which were written in the midst of the Cold War and marked by its oversimplifications and rhetoric. Only a few scattered works by Nikolai Marr have ever appeared in English, generally in publications that are now difficult to obtain, and the work of some of the most talented scholars who worked within the trend have never been translated or even discussed in any sustained fashion. There are probably good reasons that Marr's own tortuous musings have never attracted a dedicated translator, for they frequently try the patience even of native Russian speakers, but this cannot be said of all the scholars who espoused some version of Japhetic Theory. It is with this in mind that we offer Ivan Meshchaninov's 'Theses' on Japhetidology, which were published at the beginning of his 1929 book *Introduction to Japhetidology* (*Vvedenie v iafetidologiiu*), in which the author aimed to provide a systematic and accessible overview of the field. The book was published as one of a series of monographs of the Institute of the Comparative History of the Literatures and Languages of the West and East (*Institut sravnitel'noi istorii literatur i iazykov Zapada i Vostoka*) in Leningrad that included such well-known works as Pavel Medvedev's *The Formal Method in Literary Scholarship* (*Formal'nyi metod v literaturovedenii*, 1928), Valentin Voloshinov's *Marxism and the Philosophy of Language* (*Marksizm i filosofiia iazyka*, 1929) and Mikhail Bakhtin's *Problems of Dostoevskii's Art* (*Problemy tvorchestva Dostoevskogo*, 1929). Unlike these works, Meshchaninov's text was a product of the linguistics section of the institute, where Marr's ideas about language constituted an influential trend, though not yet the only acceptable theory. Meshchaninov was, at the time, a 46 year old research fellow and follower of Marr, who also held a position at Marr's Institute of Language and Thinking (*Institut iazyka i myshleniia*), and following Marr's death in 1934 he was to become the most influential linguist in the USSR and the director of the institute until it was closed following Stalin's denunciation of Marr in 1950. Even then, however, the institute became the basis of the Leningrad branch of the newly-founded, and now Moscow centred, Institute of Linguistics. This Leningrad branch retained most of the staff members and research specialities of the former Institute of Language and Thinking, and indeed such research directions as language typology, functional grammar and formal semantics are still being pursued and developed in the contemporary incarnation of the branch in the form of the Institute of Linguistic Research in St. Petersburg (see Desnitskaia 1971).

Meshchaninov was certainly a different type of figure than the young, belligerent advocates of Marrism exemplified by Valerian Aptekar´, about whom Alpatov writes in his essay for the current volume. He was also far more systematic and balanced in his approach than Marr himself, who was constantly adapting his eclectic doctrine to negotiate rather than solve its internal problems, and whose volatile temperament, intolerance and intellectual hubris dismayed many of his contemporaries. While Meshchaninov championed Marr's ideas, his own work was not marked by the dogmatism of some of his colleagues, and he was willing to combine Marrist ideas with a more general typology and historical linguistics. This openness is evident in Meshchaninov's admission that many of the designations of certain languages are still provisional and open to further consideration. His leadership in Soviet linguistics between 1935 and 1950 was also much more flexible and integral than many feared in the wake of the victory of Marrism during the so-called Cultural Revolution of 1929–32, and this allowed some of the more extreme elements of Marr's thought, such as the notorious 'four element' theory (theses 19 and 20) to be quietly sidelined in subsequent research.

Most commentaries on Marr's ideas highlight his hostility to Indo-European comparative linguistics and his one-sidedly genetic approach to language. Around the time of Stalin's denunciation of Marr in June 1950 there were a series of serious assessments of his work and the linguistics of some of his followers (Matthews 1948, 1950; Poláck 1948; Ellis and Davis 1951), but these rarely gave an impression of the various ways in which Japhetic theory has been developed or the full range of influences that were brought to bear on Japhetic theory. One full-length study of Marr's intellectual development appeared in 1957 (Thomas 1957), which is still of considerable value, showing that Marr adopted positions from a number of key figures, most notably the Russian comparative historian of literature Aleksandr Veselovskii, the French positivist anthropologist Lucien Lévy-Bruhl and the German philosopher and philologist

Ludwig Noiré. Since this time, however, Anglophone engagements with Marrism have either been in historical surveys of the low-points of Soviet linguistics (Brusche-Schultz 1993) and anthropology (Slezkine 1996) or as contextual materials for the discussion of literary scholars of the time (Perlina 2002; Brandist 2002). There has, however, been a rise in interest in Marr's earlier works on the Caucasian languages (Cherchi and Manning 2002; Tuite 2008). In the Francophone world there has been a revival of interest in Marrist linguistics, as evidenced by a conference on the subject held at the University of Lausanne, Switzerland, in 2005 (Sériot 2005) and the publication of a recent monograph on Marr's semantics (Velmezova 2007). In Russia, reassessment of the intellectual history of the 1920s and 1930s has inevitably led to rising interest in Marrism, which played such an important role at that time. This is clear from the recent republication of the 1933 textbook *Japhetidologiia* (Marr 2002) and of the work of such significant figures associated with Marrism as Freidenberg, Izrail' Frank-Kamenetskii and Konstantin Megelidze. In secondary literature there has been an emergence of a more holistic approach to Marr's career (Platonova 1998, 2002; Vasil'kov 2001) and the beginnings of a more general assessment of the achievements of Japhetic theory (Nikonova 2003).

One of the difficulties in assessing the works of Marrists is the relative unfamiliarity of today's readers with the intellectual context in which it emerged. Marr's formative years preceded the Saussurean recasting of linguistics and pertained more to the dominant type of philology and anthropology of the later nineteenth century, and about which Alpatov has relevant points to make in his contribution to this volume. Like philologists of the time, Marr did not view language as a separate object domain, but one that was closely connected to questions of ethnology, psychology and material culture. His work maintains several of the key assumptions of comparative philology, including the idea that 'Language, in the sense in which we use the word, begins with roots, which are not only the ultimate facts of the science of language, but real facts in the history of human speech' (Max Müller, 1868, quoted in van den Bosch 2002, p.221). Like Max Müller, Adolphe Pictet and others, Marr believed language could be subject to paleontological analysis until the primary roots could be ascertained, but unlike such scholars he was particularly hostile to the ideas of Aryan superiority that underlay the Indo-European paradigm. Marr's early Romantic Georgian nationalism led him to object to the proposition that linguistic palaeontology would reveal a particularly valuable Indo-European *Ur*-language that could be correlated with a superior Aryan people. In developing his ideas, Marr also developed a flawed ideology critique of orientalism that anticipated that of Edward Said decades later (Cherchi and Manning 2002; Tolz 2005, 2006). Even those philologists who opposed the direct correlation between language and race tended to assume that the original Indo-Europeans had a special place in history and that this underlay their imperial mission. Max Müller was exemplary in this regard:

> The Aryan nations… have been the prominent actors in the great drama of history, and have carried to their fullest growth all the elements of active life with which our nature is endowed. They have perfected society and morals; and we learn from their literature and works of art the elements of science, the laws of art, and the principles of philosophy. In continual struggle with each other and with Semitic and Turanian races, these Aryan nations have become the rulers of history, and it seems to be their mission to link all parts of the world together by the chains of civilisation, commerce and religion. (Müller, 1899, quoted in Voigt, 1967, p. 6)

While maintaining a commitment to linguistic palaeontology, Marr and his followers drew close to the ideas of the British evolutionary anthropologists such as Herbert Spencer and Edward Tylor, and the folklorist Andrew Lang, who held that semantic materials could be traced back until they become the objects of general ethnography. Typical forms of plot, metaphor and the like were held to have arisen in various places as a result of similar conditions. As Lang put it, '[h]olding that myth is a product of the early human fancy, working on the most rudimentary knowledge of the outer world, the student of folklore thinks that differences of race do not much affect the early mythopoetic faculty' (Lang 1884, p. 23). While many of his ideas were adopted from the work of Veselovskii, Marr regarded Spencer as perhaps the most important influence on his intellectual development (Marr 1935, p. 127), and he developed the notion of the universality of primary semantic units until it applied to the roots of language itself. The main point of mediation between the two trends was what Müller called Noiré's *synergastic theory* (van den Bosch 2002, p. 234), according to which 'the earliest meanings of verbal roots referred to human action' (Noiré 1917, p.139), while 'things are brought within the horizon of human reason, or first grow intro things, in proportion as they suffer the effect of human action and have names assigned to them accordingly' (Noiré 1917, p. 149). Here is the origin of the Marrist notion of functional semantics (thesis 25), according to which objects bear names according to the function they play in society.

While much of this is now clearly open to question, 'it was rare indeed for anyone from this period to argue that the structure of language could be paralleled anywhere else in culture' (Henson 1974, p. 19). Moreover, in combining elements from linguistic palaeontology with evolutionary anthropology, the Marrists recognised what few Western commentators contemporary with them noticed until several decades later: that in the confrontation between the evolutionists and mythologists, the latter paradigm was not simply routed but that problems with each paradigm were revealed (Dorson 1968). The resulting formulation, semantic series and semantic 'nests' or 'clusters' (theses 21–25), proved to be very provocative categories in the analysis of myth and the various literary and religious forms that emerged from them. One can find examples in the work of Frank-Kamenetskii, Freidenberg and Bakhtin among others. We thus offer Meshchaninov's *Theses* not in order to rehabilitate Marrism, but to identify Japhetidology as a complex historical phenomenon, aspects of which influenced the development of Soviet philology and, through such figures as Freidenberg, Bakhtin and Iurii Lotman, continue to exert an influence on cultural theory today.

References

Bosch, L.P. van den (2002) *Friedrich Max Müller: A Life Dedicated to the Humanities* (Leiden: Brill).

Brandist, C. (2002) *The Bakhtin Circle: Philosophy, Culture and Politics* (London: Pluto Press).

Brusche-Schultz, G. (1993) 'Marr, Marx, and Linguistics in the Soviet Union', *Historiographia Linguistica* vol. 20, Nos. 2–3, pp. 455–472.

Cerchi, M. and H.P. Manning (2002) *Disciplines and Nations: Niko Marr vs. His Georgian Students on Tbilisi State University and the Japhetidology/Caucasology Schism* (=Carl Beck Papers in Russian and East European Studies 1603).

Desnitskaia, A.V. (1971) '50 let akademicheskogo lingvisticheskogo instituta' Online at http://iling.spb.ru/pdf/des/004des.html (accessed 16/05/09).

Dorson, R. (1968) *The British Folklorists: A History* (London: Routledge and Kegan Paul).

Frank-Kamenetskii, I.G. (2004) *Kolesnitsa Iegovy* (Moscow: Labirint).

Freidenberg, O.M. (1998) *Mif i literatura drevnosti* (Moscow: Vostochnaia literatura).

Ellis, J. and R.W. Davis (1951) 'The Crisis in Soviet Linguistics', *Soviet Studies* vol. 2, no. 3, pp. 209–264.

Henson, H. (1974) *British Social Anthropologists and Language: A History of Separate Development* (Oxford: Clarendon Press).

Lang, A. (1904 [1884]) 'The Method of Folklore' in *Custom and Myth* (London: Longmans, Green and co.) pp. 10–28.

Marr, N. Ia. (1935) 'Avtobiografiia N.Ia. Marra', *Problemy istorii dokapitalisticheskikh obshchestv*, nos. 3–4, pp. 126–30.

Marr, N. Ia. (2002) *Iafetidologiia* (Zhukovskii and Moscow: Kuchkovo pole).

Matthews, W.K. (1948) 'The Japhetic Theory', *Slavonic and East European Review*, nos. 27, pp.172–192.

Matthews, W.K. (1950) 'The Soviet Contribution to Linguistic Thought', *Archivum Linguisticum* no. 2, pp.1–23 and 97–121.

Megrelidze, K.R. (2007) *Osnovnye problemy sotsiologii myshleniia* (Moscow: URSS).

Nikonova, A.A. (2003) *Problema arkhaicheskogo soznaniia i stanovlenie otechestvennoi kul'turologicheskoi mysli (20–30-e gody XXv.)* (Kandidatskaia dissertatsiia: St. Petersburg State University).

Noiré, L. (1917) *The Origin and Philosophy of Language* (Chicago and London: Open Court).

Perlina, N. (2002) *Ol'ga Freidenberg's Works and Days* (Bloomington: Slavica).

Platonova, N.I. (1998) 'Nikolai Iakovlevich Marr – arkheolog i organizator arkheologicheskoi nauki', *Arkheologicheskie vesti* no. 5, pp. 371–82.

Platonova, N.I. (2002) "' Bezzakonnaia kometa na nauchnom nebosklone". N.Ia. Marr', in *Znamenitye universanty* (St. Petersburg: Izd. Sankt-Peterburgskogo universiteta) pp.156–78.

Poláck, V. (1948) 'Present Day Trends in Soviet Linguistics', *Slavonic and East European Review*, no. 26, pp. 438–451.

Sériot, P. (ed.) (2005) *Un paradigme perdu: la linguistique marriste* (*Cahiers de l'ILSL*, no. 20).

Thomas, L.L. (1957) *The Linguistic Theories of N.Ja. Marr* (Berkeley and Los Angeles: University of California Press).

Tolz, V. (2005) 'Orientalism, Nationalism and Ethnic Diversity in Late Imperial Russia, *Historical Journal* no. 48(1), pp. 127–50.

Tolz, V. (2006) 'European, National and (Anti-)Imperial: The Formation of Academic Oriental Studies in Late Tsarist and Early Soviet Russia', in Michael David-Fox et al (eds), *Orientalism and Empire in Russia* (Bloomington: Slavica) pp. 107–34.

Tuite, K. (2008) 'The Rise and Fall of the Ibero-Caucasian Hypothesis', *Historiographia linguistica* vol. 30, nos. 1/2, pp. 23–82.

Vasil'kov, Ia.V. (2001) 'Tragediia akademika Marra', *Khristianskii vostok*, no. 2, pp. 390–421.

Velmezova, E. (2007) *Les Lois du sens: la sémantique marriste* (Bern et al: Peter Lang).

Voigt, J.H.F. (1967) *Max Müller: The Man and His Ideas* (Calcutta : Mukhopadhyay).

INTRODUCTION TO JAPHETIDOLOGY (1929)

Theses

A. The General Propositions of Japhetidology

1) *Japhetic Theory* is built on research into the fundamental questions of man in the circumstances of his social activity. The study of man as a social creator is carried out within Japhetidology, first of all, on the basis of *linguistic* material, which reflects the various epochs through which human life has passed in the most complete way.

2) In as much as language is but one of the products of common-human cultural activity, *Japhetic linguistics* retains a close connection with the studies into the history of material culture, the history of social formations, the history of the development of human thinking.

3) Japhetidology studies the *process* of the development of human activity because society is defined by an uninterrupted, changing system of relations between members of a social community.

4) Since the process of the development of various phenomena in the realms of material and spiritual culture forms the basis of Japhetidology, it also touches on *genetic* problems.

5) In the realm of the *general theory of language* Japhetidology addresses the questions of the origin of language, the interrelationships of different systems of languages (in the usual terminology 'families') in their static condition, the successive connections of linguistic systems and the evolution within and between them, both as formal typology and ideologically.

6) Japhetic investigations have a special interest in the *Japhetic languages*, that is the languages of the Japhetic system (in usual terminology the 'Japhetic family') which are distinctive in terms of their formal organization.

7) Studies of Japhetic languages (i.e. languages of the Japhetic system) have the Japhetic stage of all-human speech as their object of research. This stage was found among the prehistoric population of the whole mainland, and is studied through its remains in the historical languages that are the survivals of the Japhetic stage that preceded them and is retained to this day by its representatives in the Pamirs (the Vershiks),[1] in the Pyrenees (Basques) and in the Caucasus in numerous and various forms.

8) While studying the Japhetic languages in their static condition, Japhetidology traces the process of development both within those languages, and in connection with the common path of the process of the development of speech in general inasmuch as it is revealed in determinate parts of the languages of the Japhetic system.

9) In as much as the Japhetic condition of languages is but one of the stages of the development of speech, this in turn posits the question of the conditions preceding it and of their rebirth in languages of other systems.

10) Every phenomenon, both in lingual speech (*iazykovaia rech'*)[2] and in other regions of cultural creation [*kul'turotvorchestvo*], is studied in the condition in which it is caught, but in order to achieve its complete elucidation the study of its previous condition (*paleontological analysis*) is also carried out.

B. Theses Outlining the Propositions of General Linguistics

11) Human speech constitutes a unity in its process of development. The formation of linguistic systems, usually called 'families', represent their moving along separate inclines of formation of this single process of development.

12) The rise of human speech is conditioned by the grouping of human individuals in connection with the satisfaction of common human needs and demands on the means of communication between them.

13) The first detectable traces of a means of communication were in the language of gestures, bodily movements and facial expressions (*kinetic speech*). The period of kinetic speech is rather protracted and must have had its subdivisions.

14) The initial elements of *sound speech* accompanied kinetic speech, as reflex acts, at the first stages of the simplest social association, when human productive labour was still not delimited in the person's consciousness from magical activity.

15) The achievement of articulate sounds is not just brought about by the demands of communication, which was satisfied by kinetic speech. The origin of articulate sound speech needs to be sought in the magical

activities that were necessary for the success of productive activity and accompanied this or that collective labour process.

16) The necessity for a range of concepts to coincide with a specific sound designation (the beginning period of word creation) already pertains to the period of the strengthening of the collective activity of human community. This initial range of concepts had a cultic character, but in the special context of cultic circumstances, since in the thinking of humanity the productive act and cultic activity were not completely set apart.

17) The range of concepts became larger with the emergence of the human collective from the state of diffuse thinking and this demanded a special designation. With the enlargement of the word stock these began to be used in everyday speech, leading to a gradual shift from kinetic to lingual speech.

18) The broadening of the range of concepts demanded an increase in sound designations. For this human society utilized the stock of the primary elements of sound speech, introducing phonetic distinction and so enriching the paucity of the word stock.

19) The number of such primary elements was set at four. They were found everywhere and applied to designate every concept, i.e. they were a-semantic (having no determinate, fixed meaning).

20) The entire word stock of all humanity, in all its variety, arose from these four fundamental elements (primary sound complexes).

21) Given the feeble development of sociality and of the variety of labour activities, and in accordance with the particular way of thinking, an appellation was conferred upon a range of concepts and objects. One appellation signified a whole series of objects and concepts, and consequently, was distinguished by multiple meanings (polysemanticism). One can find a survival of this situation in historical languages in what is called *semantic nests* or *clusters*, united by the connections that we have made between them.

22) The distinction of separate objects and concepts, each needing its own appellation, is a phenomenon of later in the development of social life and, consequently, of a certain stage in the development of worldview.

23) The gradually growing need for special appellations demanded an increase in the number of separate sound complexes, already words. These were formed from previous appellations applying to the range of concepts and objects. Thus a meaning attached beyond the given word (its *semantics*) acquires an essential significance.

24) In the process of the continuing development of human speech a series of words were connected to each other according to their meanings as semantic derivatives, as they emerged from previous appellations of a range

of concepts and objects. Later they also emerged from such separate appellations, forming a series of words with their distinct meanings (*semantic series*), united by the successive changes of meaning (semantic links) and ascending to one common basis for the whole semantic series (the beginning or first link of the semantic series).

25) Shifts in the meaning of a given word depend upon the changing role of the designated object in the society that uses it. Thus a word acquires its meaning in the social milieu that surrounds it. When a function shifts from one object to another, the latter object acquires the designation of the former (*functional semantics* and semantic series).

26) The development of speech is conditioned by the process of crossing [*skreshchenie*], that is, the organic combination of fundamental elements and, subsequently, words with the same meaning. This, in turn, is the result of the crossing of separate human groupings and, later, tribes. Each of the accreted elements is can be understood as that of one of the social units that has crossed or has entered into communication and, thus, an entire crossed word can be understood by both social groups (masses) which have crossed or entered into communication.

27) The accumulation of the word stock progresses by means of the crossing and phonetic differentiation (distinction of sounds) of those four fundamental elements, and with the development of social intercourse, especially in the period of the formation of tribes, various types of these fundamental elements and their combination form particular sets of word stems (stem morphemes) (this is fundamental in tribal word-creation, and forms the bases of what is called national languages).

28) Subsequently, in the process of the development of speech, we see what are called *composite words* being formed from the combination of two or more words having different meanings for the expression of more complex concepts. Each of them could enter into different semantic series or act as different links of a single series, whereas in *crossed words*, all stem morphemes that have merged belong not only to the same semantic series, but even to one and the same link.

29) Throughout the whole period of the development of human speech which moves in coordination with the development of human collectives, and, consequently, with the development of the phenomena of cultural creation, one can identify epochs that are characterised by a dominant worldview. Such epochs are called *stages*, for instance the stage of magical perception, the stage of cosmic perception etc.

30) Characteristic features (*coordinates*) are formed in the life of language, according to which the process of development takes place. These features are multiform. One of these accompanies another, while others are

overcome by the reinforcement of others etc., for instance monosyllabism, linguistic syntheticism (the determination of the function of a word by its place in a phrase), polysemanticism and others.

31) Established languages are characterized by the complexes of *coordinates* (sums of features) that are inherent to them. Groups of languages, designated by their system (Japhetic systems, the Semitic system, Indo-European system etc) are defined by the available complex of coordinates that produce them.

32) Languages are grouped according to some or other features (coordinates) being present in them, but since languages, even fully developed ones, are but specific formations within the general process of the development of speech, then it is impossible for only those accurately named features to be present. In every language some features are active, others are dying out, a third set is being born. Grouping is therefore to a certain extent conditional and proceeds according to the availability of a specifically characteristic *sum of features* that are still actively present in them.

33) In such conditions, a series of languages appear, according to the features present in them, to belong to different systems. Such languages are denoted as being in a *transitional state* between one system and another. This designation is still conditional, since the grouping according to complexes of coordinates that has been established by Japhetidology is also conditional.

34) Language is one of the phenomena of the cultural life of the person. Therefore division into stages and systems, the establishment of coordinates, the elucidation of fundamental elements etc must also be carried out on other phenomena of cultural creation, especially in the study of the monuments of material culture and the creation of myths [*mifotvorchestvo*].

Appendix 2

GLOSSARY OF NAMES

Abaev, Vasilii Ivanovich (1900–2001) Russian linguist. Advocate of Marr's New Theory of Language in the 1920s–1940s. Among his works are publications about Ossetian and Iranian etymology, Ossetian folklore, Iranian studies and general linguistics.

Antonov-Ovseenko, Vladimir Aleksandrovich (1883–1939) Russian state, Party and Military figure. A revolutionary participant in 1917 and commanded the Ukrainian front in the Civil War. Participated in the Left Opposition 1923–7. Arrested for oppositional activity in 1938 and shot.

Aptekar´, Valerian Borisovich (1899–1937) Russian linguist and propagandist of Marr's New Theory of Language. Arrested and shot in 1937.

Avanesov, Ruben Ivanovich (1902–1982) Russian linguist, co-founder of the Moscow Phonological School, along with Nikolai F. Iakolev, Vladimir I. Sidorov and Alexandr A. Reformatskii. Known for his works on Russian phonetics, orthography and dialectology. The author of the first dictionary of Russian pronunciation (1950).

Bakhtin, Mikhail Mikhailovich (1895–1975) Russian philosopher and literary theorist.

Bally, Charles (1865–1947) Swiss linguist and co-editor of Saussure's *Cours*. Bally's book *Langage et la Vie* was required reading for linguists at ILIaZV in the 1920s.

Bartoli, Matteo (1873–1946) Italian linguist, founder of so-called 'Neolinguistics', which mapped the diffusion of linguistic elements between sign communities. Teacher of Antonio Gramsci.

Baudouin de Courtenay, Jan (Ivan Aleksandrovich Boduen de Kurtene, 1845–1929) Polish-Russian linguist. Established the Kazan and the Petersburg Linguistic Schools. Polivanov, Iakubinskii, Larin and Shcherba, inter alia, participated in the latter. He emigrated to Poland in 1918.

Bopp, Franz (1791–1867) German linguist, one of the main developers of the comparative method in linguistics. Published extensively on the comparative history of grammatical forms in Indo-European languages. Among his most influential works is *Vergleichende Grammatik des Sanskrit, Zend, Griechischen, Lateinischen, Litauischen, Gotischen und Deutschen* (*Comparative Grammar of Sanskrit, Zend (Avestan), Greek, Latin, Lithuanian, Gothic and German*), (Berlin, 1833–52).

Bubnov, Andrei Sergeevich (1884–1938) Ukrainian Party, State and Military figure. Secretary of the Central Committee 1925 and Commissar of Enlightenment 1929. Arrested and shot in 1938.

Cohen, Hermann (1842–1914) German Jewish philosopher. Founder of the Marburg School of Neo-Kantianism.

Curtius, Georg (1820–1885) German philologist whose work on classics and Indo-European languages were fundamental to the study of the Greek language.

Danilov, Georgii Konstantinovich (1896–1937) Russian linguist, specialist in African languages, and founder of the group *Iazykfront*, which opposed Marr's New Theory of

Language being granted the status of Marxism in linguistics. In 1931–2 deputy director of the Moscow-based Research Institute of Linguistics (1931–1933). He was arrested and shot in 1937.

Derzhavin, Nikolai Sevast´ianovich (1877–1953) Russian Slavist, director of ILIaZV 1923–1932, and advocate of Marr's New Theory of Language.

Doroshevskii, Vitol´d Ian (Doroszewski Witold Jan, 1899–1976), Polish linguist, specialist in Slavonic languages and dialectology.

Durnovo, Nikolai Nikolaevich (1876–1937) Russian linguist and member of the Moscow Dialectology Commission, the forerunner of the Moscow Linguistic Circle. Spent 1924–8 in Prague, working with the Prague Linguistic Circle. Worked and published on Russian dialectology, the history of Russian and Slavonic languages, Russian morphology, the theory of grammar and old Russian literature. Was arrested and shot in 1937.

Fortunatov, Filipp Fedorovich (1848–1914) Russian linguist and founder of the Moscow Linguistic School known for his formal approach to the study of linguistic data.

Frank-Kamenetskii, Izrail' Grigor'evich (1880–1937) Russian orientalist, specialist in ancient history, literature and culture of the Middle East.

Freidenberg, Olga Mikhailovna (1890–1955) Russian literary scholar, classicist, specialist in comparative ancient and medieval literature and folklore.

Frunze, Mikhail Vasil´evich (1885–1925) Soviet political figure, Party member from 1904, commander in the Red Army during the Civil War and Commissar for War 1924–5 during which time he introduced important reforms.

Galton, Francis (1822–1911) British Polymath. Among his many activities, he was the first to apply statistical methods to the study of human differences and intelligence and introduced the use of questionnaires and surveys for collecting data on human communities. This led to the development of anthropometrics and eugenics, a term Galton introduced. He founded psychometrics (the science of measuring mental faculties) and promoted differential psychology.

Gastev, Aleksei Kapitonovich (1882–1939) Russian revolutionary, poet, writer, participant in the Proletkul´t movement, proponent of the scientific organization of labour (NOT) and the director of the Central Organization of Labour. Arrested in 1938 and shot the following year.

Giese, Fritz (1890–1935) German conservative industrial psychologist, who combined psychotechnics with the metaphysics of *Lebensphilosophie*.

Gramsci, Antonio (1891–1937) Italian political theorist and activist, leader of the Italian Communist Party 1923–26 before being arrested. He then wrote his now famous *Prison Notebooks* in which the relation between language and politics plays a key role.

Grimm, Jacob (1785–1863) German philologist whose histories, grammars and dictionary of the German language, development of a theory of non-trivial sound-changes in language and collection (with his brother Wilhelm (1786–1859)) of German folktales exerted a formative influence on philology across Europe, including Russia.

Humboldt, Wilhelm von (1767–1835) German government functionary, diplomat, philosopher, particularly remembered as a linguist who made important contributions to the philosophy of language and to the theory and practice of education. His book *The Heterogeneity of Language and its Influence on the Intellectual Development of Mankind* in which he defined language as a rule-governed system that embodies a worldview was particularly influential in Russia.

Iakovlev, Nikolai Feofanovich (1892–1974) Russian linguist, played a key role in the formation of the Moscow Phonological School. Made a significant contribution to the codification of the phonetics of several Caucasian languages in the USSR and in the development of Latin scripts for those languages in the 1920s. He attempted to incorporate elements of Marr's theories into his work from the late 1920s.

Iakubinskii, Lev Petrovich (1892–1945) Russian linguist and, early in his career a literary scholar connected with OPOIaZ. His work on dialogue and the development of the Russian national language was very influential in the 1920s and 1930s. A student of Baudouin de Courtenay, he supported Marr's New Theory of Language from the late 1920s.

Il'inskii, Grigorii Andreevich (1876–1937) Russian linguist, specialist in the history and etymology of Slavonic languages. Professor at Kharkov, Saratov and the 1st Moscow Universities. Between 1899–1906 – Secretary of the Linguistic Section of the Neophilological Society of the St. Petersburg University. Staff member of the Moscow-based Research Institute of Language and Literature, member of the Dialectology Commission. Arrested in 1934 and sentenced to ten years hard labour which was subsequently commuted to exile in Slavgorod (Western Siberia); he was repeatedly arrested and eventually shot in 1937.

Jespersen, Otto (1860–1943) Danish linguist specializing in English grammar.

Karinskii, Nikolai Mikhailovich (1873–1935) Russian philologist, palaeographer, Slavist, and dialectologist. Worked on Russian regional dialects but after the Revolution increasingly connected this to sociological factors. From 1931 he was a prominent member of the Dialectology Commission at Marr's Institute of Language and Thinking.

Kerzhentsev, Platon Mikhailovich (1881–1940) Russian dramatist and theorist of the arts who was a leading member of the Proletkul't movement, and who applied his ideas about collective activity to the rationalization of labour.

Kornilov, Konstantin Nikolaevich (1879–1957) Russian psychologist, director of the Institute of Experimental psychology where he led the Marxist reform of psychology, often associated with his own theory of 'reactology'.

Kraepelin, Emil (1856–1926) German psychiatrist and follower of Wilhelm Wundt, who was particularly influential in defining schizophrenia and manic-depression.

Kruszewski, Mikolaj (1851–1887) Polish linguist who, with Baudouin de Courtenay, established the Kazan school of linguistics, and developed an innovative, systematic approach to the phonological structure of language.

Kusik'ian, Iosif Karpovich (1890–1964) Armenian linguist, specialist in the history of Armenian language, literature and folklore, advocate of Marr's New Theory of Language.

Kuznetsov, Petr Savvich (1899–1968) Russian linguist, co-founder and one of the key theorists of the Moscow Phonological School, along with Nikolai F. Iakovlev, Ruben I. Avanesov, Vladimir N. Sidorov and Aleksandr A. Reformatskii. Member of the Moscow Dialectology Commission, specialist in Russian phonetics, orthography, dialectology and the history of the Russian language.

Larin, Boris Aleksandrovich (1893–1964) Russian linguist and, in his early career, literary scholar. His work on urban dialects and argot in the 1920s was well known in the USSR.

Leont'ev, Aleksei Nikolaevich (1904–79) Russian psychologist, early colleague of Vygotskii and Luria and founder of activity theory in psychology.

Liapunov, Boris Mikhailovich (1862–1943) Russian Slavist, specialist in the history and comparative grammar of Slavonic languages, a former student of Aleksandr A. Potebnia and Aleksei I. Sobolevskii, professor at Novorossiisk and Leningrad universities. Took an active part in discussions of the post-Revolutionary Russian orthography in mid-1930s.

Likhachev, Dmitrii Sergeevich (1906–1999) Russian philologist. His early work was related to the Marrist paradigm in linguistics and was developed at the Institute of Language and Thinking in Leningrad. He later became one of the foremost researchers on the Old Russian language and literature.

Marr, Nikolai Iakovlevich (1864/5–1934) Georgian archaeologist, philologist and linguist whose controversial Japhetic Theory, later recast as the New Theory of Language, achieved considerable official support in the 1930s and 40s. Marr's dominance in Soviet linguistics was brought to an abrupt end in June 1950 when it was denounced by Stalin.

Meshchaninov, Ivan Ivanovich (1883–1967) Russian linguist, orientalist and archeologist, one of the main advocates and interpreters of Marr's New Theory of Language. An author of a number of pioneering works in the area of functional grammar, most notably, the theory of verbal systems.

Meillet, Antoine (1866–1936) French linguist and founder of the sociological school which sought to combine linguistics with Durkheimian sociology. From 1906 he was a corresponding member of the Russian Academy of Sciences and he wrote works on Slavonic languages.

Münsterberg, Hugo (1863–1916) German psychologist and developer of psychotechnics in Germany and the USA. His work of psychotechnics was translated into Russian in the 1910s and 1920s and proved influential.

Muralov, Nikolai Ivanovich (1877–1937) Soviet military and state official, a Trotskyist. During the XV Party Congress (1927) he openly criticized the government for unjust treatment and exaggerating accusations against members of the political opposition. He was subsequently excluded from the Party and commissioned to Siberia to take up various administrative posts. Arrested in 1936 and shot in 1937.

Noiré, Ludwig (1829–1889) German philosopher and philologist whose views on the origin of language had a certain influence on a number of early Soviet language theorists including Marr. In his 1877 work *Der Ursprung der Sprache*, Noiré presented the role of coordinated collective labour as crucial for the development of rudimental verbal communication.

Ozhegov, Sergei Ivanovich (1900–1964). Russian lexicographer and Director of the Institute of Russian Language of the Soviet Academy of Sciences. His major work, *The Dictionary and Culture of Russian Speech* is still widely used.

Peretts, Vladimir Nikolaevich (1870–1935) Specialist in the history of Russian and Ukrainian medieval and early modern literature, theatre and folklore. Professor at Kiev and St. Petersburg Universities, staff member of the Institute for the Comparative History of the Literatures and Languages of the West and East (ILIazV). Arrested and sent into exile to Saratov in 1934, where he died the following year.

Peshkovskii, Aleksandr Matveevich (1878–1933) Russian linguist, a former student of Filipp F. Fortunatov and an author of *Russian Syntax in Scientific Representation* (1914), a popular textbook of Russian grammar for schools, the practical and academic value of which proved to be unsurpassed for several decades. In his works Peshkovskii successfully combined formal and functional approaches to the study of language which helped to narrow the methodological gap between the two. Peshkovskii's works also contain publications on Russian post-Revolutionary orthography, stylistics and prosody.

Peterson, Mikhail Nikolaevich (1885–1962) Russian linguist who emerged from the Moscow Linguistic School, a member of the Moscow Linguistic Circle and a supporter of Saussure's linguistic theory. He is best remembered for his work on the Lithuanian language and on Russian syntax.

Polivanov, Evgenii Dmitrievich (1891–1938) Russian linguist, orientalist and opponent of Marr's New Theory of Language. He publicly opposed Marr's theory at a special session of the Communist Academy in Moscow in 1929, after which he worked in Uzbekistan. He played an important role in the codification and standardisation of several Turkic languages in the USSR, including the development of Latin scripts for those languages. He was arrested in 1937 and shot the following year.

Poppe, Nikolai Nikolaevich (1897–1991) Soviet, German and American linguist, specialist in Altaic languages spoken on the territory of the Russian Federation. Poppe is an author of some significant publications on Bashkir, Chuvash, Mongolic, Altaic, Sakha languages, to the codification of many of which he actively contributed in 1920s–30s. In 1944 he emigrated to Germany and then the USA, where he continued his research work at Washington University.

Porzhezinskii Viktor Karlovich (Porzezin'ski Jan Viktor, 1870–1929) Russian and Polish linguist, a student of Filipp F. Fortunatov and a specialist in Baltic languages. Co-founder and the first Chairperson of the Moscow Linguistic Society (1918–1923). Mikhail N, Peterson, Mikhail M. Pokrovskii, Dmitrii N. Ushakov, Gustav G. Shpet, Afanasii M. Selishchev, Rozaliia O. Shor were among the members of the Society whose main objectives were the advancement of language theory in general and its practical application in language teaching in particular.

Rask, Rasmus (1787–1832) Danish philologist who established the connection between Northern and Gothic languages with Lithuanian, Slavonic, Greek and Latin.

Shcherba, Lev Vladimirovich (1880–1944) A former student of Baudouin de Courtenay, a founder of the Leningrad Phonetic School, professor at St. Petersburg/Leningrad University and a school pedagogue, Shcherba published extensively on the sound systems of Slavonic and other European languages, as well as on the general questions of language theory and practice. Similar to Baudouin, he was also interested in the problem of mixing of non-related or distantly related languages. Shcherba actively contributed to the process of codification of the post-Revolutionary Russian.

Schleicher, August (1821–1868) German linguist best known for his *Compendium of the Comparative Grammar of the Indo-European Languages*, in which he attempted to reconstruct the Proto-Indo-European language.

Selishchev, Afanasii Matveevich (1886–1942) Russian linguist and philologist, worked on the history of Russian language, the comparative grammar of Slavonic languages, Slavonic dialects in the Balkans and on Slavonic palaeography. In the early years after the Revolution he was best known for his study of changes in the Russian language in the wake of the World War, Revolution and Civil War. He was arrested in 1934, but returned to Moscow three years later.

Shakhmatov, Aleksei Aleksandrovich (1864–1920) Russian philologist and historian who worked to establish the historical study of Russian language and old Russian literature. Though a member of the Moscow Linguistic School, in later years Shakhmatov moved to St. Petersburg where he participated in the post-Revolutionary orthographic reforms of the Russian language and worked on questions of language and thought, which culminated in his posthumously published book *Russian Syntax* (1925).

Shor, Rozaliia Osipovna (1894–1939) Russian linguist, literary historian and orientalist. Her main works were on German and ancient Indian linguistics, general linguistics and the history of linguistics. She initiated the publication of a series of translations of Western linguists in the 1930s, leading to the first Russian publications of Sapir, Vendryes and Saussure.

Shpet, Gustav Gustavovich (1979–1937) Russian philosopher, psychologist, theoretician of the arts and translator. He studied under, inter alia, Edmund Husserl and went on to develop a somewhat idiosyncratic, phenomenological approach to language that was to have a significant influence in the early USSR. He was arrested for alleged participation in an anti-Soviet organization and shot in November 1937.

Shpil'rein, Isaak Naftulovich (1891–1937) Russian psychologist and leader of psychotechnics in the USSR. The author of a significant number of works about applied psychology, most notably *The Language of the Red Army Soldier* in 1928. He was arrested and shot as a Trotskyist in 1937.

Sobolevskii, Aleksei Ivanovich (1856/7–1929) Russian Slavist, specialist in Russian ethnography, palaeography, the history of the Russian literary language, historical dialectology of Slavonic languages.

Spitzer, Leo (1887–1960). Austrian Romance philologist. A member of the Vossler school of literary stylistics before emigrating in 1933. Spitzer's stylistics was influential on literary scholars in Russia in the 1920s and some of his articles were translated into Russian.

Stern, William (1871–1938) German philosopher and psychologist. Founder of psychotechnics.

Tomson, Aleksandr Ivanovich (1860–1935) Russian linguist, a member of Fortunatov's Linguistic Circle, a specialist in diachronic and experimental phonetics, the history of Slavonic and Armenian languages and Russian orthography.

Trubetskoi, Nikolai Sergeevich (1890–1938) Russian linguist who emigrated to Prague after the Revolution, where he introduced the discipline of phonology. He was also involved in the Eurasian movement.

Tynianov, Iurii Nikolaevich (1894–1943) Russian novelist, literary critic, theorist and translator. Tynianov became perhaps the leading figure in the development of the so-called 'formal method' in the late 1920s in Leningrad developing, inter alia, an influential theory of literary evolution.

Ushakov, Dmitri Nikolaevich (1873–1942) Russian linguist, a member of Fortunatov's Linguistic Circle, Head of the Moscow Dialectology Commission (later – the Dialectology Commission at Narkompros), a member of the Orthography Commission at Narkompros, the author of the first post-Revolutionary dictionary of the Russian language, also known as The Ushakov Dictionary (1935–1940). Ushakov played a key role in the codification of the Russian language in 1930s. In his works on the topic he argued for the importance of a balanced combination of the new linguistic elements of the Soviet period with the well-established classical traditions of the Russian literary language.

Vendryes, Joseph (1875–1960) French linguist who developed the ideas of the French sociological school that had been established by Meillet.

Vinokur, Grigorii Osipovich (1896–1947) Russian linguist and literary scholar who was particularly concerned with the stylistics of Russian language and its relationship to socio-historical factors. Vinokur was an early member of the Moscow Linguistic Circle and went on to work at a number of significant Moscow institutes.

Volodarskii, V. (pseudonym of Moisei Markovich Goldshtein, 1891–1918) Russian revolutionary and renowned orator. Became a Bolshevik in July 1917 and was assassinated in June 1918.

Voloshinov, Valentin Nikolaevich (1895–1936) Russian linguist and literary scholar. A member of the Bakhtin Circle and senior researcher at ILIaZV 1925–32. Best known for his 1929 book *Marxism and the Philosophy of Language* in which verbal interaction is foregrounded.

Vossler, Karl (1872–1934) German linguist and specialist in Romance philology. Several of his works were translated into Russian in the period before 1929 and his development of literary and linguistic stylistics proved influential for a number of Russian scholars including Viktor Zhirmunskii and members of the so-called Bakhtin Circle.

Vygotskii, Lev Semënovich (1896–1934) Russian psychologist and leader of the so-called 'cultural-historical school'. Vygotskii's work on psychological theory, child development, 'defectology' (disability studies), and the psychology of language were key developments in Soviet psychology and continues to exert a significant influence in the discipline on an international basis.

Wundt, Wilhelm (1832–1920) German psychologist and philosopher.

Appendix 3

LIST OF CONTRIBUTORS

- **Vladimir Alpatov** is a Corresponding Member of the Russian Academy of Sciences and Deputy Director of the Institute of Oriental Studies in Moscow, Russia.

- **Craig Brandist** is Professor of Cultural Theory and Intellectual History, and the Director of the Bakhtin Centre at the University of Sheffield, UK.

- **Katya Chown** is Lecturer in Russian at Nottingham University and Honorary Research Fellow of the University of Sheffield, UK.

- **Kapitolina Fedorova** is Assistant Professor at the Department of Ethnology of the European University at St. Petersburg, Russia.

- **Michael Gorham** is Associate Professor of Russian Studies at the University of Florida, USA.

- **Viktoria Gulida** is a Docent in the Philology Faculty of St. Petersburg State University, Russia.

- **Mika Lähteenmäki** is Senior Researcher in the Department of Languages at the University of Jyväskylä, Finland.

- **Vladislava Reznik** has worked as Lecturer in Russian at Durham University and collaborated on a number of research projects at the London School of Slavonic and East European Studies and the University of Lausanne in Switzerland.

- **Michael Smith** is Associate Professor in the Department of History at Purdue University, USA.

NOTES

Chapter 1. Introduction

1 The project was funded by the Arts and Humanities Research Council, and additional funding for the conference was provided by the British Academy. The first collection of materials from the conference was published in Brandist ed. (2008).

2 See, for instance, Edgar (2004, pp. 129–64).

3 In Marr's work the alleged category mistake was the notion that languages evolved from a common proto-language rather than from plurality towards linguistic unity.

4 It is now clear that Said was also prone to overgeneralizations from a legitimate starting point, on which see, for instance Ahmad (1992, pp. 159–242). Vera Tolz (2006) has helpfully shown that one of the authors whose ideas Said developed, Anouar Abdul-Malek, borrowed directly from Russian scholarship of the late 1920s and the early 1930s, and particularly, from Sergei Ol´denburg and Marr.

5 While Zhukov's work is rich in valuable information, much of it based on archival research, his thesis that Stalin sought to democratize the USSR, repeatedly thwarted by the remnants of the opposition, and that he bore no responsibility for the large-scale repressions among the intelligentsia and elsewhere is difficult to accept.

6 Bukharin's *Istoricheskii materializm: Populiarnyi uchebnik marksistskoi sotsiologii* was adopted by Party and state institutions alike. It was, for instance, mandatory reading for all social science institutes that came within the orbit of the Russian Association of Social Science Research Institutes from 1926 (TsGALI SPb 288/1/17/13).

7 This discussion is based on the principles discussed in Bourdieu (1981).

Chapter 2. Soviet Linguistics of the 1920s and 1930s and the Scholarly Heritage

1 These Polish-Russian linguists are known as Nikolai V. Krushevskii and Ivan A. Boduen de Kurtene in Russia (trans.).

2 A political doctrine developed by the writer and political activist Jan-Waclaw Makhaiski (1866/7–1926) who established a group of workers to struggle against the 'perfidious socialist intelligentsia' (trans.).

3 'The fundamental supra-dialect form of existing language, characterised by a greater or lesser degree of having been worked out [*obrabotannost´*], polyfunctionality, stylistic differentiation and tendency toward regulation. According to its cultural and social status, the literary language is counterposed to territorial dialects, various types of

everyday koinè and non-standard speech – as a higher form of existing language.' (Iartseva 1990, p. 270) (trans.).

4 From Maiakovskii's 1926 poem, *Razgovor s fininspektorom o poezii* (*Conversation With a Tax Inspector About Poetry*) (trans.).

5 OPOIaZ was an acronym for *Obshchestvo izucheniia poeticheskogo iazyka* (Society for the Study of Poetic Language) active in St. Petersburg c.1914–27, and incorporating Viktor B. Shklovskii, Osip M. Brik, Lev P. Iakubinskii, Evgenii D. Polivanov, Boris M. Eichenbaum, Iurii N. Tynyanov, Boris V. Tomashevskii and Viktor M. Zhirmunskii,

6 An opera (subtitled a 'national music drama') in five acts by Modest Musorgskii (1839–81), written between 1872 and 1880 with a libretto based on historical sources. It is set during the Moscow Uprising of 1682, and concentrates on the struggle between progressive and reactionary political factions early in the reign of Peter the Great, and the passing of old Muscovy before Peter's westernizing reforms. The opera was left unfinished upon the composer's death, and was performed posthumously, in 1886 (trans.).

7 The author here alludes to Lenin's 1897 article 'The Heritage We Renounce' in which the propositions of the embryonic Marxist movement were contrasted to the tradition of Russian Populism (trans.).

8 The Russian '*kateder-grammatiki*' is a play on '*kateder-sotsializm*', from the German *Kathedersozialismus*, or 'professorial socialism' (trans.).

9 We do not regard the attribution of *Marxism and the Philosophy of Language* entirely to Bakhtin to be justified, although the ideas in the book may have been worked out with some of his participation (Alpatov 2005, p. 94–110).

Chapter 3. 'Sociology' in Soviet Linguistics of the 1920–30s: Shor, Polivanov and Voloshinov

1 For discussion, see Day 1976.

2 One of the representatives of the mechanists was Ivan Skvortsov-Stepanov (1870–1928) and, as pointed out by Joravsky (1961, p. 49), Bukharin was not directly linked with the mechanist school, although his natural-scientific understanding of sociology was close to the views held by the mechanists.

3 The widely accepted opinion about Durkheim's influence on Saussure has been contested in Koerner (1973).

4 The first Russian translation of Saussure's Cours de linguistique générale (1933) as well as Meillet's *Introduction à l'étude comparative des langues indo-européennes* and Vendryes' *Langage* was edited and commented by Shor. The Russian translation of Sapir's *Language* appeared in the series *Iazykovedy Zapada* (Linguists of the West) edited by Shor.

5 Baudouin de Courtenay's possible influence on Saussure linguistic ideas has been discussed in detail in Koerner (1973). For a discussion of Saussure and Mikolai Kruszewski (1851–1887), see Williams (1993).

6 In concordance with Saussure (1959, p. 74), Polivanov holds that language structure as such is conservative and resists change, which clearly distances him, for instance, from Lev Iakubinskii (1986) who criticised Saussure's idea of the immutability of the linguistic sign (for discussion, see Lähteenmäki 2006).

Chapter 4. Theoretical Insights and Ideological Pressures in Early Soviet Linguistics: The Cases of Lev Iakubinskii and Boris Larin

1 Quoting Tomson on the concept of 'obshchenarodnyi' ('all people's') language and demonstrating the author's inconsistencies in allocating its constituent parts, Iakubinskii deplores Tomson's obviuos confusion of distinctions between the language of literature and 'literaturnyi' (standard) language, 'ustnaia' (oral) speech and 'razgovornaia', everyday spoken language, literary language and written language (varieties). (1986[1923], p. 21–22). Given Tomson's fine-tuned sensitivity to phonetic differences Iakubinskii attributes this lack of discrimination with respect to functional language varieties to a generally inadequate level of current academic linguistics in this area.

2 Interestingly, Schegloff & Sacks' term 'speech exchanges' corresponds exactly to a Russian term 'rechevoi obmen', used by Iakubinskii.

3 The term 'multilingual' refers, in the sociolinguistic usage, to both different ethnic languages and social dialects of one ethnic language.

4 In his 'Autobiography' Larin mentions annual expeditions with dialectology students that he supervised between 1924 and 1940, and the studies of working class speech, as well as textile, print and ceramic workers' terminology, in 1926–1931 (Larin,1977, p. 214).

5 'Argot' here *pace* Jules Gilleron (1854–1926): a non-codified working class dialect.

6 He discusses M. Cohen's 1919 article 'Notes sur l'argot' and L. Sainéan's 1920 book *Le langage parisien au XIX-e siecle* (Larin B.A. 2003 [1928a] p. 308, 309).

Chapter 5. Early Soviet Linguistics and Mikhail Bakhtin's Essays on the Novel of the 1930s

1 Nikolai Pan´kov has discovered an alternative typescript of the essay from the archive of Boris Zalesskii which contains references absent in the published version. He confirms that the reference to Iakubinskii was excised from the given passage (personal communication, 5. Nov. 2003).

2 See, Hirschkop (1999, p. 123). The existence of the reference to Marr has also been confirmed by Nikolai Pan´kov (see footnote 1).

3 In the 1963 version of the Dostoevsky book (Bakhtin 2002 [1963], p. 226), 'social group' [sotsial´naia gruppa] has been replaced by 'trend' [napravlenie] which indicates that Bakhtin wanted to distance himself from the earlier manifestly sociological position.

4 The reference is to Marr's correlation of stages of language development with forms of social differentiation, on which see Thomas (1957, pp. 117–134) This also corresponds to Bukharin's definition of ideology as 'certain unified systems of forms, thoughts, rules of conduct etc' such as 'science and art, law and morality, etc.', which was adopted by Voloshinov and Medvedev. See Bukharin (1926 [1921], p. 208). Voloshinov and Medvedev both regard the philosophy of language and literary scholarship as branches of a 'science of ideologies'. See, for example, Medvedev (1993 [1928] p. 45; 1978 [1928] p. 37) On Voloshinov's debt to Bukharin see Tihanov (2000, pp. 85–95).

5 Iakubinskii's colleague at ILIaZV Lev Shcherba (1958 [1915] p. 36) had already made the same point as early as 1915: 'Every monologue is in essence a rudimentary form of the "common", normalised, widespread language; language "lives" and changes by and large in dialogue'. See also Shcherba (1957).

6 Voloshinov (1995 [1929] pp. 314–5; 1973 [1929] pp. 96–97) briefly used the term 'discursive genre' in 1929, but it remained relatively undeveloped and certainly not linked to historical considerations.

7 Bakhtin (1996 [1951–53], p. 165; 1986 [1951–53], p. 65). Marr argued that 'language acts as a drive belt [*privodnoi remen*] in the region of the superstructural categories of society', Quoted in Alpatov (2004, p. 35).

8 Similar observations were made by N.M. Karinskii as early as 1903 in an article (Karinskii, 1903) about the peasantry's conscious move towards the common-urban language. He discusses various cases of dialectal mockery and made an interesting observation on the significant influence of travelling salesmen on linguistic changes in rural communities. According to him, even the influence of village schools on the language of peasants could be compared to that of '*byvalye ludy*' or '*korobeiniki*' (travelling salesmen) who were very familiar with the vernacular of both Moscow and St. Petersburg and were treated with respect by villagers.

9 See Veselovskii (1939; 1940). It may be significant that Veselovskii was an important and acknowledged source for Marr's work and that Zhirmunskii was the editor and wrote the introduction to these editions. See also Misch (1950, vol. 1, p. 69); Tihanov (2000, pp. 149–50); Tamarchenko (1998); Brandist (1999, pp. 19–24).

10 Bakhtin may have been following Zhirmunskii (1936) in the later 1930s, for the latter had attempted to establish a methodology for 'comparative literary studies' on the basis of Marr's notion of the 'single glottogonic process' (pp. 383–4). On the significance of this article see A.V. Desnitskaia (2001).

Chapter 6. Language as a Battlefield – the Rhetoric of Class Struggle in Linguistic Debates of the First Five-Year Plan Period: The Case of E.D. Polivanov vs. G.K. Danilov

1 It should be noted that this term in the language of Soviet debates of the time is rather confusing. Its use by the 'Language Front' group differs in some aspects from the one customary in ideological polemics in the 1920s. There is a significant amount of literature on the debates between the 'mechanists and Deborinites', and how official condemnation of the mechanists in 1929 led the term to be used as a term of abuse in the polemics of the time. Among the most significant are Somerville (1946); Joravsky (1961); Ksenofontov (1975); Iakhot (1981) and Bakhurst (1991, pp. 25–58).

2 Throughout I will use the term 'Cultural Revolution' in the sense elaborated by Fitzpatrick, as the period of the First Five-Year Plan of 1928–1932 when 'the class war on the cultural front' was launched. It began with the trial of Shakhty engineers charged of sabotage and conspiracy (see Fitzpatrick 1974). The main slogan at the beginning of the political campaign was 'tearing of the masks from class enemies', and as such many elements of Danilov's rhetoric discussed in this article can be traced back to the polemics around Shakhty trial. It should be noted, however, that Fitzpatrick's use of the term 'Cultural Revolution' has been challenged by Michael David-Fox (1999).

3 See the following sources for the respective biographies of Polivanov: Leont'ev (1983); Lartsev (1988) and Ashnin and Alpatov (1997). On Danilov see Ashnin and Alpatov (1994).

4 Since the actual language of the texts is very important and significant phenomena of the spirit of the age can be lost in translation, I will quote th Russian passages and provide translations of them.

5 Polivanov refers here to Marrists' criticism of Indo-European studies for being concentrated on Indo-European languages, and, hence, neglecting the languages of Russian ethnic minorities, such as Chuvash (one of the Turkic languages) and some others (Polivanov 1931b, p. 16. – *ed.*)

6 The indexes elaborated by A. Zhuravlev (Zhuravlev 1988) have been used for comparison of different registers on the base of J. Greenberg's indexes for the comparison of different languages.

Chapter 7. The Tenacity of Forms: Language, Nation, Stalin

1 Several recent, broadly interpretive studies of these Platonic questions include: Clay 2000; Dancy 2004; and Grabowski 2008.

2 Montefiore (2007, p. 63) discussed Stalin's early readings, including Plato. van Ree (1994, pp. 214, 232) argued that Stalin understood nations as "tenacious things," that he always respected "the resilience of national life." Molotov (1993, p. 167) noted that "Stalin had a very good knowledge of antiquity and mythology. It was a strong point of his."

3 Montefiore (2007, pp. 265–266, 277–297) who also noted that Stalin wrote a supplement to the 1913 article, 'Cultural-National Autonomy', sent westward from his Siberian exile later in 1913, seemingly lost in the mail.

4 The parallels between Lenin's and Stalin's views on the language and national questions have been well-documented. See Kaiser 1994, pp. 96–113; Kemp 1999, pp. 45–56.

5 For the influence of Kautskii, Lenin, and the Austro-Marxists upon Stalin, see Pipes 1964, pp. 21–41; Agnelli 1969, p. 31; Tucker 1973, p. 153; Nimni 1991, pp. 91–92; Carrere D'Encausse 1992, pp. 13–39; and van Ree 2002, pp. 66–67, 191, 292.

6 I am indebted to Nimni 1991 and Gellner 1983 for my approach to Renner, Bauer, and their concepts of the nation.

7 Swietochowski 1985, pp. 60–62, 89–92. On Stalin's original sympathies for the Georgian national cause, represented by Ilia Chavchavadze and Georgii Tsereteli, see van Ree 2007, pp. 52–53.

8 Stalin first raised the formula in 1925, again at the party congress of 1930, in his comments upon the new Soviet constitution of 1936, in many letters and speeches, and yet again in 1950. Connor (1984, pp. 240–241), finds the origins of the phrase in Karl Marx's remark in *The Communist Manifesto*, that the "class struggle is national, not in substance, but … in 'form';" and in V.I. Lenin's theory of two cultures (bourgeois and proletarian) in every national culture.

9 'The National Question and Leninism', in Stalin 1954, vol. 11, pp. 351–355. This 1929 work was only published after 1945.

10 These terms are from a variety of sources, in Stalin 1942 [1934], pp. 72, 79, 82–85, 93, 132–136, 139, 144, 153, 194.

11 Blank 1988; Alpatov 2000; Smith 1998.

12 There is a growing and diverse literature on script reform and Latinization, as represented by Baldauf 1993, Smith 1998, Martin 2001, and Frings 2007.

13 Stalin 1942 [1934], pp. 192–200; 'The National Question and Leninism', in Stalin 1954, vol. 11, pp. 356–364. 'Reply to the Discussion on the "Political Report of the Central Committee to the Sixteenth Congress of the CPSU(b)"' in Stalin 1954, vol. 13, p. 7.

14 'The National Question and Leninism', in Stalin 1954, vol. 11, pp. 359, 363, 367–370. 'Political Report of the Central Committee to the Sixteenth Congress of the CPSU(b)' on 27 June 1930, in Stalin, 1954, vol. 12, p. 374.

15 Slezkine (1996, p. 861) discussed "ethnoracial genealogies and national essences." Martin (2000, p. 357) saw nationality as "primordial and essential." Suny (2001, p. 867), wrote of nationality as "fixed," "primordial," "biologically determined."

16 "Form has become saturated with national content," wrote Connor (1984, p. 497). "The national form seemed to have become the content and ... nationalism did not seem to have any content other than the cult of form," claimed Slezkine (1994, p. 451). "Rather than a melting pot, the Soviet Union became the incubator of new nations." (Suny 1993, p. 87).

17 Hirsch (2005, p. 317) has discussed the rise of a "Soviet-Russian nation," an amalgam of Russian and non-Russian national factors. Blitstein (1999, pp. 3–8) has argued that the USSR was on track for "modernizing nationhood," becoming more like a "centralized nation-state."

18 Talmon (1981, p. 27) confirms the insight, that Marx's future classless society would "theoretically" embody the "real nation," if now representing values of proletarian equality, of universal justice rather than particularist pride.

19 See Bellamy 1960 [1888], pp. 110–114; and Vail 1889, p. 25.

20 Bukharin 1925, pp. 151, 294–295. I say "toyed" because Bukharin was equivocal and uncertain about the role of the nation in history, seeing its peculiarities as more malleable (dependant upon the economic base) than tenacious. True Marxists "do not overestimate these peculiarities." Such a barb might very well have stung at Stalin's pride. (Bukharin 1925, p. 212. The quote in the text is from Shpet 1989 [1927], p. 574).

21 On the other hand, the model of a future Soviet society free of national characteristics is a powerful one in the scholarship. Suny (1993, p. 112) wrote of a coming "supranational ideology;" Kaiser (1995, p. 97), of an "anational communist people;" and Martin (2000, p. 354) of the "long term Soviet goal of transcending national identity."

22 For a model treatment of the Lysenko controversies, see Joravsky 1970. For informed opinion valuing Stalin's essay on linguistics, see Althusser 1997 [1968], p. 133; Althusser 1969, p. 22; Della Volpe 1978, p. 181; and Dupre 1983, p. 228.

23 See Smith 1998, pp. 161–173 for these arguments; and Blitstein 1999, pp. 91–188, for the broader context.

24 See Wells 1933 [2005], p. 138; and Popper 1962, vol. 2, pp. 31, 319.

25 Bourdieu (1991, p. 288). Popper (1962, vol. 2, p. 238) also discussed totalitarian rule by "'science'," by "a Platonic, a pseudo-rational authority." And Levy (1980, p. 145), similarly wrote, "The totalitarian state means not police but scientists in power, not unleashed violence but truth in chains, not brutal repression but science and rigor."

Chapter 8. The Word as Culture: Grigorii Vinokur's Applied Language Science

1 For an excellent analysis of this, see Gorham (2003).

2 Vinokur commented: 'Nowadays philology is out of fashion. This can be explained by the fact that no one exactly knows what philology is.' (Vinokur 1925, p. 214).

3 Vossler distinguished style as individual language usage as opposed to general language use. Language usage that has become a rule, a convention, is opposed to language usage as individual creativity, and the two types are correspondingly studied by syntax and stylistics.

4 It has been repeatedly emphasized by various commentators on Vinokur's work that his understanding of *langue* as the societal norm is not the same as Saussure's original, but Vinokur's own innovative elaboration of his predecessor's thought (Shapir 1990, p. 275). At the MLC Saussurean discussion, the first translator of the *Course* Aleksandr Romm

remarked that the concept of norm is absolutely alien to Saussure, and is found only once in the entire book (Toddes and Chudakova 1981, p. 244).

5 Emphasis in the original. It should be added that Vinokur's recourse to the technological metaphor came from the influence of the 'industrial' wing of *LEF*, which included such apologists of 'industrial art' as Osip Brik and Boris Kushner, who aspired to create new 'inventions' in language, and who sought to overcome the barrier between poetic and everyday speech. It is worthy of note that the terms 'language policy' and 'language culture' first appeared in Kushner's and Brik's reports at the MLC meetings in December 1919 (Shapir 1990, p. 264).

6 On poetry as the highest form of language culture, capable of overcoming the inertia of language norms, organizing and inventing new linguistic phenomena, see Vinokur's article 'Futuristy – stroiteli iazyka' [Futurists – Constructors of Language] (1923d). For a more comprehensive analysis of the Futurists' linguistic experimentation, which reflects Vinokur's relationship with Formalism and the evolution of his thought on poetic language, see his 1943 book *Maiakovskii – novator iazyka* [Maiakovskii – An Innovator of Language].

7 Vinokur's lectures are collected in *Vvedenie v izuchenie filologicheskikh nauk* [Introduction into Philological Scholarship] (2000).

Chapter 9. Language Ideology and the Evolution of *Kul´tura iazyka* ('Speech Culture') in Soviet Russia

1 Vladimir Alpatov gives two reasons for the relative lack of impact of Marr's teachings – the sheer utopian nature of his proscriptions (such as doing away with grammar) and the predominantly negative nature of his proposals (Alpatov 1991, pp. 106–108).

Chapter 10. Psychology, Linguistics and the Rise of Applied Social Science in the USSR: Isaak Shpil´rein's *Language of the Red Army Soldier*

1 On Shpil´rein more generally, see especially V.A. Kol´tsova et al, (1990). 'Psychotechnics' or 'psychotechnology' (German: *Psychotechnik*; Russian: *psikhotekhnika*) is now often regarded simply as 'a sometime synonym for applied psychology' (Reber 1985, p. 598) but, as we shall see, the term was used much more specifically in the 1920s.

2 See, for instance, Shor (1926), Bühler (1927), Vygotsky (2004 [1926–7]), Vygotsky (1997 [1926–7]).

3 On Vygotsky's relationship to psikhotekhnika see Noskova (1981) and Munipov and Radzikhovskii (1981).

4 See the excellent discussion in Noskova (1998, pp. 191–96).

5 Stern's ideas were also combined with the metaphysics of *Lebensphilosophie* in the work of the German psychotechnician Fritz Giese (1890–1935), which ultimately became highly conducive to the Nazis. On Giese see Rabinbach (1992, pp. 271–88) and Killen (2007, pp. 48–71).

6 Münsterberg's work had also been complemented in Germany by that of Emil Kraeplin (1856–1926), who developed testing for fatigue and performance. On this see Rabinbach (1992, pp. 189–95).

7 See also Bailes (1977) Sochor (1981) and Stites (1989, pp. 145–59).

8 Shpil´rein also contributed the programmatic article (Shpil´rein 1924).
9 See also Trotsky (1973 [1926], pp. 233–4).
10 This position was rethought under some pressure at the beginning of the 1930s (Kol´tsova et al 1990, pp. 120–21).
11 During the Civil War political education in the Red Army was often aimed at halting atrocities. Success was limited but the very attempt distinguished the Red from the White Armies. See Brown (1995).
12 On the preceding period see also Benvenuti, (1988, pp. 175–94).
13 See also Deutcher (2003, pp. 98–102).
14 On the Frunze reforms see Hagen (1990, pp.183–267). Frunze was subsequently succeeded by another opponent of Trotsky, Kliment Voroshilov (1881–1969).
15 See also Figes (1990).
16 Iurovskaia was clearly familiar with the preliminary reports of Shpil´rein's findings in 1924 (1928, p. 30 n. 1).
17 The new approach is signalled in KPSS (1984, pp. 261–63). See also Brandist (2007, p. 66)
18 On this see, especially, Ives (2004, pp. 40–51).
19 On Gramsci's sources see Lo Piparo (1979) and Ives (2004, pp. 16–52). Meillet also had a considerable influence in Russia at the same time, on which see Brandist (2003) and Shcherba (2007). Gramsci spent much of the crucial period 1922–26 in Russia working with the Komintern, during which time he had close contacts with Bolshevik leaders and made considerable progress in reading Russian texts, among them Trotsky's *How the Revolution Armed*. On this see Grigor´eva (1998, pp. 108–9). He was also evidently aware of Trotsky's involvement in the Soviet Taylorist movement and his essays on the problems of everyday life (*byt*), on which see Gramsci (1971, pp. 301–2). On Gramsci's complex relations with Trotsky more generally see Rosengarten (1985). Shpil´rein joined the Party as early as 1920 (Kol´tsova et al 1990, p. 124, n. 24) and so was exposed to all the same political debates as Gramsci. No evidence of any meeting has been found.

Appendix 1. Introduction to Japhetidology: Theses

1 The reference is to Burushaski, a seemingly isolated language spoken by the Burusho people of northern Pakistan. Attempts to connect the language with certain languages of the Caucasus are still ongoing. See John Bengtson, 'Ein vergleich von buruschaski und nordkaukasisch', *Georgica* 20, 1997, 88–94 (trans.).
2 The term '*iazykovaia rech´*' is here translated as 'lingual speech', i.e. speech pertaining to the tongue, since it is contrasted with 'kinetic speech' or 'gesture language', which is conveyed through bodily movement. The Russian 'iazyk' equally applies to the tongue and to language. This is also related to the term '*zvukovaia rech´*', literally 'sound speech', which is contrasted with visually conveyed speech (trans.).

INDEX OF NAMES